THE
EVERYTHING
BUSY MOMS' COOKB[...]

Dear Reader,

Four years ago, after the birth of my only son, I took a leap and decided to become a stay-at-home mom. Little did I know it would be the toughest job I ever had! Despite previous jobs in the food and beverage industry, and despite owning my own business, nothing prepared me for the challenges I faced in becoming a homemaker. The toughest part? Meals! I had no knowledge of cooking or baking, no experience in the kitchen other than knowing how to artfully decorate a fruit and cheese display for a party!

So I turned to the world of food blogs and found a plethora of dishes to try out almost immediately. I began a small blog of my own, *www.dough messtic.com*, and over the next few months began baking multiple times a week and preparing meals that surprised not only me, but my family as well!

Today my food blog is thriving, and I have become a full-time professional blogger, a recipe developer for multiple companies, and a freelance writer and food photographer. I work on average twelve hours a day (even weekends), and all the while, I have my son here at home with me! Of course, we all have our own unique work challenges, but I do know how it feels to be a busy mom (even you stay-at-home moms, I know for a fact you are busy!). I hope that you'll find some comfort in knowing you are certainly not alone, and that this cookbook will lend you a hand in keeping it all together.

Enjoy!

Susan Whetzel

Welcome to the EVERYTHING® Series!

These handy, accessible books give you all you need to tackle a difficult project, gain a new hobby, comprehend a fascinating topic, prepare for an exam, or even brush up on something you learned back in school but have since forgotten.

You can choose to read an Everything® book from cover to cover or just pick out the information you want from our four useful boxes: e-questions, e-facts, e-alerts, and e-ssentials.

We give you everything you need to know on the subject, but throw in a lot of fun stuff along the way, too.

We now have more than 400 Everything® books in print, spanning such wide-ranging categories as weddings, pregnancy, cooking, music instruction, foreign language, crafts, pets, New Age, and so much more. When you're done reading them all, you can finally say you know Everything®!

QUESTION

Answers to common questions

FACT

Important snippets of information

ALERT

Urgent warnings

ESSENTIAL

Quick handy tips

PUBLISHER Karen Cooper

MANAGING EDITOR, EVERYTHING® SERIES Lisa Laing

COPY CHIEF Casey Ebert

ASSOCIATE PRODUCTION EDITOR Mary Beth Dolan

ACQUISITIONS EDITOR Lisa Laing

ASSOCIATE DEVELOPMENT EDITOR Eileen Mullan

EVERYTHING® SERIES COVER DESIGNER Erin Alexander

Visit the entire Everything® series at *www.everything.com*

THE
EVERYTHING®
BUSY MOMS'
COOKBOOK

Susan Whetzel

Avon, Massachusetts

An Everything® Series Book.
Everything® and everything.com® are registered trademarks of F+W Media, Inc.

Published by Adams Media, a division of F+W Media, Inc.
57 Littlefield Street, Avon, MA 02322 U.S.A.
www.adamsmedia.com

ISBN 10: 1-4405-5925-2
ISBN 13: 978-1-4405-5925-9
eISBN 10: 1-4405-5926-0
eISBN 13: 978-1-4405-5926-6

Printed in the United States of America.

10 9 8 7 6 5 4 3 2 1

Always follow safety and common-sense cooking protocol while using kitchen utensils, operating ovens and stoves, and handling uncooked food. If children are assisting in the preparation of any recipe, they should always be supervised by an adult.

This book is available at quantity discounts for bulk purchases.
For information, please call 1-800-289-0963.

Contents

Introduction

FIFTY YEARS AGO, when women were fighting their way into the working world, they not only had to raise their families while climbing the corporate ladder; they had to do so without the aid of multiple automobiles, cell phones, many household appliances, and computers. Despite the lack of these modern accessories, women were still expected to keep dinner on the table, lunches packed, and kids tucked carefully in bed.

In today's world, moms no longer have to fight for a position in the workplace. In fact, most moms are expected or even required to work to make ends meet. Gone are the leisurely days of book clubs and Tupperware parties, and in their place are conference calls and business lunches. It's not easy to keep work and home under control, and more often than not, it still falls on mom to keep everything balanced.

On top of everything, children are also much busier than in the past. Multiple sports for both boys and girls keep kids after school for extra hours each day; games are scheduled out of town multiple nights a week; and other extracurricular activities tie up precious family weekends. With music practices, study groups, and advanced classes (often on the collegiate level) cutting into family time, how can you expect to keep your family together, healthy, and engaged with one another?

Mealtimes.

Nothing brings the family together like a shared meal, and despite busy schedules, it is important to remember that there is still time to dine together several times a week as long as a little effort is made. Prep work on a Sunday afternoon can lead to no prep on a busy Wednesday night; a batch of muffins made on Saturday morning before soccer practice can be frozen and reheated for a quick grab-and-go breakfast on Friday. Bringing the family together for a Sunday breakfast of waffles can be a great way to start the impending action-filled week. A surprise picnic down by the lake later in the day can turn into a lasting memory for you and your children.

The important part is the preparation. Arming yourself with an arsenal of quick, family-friendly meals and desserts is a timesaving strategy. Simple ingredients that even your picky eaters will appreciate, basic cooking techniques, and a smartly stocked pantry are all key in making family meals work. It also helps to spend fifteen minutes or so making a menu plan for the upcoming week in order to save yourself from hours of indecision later on. It is this menu plan that can lead to a detailed shopping list, which will surely save you multiple visits to the grocery store (and money). With a few tips and tricks, and a little perseverance, you'll find yourself becoming an old pro at managing both work and home life.

Enjoy your family, and enjoy your children while you can. They grow up so fast! Though they have so much on their young plates already, the meals you prepare and eat together will stick with them throughout their lives, bonding you forever.

CHAPTER 1

Tips and Tricks for Busy Moms

When it comes to being a mom, one of today's biggest challenges is finding time. Time for the children's homework, baths, sports, school, and of course, eating. So often our meals become a matter of convenience versus nutrition, and on stressful nights, a trip to the drive-through wins out over a home-cooked meal. However, this doesn't have to be the case! The meals in this book can all be prepared in about the same amount of time as it takes to put on your shoes, head out to the car, and make a trip into town. If you start using some of the strategies found throughout this chapter, meals can be a breeze. Thirty minutes is all it takes from start to finish!

Busy Mom Challenges

We all face challenges as parents, whether we work outside the home or from within. There just never seems to be enough time to get it all done! Obstacles such as nonstop schedules, picky eaters, and staying within your household budget can all prevent your family from having nutritious family meals. But you'll find that with a couple of deep breaths and a few tips and tricks, you'll be on your way to domestic bliss in no time!

Eating as a Family

It's so difficult to find time to come together as a family for more than a few minutes, especially for a meal. It is important to plan ahead and be prepared for just such occasions. A few simple preparations and a list of quick, family-friendly recipes can reduce stress and make mealtime as a family much easier. There is nothing more satisfying than a Saturday morning filled with your loved ones around the breakfast table, or a thoughtful family meal after a difficult day at the office. Children find comfort in family meals, and will grow to treasure this family time later on in life. Get the kids involved: ask your daughter to help stir the pasta, or have your young son set the table. Turn off those televisions, share the happenings of the day, and eat together as often as possible!

ESSENTIAL

Sitting down for a meal with your children can help everyone unwind from their hectic schedules. Even little questions such as "Did you have fun at soccer practice?" or "How do you like your science teacher?" can prompt longer, more in-depth conversations that both you and your children will look forward to.

Staying on Budget

Staying on a budget is critical, but is also a very difficult thing to achieve. Cooking at home is an easy way to save money, especially if you are a smart shopper. Coupons, online discounts, and store specials are great ways to curb spending, and shopping with a list will shave more off of your total bill than you may think. Make a list, and stick to it!

Even if you aren't able to avoid buying that package of ice cream sandwiches from time to time, the money saved by shopping smart and cooking at home will far outweigh the money spent on fast food. The average fast food meal of burgers and fries for a family of four comes in at over $20, whereas a similar meal prepared at home is only $7. Dinner for four at a popular steakhouse can easily drain your wallet of $80 or more, whereas steaks and baked potatoes at home will only cost around $20. It's money well saved, not to mention faster than waiting in line for a table!

Breakfast and Lunch for the Kids

The majority of children detest getting up in the morning, especially those growing teenagers! That can make feeding them a good breakfast even harder than it has to be. Make it easier on yourself by not fighting the inevitable! While they are getting dressed, try whipping up a quick breakfast fajita and wrapping it for them to eat on the way to school.

No time to cook in the morning? Prepare a double batch of pancakes over the weekend and freeze the leftovers to reheat in the microwave on those rushed mornings. It's also easy to spend a little time the night before making a batch of muffins for the next day. There's nothing easier than grabbing a blueberry muffin and heading out the door on the way to the bus stop! If all else fails, having a bowl of fresh fruit sitting out on the counter is always a great alternative for an easy on-the-go breakfast.

Packing lunches is also a challenge for many of us. There is a lot of talk today about the quality of school-prepared lunches and whether those lunches are providing children with enough nutritional value. Many schools are adding healthier foods to their lunch menus, but removing all the unhealthy options is still a work in progress. By packing, we can make sure our children are getting the healthy grains, fruits, and vegetables they need, without the added fats. Know what your children are eating!

On the Run

Between ballgames, cheerleading, band practice, study sessions, and more, children today are incredibly busy, and this can make dinnertime a true challenge. With a little forethought, however, a grab-and-go meal from home will be just as quick and easy as ordering takeout, not to mention healthier! A premade wrap can be quickly microwaved and ready in a flash for that busy teen, or a pizza burger and homemade microwave potato chips can be packaged up in a lunchbox for a quick meal on the way to practice. Mix it up, and keep it fun.

Healthy Eating

Everyone knows that fast food is bad for you, and yet many people continue to eat it. Why? It's easy. It's convenient. But healthy? It certainly is not. There are many ways to make convenient meals healthier at home, such as replacing fatty meats with lower-fat alternatives like turkey or veggie burgers. Consider packaged applesauce or other single serving fruits as side dishes for packed lunches or snacks. Smoothies and fresh juices make wonderful after-school snacks, can be prepared in minimal time, and will provide hours of energy for your growing child in a healthy way.

FACT

According to the nutritional information published on their website, one McDonald's Big Mac has 550 calories and 29 grams of fat. When you and your family do eat fast food, look for healthier options such as grilled chicken sandwiches or salads.

Picky Eaters

You likely have one in your home right now: a picky eater. The child that will only eat macaroni, or the teen that only wants pizza. If your child is picky, try to determine why, and instead of punishing them for it or forcing unwanted foods upon them, try catering to their wishes instead. For example, start adding a few proteins into your macaroni lover's dinner. Sliced chicken breast hidden among the noodles is an excellent strategy. You can also add in steamed broccoli, or slices of pepperoni. Eventually, their picky palate will grow, and they may even start requesting such additions. Don't be discouraged if they pick out those unwanted additions; just give them time, and they will likely come around. Just keep trying!

Pizza is another easy and fun way to develop new tastes for your picky eaters, or even those who aren't so picky but are reluctant to try new things. Add pineapples, a variety of cheeses, potatoes, peas, and fresh greens to their favorite pizzas. Again, you may be met with some resistance, but pizza is a comfort food and a great way to introduce new items into their diets.

Timesavers

Sometimes just deciding what to make for your family can derail your meal plan. With multiple family members, all with different taste preferences, how will you ever settle on a dish everyone will enjoy? By being prepared! Doing small things like making a shopping list or planning the week's menu are quick tricks you can use to not only tackle indecision, but cut down on the amount of time it takes to get a nutritious meal on the table.

Shopping for the Week

Planning out a week's worth of menus in advance is a helpful tool for creating extra time. Knowing what to expect each day takes away the indecision you may face on a nightly basis when the kids are hungry and you are at a loss for what to prepare. A weekly menu plan also allows you to shop, list in hand, so that you are prepared for each meal. There is nothing worse than setting out to make a dish only to find you are missing one essential ingredient. Be prepared; it saves time!

Take Advantage of Your Grocer

Many supermarkets today are increasing the amount of convenience foods they offer. Rotisserie chicken, salad bars, prepared vegetables, and desserts can make your life much easier, and sometimes more affordable. Deli chicken is often less expensive than buying an uncooked chicken and preparing it yourself. Take advantage! You should also spend more time in the freezer section of the market; frozen vegetables are already cleaned and are preserved at their most nutritious. If chopping and dicing is the last thing you want to do, look no further than the freezer aisle! Prepared puff pastry and pie crusts found in the freezer section are also wonderful timesavers, and rival homemade quality in many cases.

Save Time with Advanced Prep

Upon your return home from the grocery store with the week's menu items, you can save time by preparing many of the items as you put them away. Fresh vegetables can be cleaned and chopped immediately based on the amounts needed for the recipes you plan to prepare; simply clean, chop, and then store the proper amounts in plastic bags for a quick grab when needed.

ALERT

In order to avoid food-borne illnesses, always follow the four "Cs" of food hygiene: Make sure your hands and work area are clean before you begin cooking. Cook food through to the required level of doneness. Make sure food is chilled at the correct temperature. Finally, avoid cross-contamination by keeping cooked and raw food separate, and by using different cooking equipment and work surfaces for raw and cooked foods.

Make Use of Leftovers

Leftovers are a true luxury, and should be viewed as such. It is just as easy to prepare double quantities of many items, such as rice or pasta, for use in a meal later in the week. Simply prepare the night's meal, putting half of the doubled recipe aside and then refrigerating or freezing it until needed. Meats can be prepared in the same fashion. It takes just as much time to prepare eight chicken breasts or hamburgers as it does four, and having the leftovers ready to go later in the week is wonderful when you aren't in the mood to cook.

It is very important to label and store each item appropriately. Many foods can easily be stored in the freezer for later use, but a proper label is critical. Mark each container with what it is and the date it was prepared.

Plastic freezer bags are a wonderful convenience in this way, and many have a nice area just for such labeling. Be sure to properly store all items and follow basic hygiene rules for storing and reheating these foods.

Timesaving Tools

Thanks to modern technology and big-box stores on every corner, there is no excuse for not having a well-equipped kitchen. Manufacturers offer small appliances that can shave precious moments off of your busy days, and those minutes will add up to less stress and more family fun. Many of these products are child friendly, and with your assistance, the kids can even lend you a hand at mealtime.

The Microwave Oven

Throw out what you think you know about your microwave oven . . . it does so much more than reheat and defrost! Cooking many of your foods in the microwave versus in a conventional oven, or even on the stove, has several advantages. Namely, cooking time is much shorter. In addition, the microwave oven uses less energy than a conventional electric oven, and just as important, it doesn't add extra heat to the kitchen. This becomes a lifesaver when you are sweating through the summer months! Even though consumers have been using microwaves for over half a century, most of them are still only using this appliance as a way to reheat versus cook. It can do so much more than reheat a lukewarm cup of coffee, and you'll find it saves quite a bit of time in preparing many meals.

A microwave oven cooks food when the microwaves hit the food, causing water molecules in the food to vibrate and produce heat. This makes it perfect for cooking food with a high liquid content, such as soups and casseroles, or for boiling rice and vegetables.

No two microwaves are the same, and for that reason, use caution when it comes to cooking times. Differences in wattage, size, and even how often you stir can affect the results of microwaved foods. To be safe, start with the shortest amount of recommended cooking time and work your way up from there.

Countertop or Toaster Oven

Countertop ovens, while very popular in the past, lost appeal in the late 1980s and 1990s. However, they are beginning to make a definite resurgence in the kitchen. Better technology and design has made these ovens very useful, especially to busy cooks. For example, a pizza can be cooked just as well (or even better) in a countertop oven, and in less time than it takes to preheat a conventional oven. It also takes less energy and doesn't heat up the kitchen.

Food Processor and Blender

A blender is a wonderful appliance to have in a busy kitchen. Purée-ing fruits and vegetables for baby food, smoothies, ice cream toppings, and mixed drinks is made substantially easier with the blender. The same is true for the food processor, though this machine can do so much more, depending on the model. Food processors are a true timesaver for chopping vegetables and nuts, pulling together pie crusts, and even making cookie dough. Some of the larger, more expensive models will even julienne and evenly slice vegetables for quick dinner preparation.

Mandoline Slicer

Quality truly makes a difference when it comes to mandoline slicers. The plastic versions featured on many infomercials may work fine for small jobs, but a more expensive metal version will last longer and produce much better results, especially for larger meals. Variable blades and thicknesses will allow for a diverse amount of usage, from thinly sliced potatoes for potato chips to thicker cuts of vegetables for salads and stews.

Juicer

Without a commercial juicer, it is next to impossible to extract juices from many fruits and vegetables. There are many quality machines on the market. Avoid the cheapest models and opt instead for one with good consumer reviews. Despite the initial investment, you will find the cost is quickly countered by the money saved by juicing at home. Plus, it's healthier and has no unwanted ingredients!

A Well-Stocked Kitchen

Being prepared is half the battle when it comes to saving time and energy in the kitchen. Just a few staples will keep you organized and ready to go on those evenings when cooking is the last thing you want to do.

Quality Cookware

A set of stainless steel pots and pans makes meal preparation a breeze. Heavier-bottomed versions are more expensive, but offer more even cooking and easier cleanup than their cheaper counterparts. If your set does not include a wok, consider buying one for stir-fry.

Heatproof Utensils

A spatula, large spoon, and whisk made out of heat-resistant silicone are a blessing in the kitchen. The soft bottoms do no damage to cookware; there is minimal sticking; and the cleanup is quick and easy.

Bakeware

Invest in at least two good cookie sheets with rimmed edges. While certainly great for cookies, the rimmed edges are also useful for containing juices should you opt to bake meats on them. For larger cuts of meat, and roasts, a roasting pan is essential. Buy one with a removable rack for easy cleanup and better roasting results.

Plastic Wrap, Plastic Bags, and Sealable Containers

Plastic bags are the most convenient way to store leftovers, or to contain prepared chopped vegetables and fruits for later use. However, for reusable storage, plastic containers with tight-fitting lids are a necessity for large amounts of leftovers. Plastic wrap is also a helpful tool for covering dishes when a lid goes missing, or for keeping splatters from escaping as you micro-wave many foods.

Knives

A sharp set of knives, especially a set contained in a knife block, makes for quick and easy food preparation, as you always know where the knives are located. It is also safer than keeping loose knives in drawers, where little hands can unknowingly grasp them when you aren't looking.

ESSENTIAL

It may sound contradictory, but a sharp knife is safer than a dull one. Trying to cut food with a dull knife forces you to use more pressure, increasing the chances of slippage. To avoid accidents, have your knives regularly sharpened by a professional, or consider buying a sharpening steel. Many knife blocks include a sharpening steel, especially those from higher-end manufacturers.

Mixing Bowls

A set of different-sized mixing bowls, especially those that nest, is a functional and timesaving kitchen necessity.

Measuring Cups and Spoons

Every recipe benefits from a standard set of measuring cups and spoons. Many take up little drawer space and remain attached, making them easy to find on busy evenings.

A Well-Stocked Pantry

Every pantry should contain the kitchen staples, from flour, to rice, to canned vegetables. Despite every effort on your part to stick to a prepared meal plan, life tends to throw curve balls, so having a well-stocked pantry is an excellent way to combat those challenges. Be prepared!

Flour

All-purpose flour is a blended wheat flour that can be used for most types of baking. Many other flours are available, from whole grain to cake and bread flours, as well as rice flour, almond flour, and other gluten-free varieties. For those with an unrestricted diet, all-purpose flour is the most useful.

Baking Powder and Baking Soda

Staples in any kitchen, these are essential for many baking recipes. If you like to bake, you may as well stock up!

Sugar

Regular granulated sugar (or white sugar) and brown sugar are sweetening essentials. Be sure to measure each appropriately.

Olive Oil

Extra-virgin olive oil is used in cases where it will not be cooked, such as dressings or marinades. Less expensive, regular olive oil can be used for sautéing and basting.

Vegetable Oil

Vegetable oil is great for stir-fry and for baking, as there is minimal flavor, so it does not compete with the dishes you may be preparing.

Dried Spices

While fresh spices are delicious, they are also a luxury. Dried spices make meal prep much easier, as they are always ready. You will find yourself using certain spices more than others, such as dried basil, sage, bay leaves, dried parsley, dried oregano, ground cinnamon, ground nutmeg, ginger, paprika, red pepper flakes, and chili powder. Of course, salt and pepper are always must-haves!

Rice

Instant rice is a great timesaver for nights when you don't have time or energy to cook rice on the stovetop or in a rice cooker. It is especially useful for adding to stir-fries, as it will take on the flavors in the dish. There are more flavorful varieties of instant rice available in many supermarkets, Asian markets, and even online if you find the instant white rice to be too bland for your liking.

Be sure to also keep regular long-grain white rice and scented jasmine rice on hand to cook ahead of time and reheat, or for nights when you have at least thirty minutes to cook dinner.

Pasta

In a house with children, pasta such as spaghetti, elbow macaroni, and shell-shaped pasta should always be on hand. Lasagna noodles, angel hair, and other long varieties are also very useful. To keep it even more fun for the kids, there are colorful and festively shaped noodles that will keep their pasta cravings coming.

Canned Vegetables

A well-stocked pantry can only benefit from a nice assortment of canned vegetables for quick meal preparations. Canned green beans, potatoes, beans, and corn are excellent in soups and stews (or as side dishes), and canned tomatoes are perfect for grab-and-go sauces, stocks, and more.

Ingredient	Maximum Storage
Flour	1 year
Baking powder	1 year
Baking soda	1 year
Granulated sugar	18 months
Brown sugar	6 months
Rice	2 years
Dried spices	2 years

CHAPTER 2

Breakfast

Scrambled Eggs with Cheese

Scrambled eggs are best served hot, right from the skillet, so have your family waiting for the eggs rather than holding the eggs for them. Serve along with hot, crisp bacon and buttered toast.

INGREDIENTS | SERVES 6

12 eggs, beaten
¼ cup light cream
¼ cup mascarpone cheese
½ teaspoon salt
⅛ teaspoon white pepper
¼ teaspoon dried marjoram leaves
3 tablespoons butter
1 cup shredded Havarti or Swiss cheese

Cheese Substitutions

Most cheeses can be substituted for each other in recipes. Ricotta cheese is a good substitute for mascarpone, as is softened or whipped cream cheese. Gruyère and Swiss are good substitutes for Havarti, and Colby cheese works well in place of Cheddar. Cotija, a Mexican hard cheese, is a great substitute for Parmesan cheese.

1. In a large bowl, combine eggs with cream, mascarpone cheese, salt, pepper, and marjoram. Beat with egg beater or hand mixer until smooth.

2. Heat butter in large skillet over medium heat. Add egg mixture. Cook eggs, stirring occasionally, until they are set, about 10–12 minutes. Add Havarti cheese, cover pan, and remove from heat. Let stand for 2–3 minutes, then remove lid, stir cheese gently into eggs, and serve.

Easy Cheese Frittata

*The Italian version of an omelet, a frittata is served open-faced instead of folded over.
A blend of shredded Italian cheeses would be ideal for this recipe.*

INGREDIENTS | SERVES 4

6 eggs

¼ teaspoon nutmeg

Salt and black pepper to taste

2 cups shredded cheese, divided

2 teaspoons olive oil

Flipping a Frittata

Traditionally, a frittata is flipped over before adding the cheese topping. To flip over the frittata, cover the skillet with a plate and then turn the pan over so that the frittata falls on the plate. Set the skillet back on the stove element, and carefully slide the frittata off the plate and back into the pan. Sprinkle the cheese over the top. Cook for 1–2 more minutes, until the cheese has melted.

1. In a large bowl, whisk the eggs with the nutmeg, salt, and pepper. Stir in 1½ cups cheese.

2. Heat a medium-sized skillet over medium-high heat. Add the oil, tilting so that it covers the bottom of the pan. Pour the egg mixture into the pan. Cook the frittata on low-medium heat, using a heatproof turner to lift the edges occasionally so that the uncooked egg flows underneath.

3. When the frittata is firm on top, remove from the pan, turn it, and slide it back into the pan.

4. Sprinkle the remaining cheese on top and cook for a few more minutes, until the cheese is melted and the frittata is cooked through.

Mini Popovers

Popovers "pop" without any leavening in the batter because it contains lots of gluten and liquid. When the popovers are placed in the hot oven, the batter almost explodes with steam, and the gluten keeps the shell together.

INGREDIENTS | YIELDS 24 POPOVERS

2 eggs
⅔ cup milk
⅔ cup flour
1 tablespoon oil
¼ teaspoon salt

1. Preheat oven to 425°F. Spray mini muffin pans with baking spray and set aside.

2. Combine all ingredients in medium bowl and beat well with wire whisk until batter is blended and smooth. Pour 1 tablespoon of batter into each prepared muffin cup. Bake for 15–22 minutes or until popovers are puffed and deep golden brown. Serve immediately.

Caramel Rolls

You could add chopped pecans or dark raisins to this easy recipe if you'd like. Place them on the topping before adding the rolls.

INGREDIENTS | YIELDS 12 ROLLS

¼ cup caramel fudge ice cream topping
2 tablespoons and ¼ cup brown sugar, divided
2 tablespoons heavy cream
¼ cup butter, softened
½ teaspoon cinnamon
1 (8-ounce) can refrigerated crescent roll dough

1. Preheat oven to 375°F. Spray a 9-inch round cake pan with nonstick baking spray.

2. In a small bowl combine ice cream topping, 2 tablespoons brown sugar, and heavy cream and mix well. Spread mixture evenly in the prepared cake pan.

3. In another small bowl, combine butter, ¼ cup brown sugar, and cinnamon and mix well.

4. Unroll dough and separate into 4 rectangles. Press seams to seal. Spread butter mixture over rectangles. Roll up dough, starting at the short edge, and pinch edges of dough to seal. Cut each roll into 3 slices and arrange the twelve rolls on the topping in the cake pan.

5. Bake for 15–20 minutes, until dough is deep golden brown. Invert pan onto serving plate and remove pan. If any caramel remains in pan, spread onto rolls. Serve warm.

Sausage Rolls

*Cheese, sausage, thyme, and some puff pastry make delicious little rolls
that are perfect for breakfast on the run. Bake them ahead of time, freeze them,
and then microwave each on high for 1–2 minutes until hot.*

INGREDIENTS | YIELDS 24 ROLLS

24 pork sausage links
1 (17-ounce) package frozen puff pastry, thawed
1 cup grated Cheddar cheese
½ cup grated Parmesan cheese
1 teaspoon dried thyme leaves
1 egg, beaten
¼ teaspoon salt

Puff Pastry

Puff pastry is found frozen near the pie shells and cakes in your supermarket. Follow the directions for thawing and using the pastry. Many brands require thawing overnight in the refrigerator so the butter that is encased in the layers of pastry doesn't melt. Keep a couple of boxes on hand to make easy snacks.

1. Preheat oven to 400°F. Line cookie sheets with parchment paper and set aside.

2. In a heavy skillet, cook pork sausage links over medium heat until golden brown and cooked, about 5–7 minutes. Remove and place on paper towels to drain.

3. Unfold puff pastry sheet and place on a lightly floured surface. In a small bowl, combine cheeses and thyme leaves and toss to combine. Sprinkle this mixture over the puff pastry and gently press cheese mixture into pastry; roll to a 12" × 18" rectangle. Cut into three 12" × 6" rectangles, and then cut each rectangle in half to make 6 squares. Cut each square into four 3" × 3" squares.

4. Place a cooked and drained sausage on the edge of each square and roll up to enclose sausage; press pastry to seal.

5. In small bowl, beat egg with salt and brush over sausage rolls. Place on prepared cookie sheets and bake for 12–18 minutes until puffed and golden brown. Serve hot.

Stuffed French Toast

*Broiling French toast helps significantly cut the cooking time
and ensures that the bread will be crisp.*

INGREDIENTS | SERVES 4

4 tablespoons melted butter, divided
½ cup mascarpone cheese, divided
¼ cup strawberry preserves
8 slices cracked wheat bread
2 eggs
1 teaspoon vanilla
¼ teaspoon cinnamon

Broiling

When broiling foods, be sure to watch the food carefully as it burns easily. Most foods should be placed about 4–6 inches away from the heated coils, and most ovens require that the oven door be slightly open when broiling. Use the broiler pan that came with your oven, or a heavy-duty stainless steel pan that won't buckle under the high heat.

1. Preheat broiler. Spread 3 tablespoons melted butter in a 15" × 10" jelly-roll pan and set aside.

2. In a small bowl, combine ¼ cup mascarpone cheese and preserves and mix.

3. Spread preserves mixture on 4 bread slices and top with remaining slices. Cut these sandwiches in half to make triangles.

4. On a shallow plate, beat remaining ¼ cup mascarpone cheese until fluffy; then add eggs, remaining 1 tablespoon melted butter, vanilla, and cinnamon and beat until smooth. Dip sandwiches in egg mixture, turning to coat. Place coated sandwich triangles in butter on jelly-roll pan.

5. Broil 6 inches from heat source for 4–5 minutes; then carefully turn the sandwiches and broil for 3–5 minutes longer on second side until golden brown and crunchy. Serve immediately.

Instant Granola

Be sure that the melted margarine covers the bottom of the cooking dish, and to spread out the granola mixture so that it doesn't burn. You can increase the brown sugar to 3 tablespoons if desired.

INGREDIENTS | SERVES 2

3 tablespoons margarine
1 cup quick-cooking oats
¼ cup vegetable oil
2 tablespoons brown sugar
2 tablespoons apple juice
½ cup dried fruit and nut mix

1. Place the margarine in a 1-quart microwave-safe casserole dish. Heat the margarine in the microwave on high heat for 15 seconds, or until it is melted.

2. In a medium mixing bowl, stir together the quick-cooking oats, vegetable oil, and brown sugar. Spoon the oat mixture into the casserole dish, spreading it out evenly.

3. Microwave on high heat for 1 minute. Add the apple juice and the dried fruit and nut mixture, stirring to mix thoroughly into the oats.

4. Give the dish a quarter turn and microwave on high heat for 1 more minute, then another 30 seconds if needed, until the granola is cooked, stirring the granola and making another quarter turn. Be sure not to overcook the fruit. (Do not worry about foaming at the top of the granola.)

Basic Blender Pancakes

If desired, you can replace the yogurt with 2½ cups of either small curd cottage cheese or ricotta cheese.

INGREDIENTS | SERVES 12

2 cups plain yogurt

2 large eggs

3 tablespoons vegetable oil

2 tablespoons granulated sugar

2 tablespoons brown sugar

2 cups all-purpose flour

½ teaspoon salt

4 teaspoons baking powder

Water, as needed

How to Freeze Pancakes

Got leftover pancakes? To freeze, place a sheet of wax paper between each pancake to keep them separate, and wrap in a resealable plastic bag. To reheat the pancakes, unwrap, remove the wax paper, and cook the pancakes in stacks of two in a microwave on high heat for 1–1½ minutes, or in a 375°F oven for 10–15 minutes.

1. Preheat a griddle or skillet over medium-high heat.

2. In a blender or food processor with knife blade attached, blend the yogurt, eggs, and vegetable oil. Add the sugars, flour, salt, and baking powder. Blend until smooth, adding as much water as needed until you have a pancake batter that is neither too thick nor too runny.

3. Grease the griddle or skillet as needed.

4. Pour the batter in ¼-cup portions into the pan. Cook the pancakes until they are browned on the bottom and bubbles start forming on top. Turn the pancakes over and cook the other side.

5. Continue cooking the remainder of the pancakes, adding more oil or margarine to grease the pan as needed.

Peach Pancakes

Serve these wonderful pancakes on warmed plates with maple syrup, peach jam, and some powdered sugar sprinkled on top, along with Canadian bacon and orange juice.

INGREDIENTS | SERVES 4

2 ripe peaches, peeled and diced

4 tablespoons sugar, divided

¼ teaspoon cinnamon

¾ cup flour

1 teaspoon baking powder

1 egg, separated

¾ cup milk

1 teaspoon vanilla

2 tablespoons butter

Cooking Pancakes

Use a ¼-cup measure to scoop out the batter, and pour onto a hot, greased skillet. Cook pancakes until the edges start to look dry and cooked and bubbles form on the surface, about 2–4 minutes. Carefully flip the pancakes and cook until the second side is light brown, 1–2 minutes longer.

1. In small bowl, toss peaches with 2 tablespoons sugar and cinnamon.

2. In medium bowl, combine flour, remaining 2 tablespoons sugar, baking powder, egg yolk, milk, and vanilla and stir just until combined.

3. Beat egg white until stiff; fold into flour mixture, and then fold in peach mixture.

4. Grease a skillet heated to medium with butter and cook pancakes, flipping once, until done.

Orange-Glazed Blueberry Muffins

These mini muffins are the perfect quick breakfast for families on the run.
They are tender, sweet, and very delicate; kids love them. Serve warm for best flavor.

INGREDIENTS | YIELDS 44 MUFFINS

1 (9-ounce) package blueberry quick-bread mix

5 tablespoons orange juice, divided

¾ cup milk

¼ cup oil

1 egg

½ cup powdered sugar

Reheating Muffins

You can make muffins ahead of time and store in airtight containers; then reheat for best taste and texture. To reheat, place a few muffins on a microwave-safe plate, cover with microwave-safe paper towels, and heat for 10 seconds per muffin, until warm.

1. Preheat oven to 375°F. Line 44 mini muffin cups with paper liners and set aside.

2. In large bowl combine quick-bread mix, 4 tablespoons orange juice, milk, oil, and egg and stir just until dry ingredients disappear. Fill prepared muffin cups two-thirds full of batter. Bake for 10–15 minutes or until muffins spring back when gently touched with finger. Cool for 3 minutes, and then remove to wire rack.

3. In small bowl combine powdered sugar and 1 tablespoon orange juice; drizzle this mixture over the warm muffins and serve.

Basic Banana Muffins

Freshly baked banana muffins have a sweet flavor. For an extra touch of flavor, add 2–3 tablespoons of sweetened coconut flakes to the muffin batter.

INGREDIENTS | YIELDS 12 MUFFINS

1 cup milk

1 large egg

⅓ cup vegetable oil

1 teaspoon vanilla extract

3 medium bananas, peeled and mashed

2 cups all-purpose flour

½ teaspoon baking soda

1¼ teaspoons baking powder

½ cup granulated sugar

½ teaspoon salt

½ teaspoon ground cinnamon

Muffin Cooking Tips

Muffins are easy to make if you follow a few simple steps. Don't overbeat the batter—a good muffin batter has a few lumps. Once the batter is mixed, fill the cups and put the muffins in the oven immediately. Be sure not to fill the cups over two-thirds full, or the muffins will have an uneven shape. Remove the muffins from the oven when a toothpick inserted in the middle of a muffin comes out clean.

1. Preheat the oven to 375°F. Grease one muffin tin.

2. In a medium mixing bowl, whisk together the milk, egg, vegetable oil, vanilla extract, and mashed banana.

3. In a large mixing bowl, stir together the flour, baking soda, baking powder, sugar, salt, and ground cinnamon, mixing well.

4. Pour the milk mixture into the dry ingredients. Stir until the mixture is just combined and still a bit lumpy (do not overbeat).

5. Fill each muffin cup about two-thirds full with muffin batter. (If you have leftover muffin batter, refrigerate and use within a few days.) Bake the muffins for 20–25 minutes, until they are a light golden brown and a toothpick inserted in the middle comes out clean.

Chocolate Chip Muffins

Easy-melting semisweet chocolate chips are perfect for baking!

INGREDIENTS | YIELDS 12 MUFFINS

1 cup milk
1 large egg
⅓ cup vegetable oil
2 cups all-purpose flour
⅓ cup granulated sugar
½ teaspoon salt
2 teaspoons baking powder
1 cup semisweet chocolate chips

1. Preheat the oven to 375°F. Grease one muffin tin.

2. In a medium mixing bowl, whisk together the milk, egg, and vegetable oil.

3. In a large mixing bowl, stir together the flour, sugar, salt, and baking powder, mixing well. Gently stir in the chocolate chips.

4. Pour the milk mixture into the dry ingredients. Stir until the mixture is just combined and still a bit lumpy (do not overbeat).

5. Fill each muffin cup about two-thirds full with muffin batter. (If you have leftover muffin batter, refrigerate and use within a few days.) Bake the muffins for 20–25 minutes, until they turn a light golden brown and a toothpick inserted in the middle comes out clean.

Pumpkin Bread

It's important to use pumpkin pie filling, not canned pumpkin purée, in this easy recipe, because it contains spices and emulsifiers that flavor the bread and add to its texture.

INGREDIENTS | YIELDS 1 LOAF

1 cup flour

¼ cup whole wheat flour

¾ cup sugar

½ teaspoon ground cinnamon

1 (3-ounce) package instant butterscotch pudding mix

½ teaspoon baking soda

½ teaspoon baking powder

½ cup butter, melted

2 eggs

1 cup canned pumpkin pie filling

Quick Breads

Quick breads use baking soda or baking powder for leavening; they are quick to stir up and quick to bake. For best results, measure all ingredients carefully and be sure to mix the wet and dry ingredients just until combined. Overmixing will make the bread tough, with large tunnels running through it.

1. Spray a glass 9" × 5" loaf pan with baking spray and set aside.

2. In a large bowl, combine flour, whole wheat flour, sugar, cinnamon, pudding mix, baking soda, and baking powder and stir to blend. Add melted butter, eggs, and pumpkin pie filling and stir just until blended. Pour into prepared pan.

3. Microwave the pan on 75 percent power for 8 minutes; then rotate the pan one-half turn and continue microwaving for 8–10 minutes on 75 percent power, or until a toothpick inserted in the center comes out clean. Let stand on a flat surface for 5 minutes; then remove from pan and cool completely on wire rack.

Fun French Toast Sticks with Cinnamon

Kids love making this fun twist on traditional French toast. While maple syrup is the traditional French toast topping, these also taste delicious topped with jam or powdered sugar.

INGREDIENTS | SERVES 4

8 slices raisin bread
4 eggs
1 cup milk
¼ teaspoon salt
¼ teaspoon ground cinnamon
½ teaspoon vanilla extract
2 tablespoons margarine
½ cup maple syrup, or as needed

1. Cut each piece of bread lengthwise into 4 equal pieces.

2. In a small bowl, whisk the eggs with the milk, salt, cinnamon, and vanilla.

3. Heat the margarine in a skillet on medium to low-medium heat.

4. One at a time, dip the bread slices in the egg mixture, coating well. Only dip as many pieces of bread in the mixture as you are cooking at one time.

5. Lay the soaked bread pieces in the skillet. Cook on one side for about 2 minutes until browned; then turn over and cook the other side.

6. Serve the French toast sticks with the maple syrup.

Marshmallow Breakfast Bars

Breakfast bars make a fun change from regular breakfast cereal.
Be sure to keep an eye on the marshmallow mixture so that it doesn't burn.

INGREDIENTS | SERVES 6

4 tablespoons margarine
½ cup peanut butter
2 cups mini marshmallows
½ cup sugar
½ cup milk
2 cups quick-cooking oats
½ cup raisins
¼ cup dried cranberries

Replacing Marshmallows with Mini Marshmallows

Replacing regular-sized marshmallows with mini marshmallows gives you a greater assortment of colors. Use 10 mini marshmallows for every regular-sized marshmallow called for in a recipe.

1. In a heavy medium-sized saucepan, melt the margarine on low-medium heat. Add the peanut butter, stirring. Turn the heat down to low and add the marshmallows. Continue cooking over low heat, stirring occasionally, until the peanut butter and marshmallows are almost melted.

2. While melting the marshmallow and peanut butter, heat the sugar and milk to boiling in a separate small saucepan, stirring to dissolve the sugar.

3. Stir the oats into the melted marshmallow and peanut butter mixture. Stir in the heated milk and sugar, raisins, and cranberries.

4. Spread the mixture in a greased 9" × 9" pan, using a spatula or your hands to press it down evenly.

5. Chill for at least 15 minutes. Cut into bars.

Nutty Apple Muffins

Delicious muffins—top with low-fat ice cream for a light, sweet dessert.

INGREDIENTS | SERVES 12

1 egg
½ cup orange juice
¼ cup canola oil
1½ cups apples, peeled and diced
1½ cups flour
½ cup sugar
2 teaspoons baking powder

Topping:

1 teaspoon cinnamon
¼ cup brown sugar
¼ cup walnuts (optional)

1. Preheat oven to 400°F.

2. Spray 12-cup muffin tray with nonstick cooking spray, or insert paper baking cups into tray.

3. Combine egg, orange juice, canola oil, apples, flour, sugar, and baking powder in a large mixing bowl. Mix thoroughly, until well blended.

4. Pour batter into prepared muffin tray.

5. Prepare topping in a small bowl by combining cinnamon, brown sugar, and walnuts (if using). Sprinkle topping over each muffin.

6. Bake for 20–25 minutes, until toothpick comes out dry.

Quick Hot Oatmeal

Most oatmeal recipes call for using water; however, you can always substitute milk for a power breakfast with more protein and more calcium. If you are in a rush in the morning, feel free to use the microwave!

INGREDIENTS | SERVES 1

½ cup cooked oats, dry
1 cup low-fat milk
½ teaspoon vanilla extract
1 teaspoon sugar (optional)

1. Pour the oats into a microwave-safe bowl.

2. Add milk and vanilla extract.

3. Microwave for 1 minute, 30 seconds, or until thick and creamy.

4. Sweeten with sugar if desired.

Not a "Real" Breakfast Food Eater?

Try any sandwich in the morning with a glass of low-fat milk and a piece of fruit. For example, 2 slices whole grain bread, 2–3 slices turkey, roast beef, or ham, and 1 teaspoon of light mayonnaise or mustard if desired. That works just fine as breakfast.

Dutch Baked Apple Pancake

Not only are these pancakes worth the work; they're fun for the whole family!

INGREDIENTS | SERVES 3–4

Apple filling:

2 tablespoons trans fat–free margarine

3–4 Granny Smith apples, peeled, cored, and sliced thinly

6 tablespoons sugar

1 teaspoon cinnamon

Pancake batter:

3 eggs

½ cup flour

½ cup low-fat milk

1 tablespoon low-fat plain yogurt

1 teaspoon lemon zest, grated

Powdered sugar, to garnish

A Fun Breakfast—Loaded with Vitamin C

Add either an 8-ounce container of any flavor low-fat yogurt, or a glass of low-fat milk and some fresh fruit salad, and this becomes a perfect well-rounded breakfast for all.

1. Preheat oven to 400°F.

2. In a skillet, melt the margarine.

3. Add sliced apples, sugar, and cinnamon. Sauté and continue stirring until apples are soft. Remove from heat, transfer apples to a large round pie pan, and set aside.

4. Mix eggs until foamy.

5. Add flour, milk, yogurt, and lemon zest and beat until smooth.

6. Pour pancake batter over apples.

7. Place in the oven for 25 minutes, until puffy and golden brown.

8. Using a sieve, dust powdered sugar over the top before serving.

Traditional Belgian Waffle

There are lots of topping options for these waffles including: fresh berries, raisins, jam, a few mini chocolate chips, low-sugar pancake syrup, and powdered sugar.

INGREDIENTS | SERVES 8

2 cups all-purpose flour

2 teaspoons baking powder

3 tablespoons confectioners' sugar

1 tablespoon canola oil

2 cups low-fat milk

3 eggs, separated

2 teaspoons vanilla extract

¼ teaspoon salt

Nonstick cooking spray

Round Out This Easy Breakfast

Add a serving of protein, e.g., scrambled eggs, low-fat cottage cheese, or a glass of low-sugar chocolate milk, for a fast and complete breakfast.

1. Combine flour, baking powder, confectioners' sugar, oil, milk, egg yolks, vanilla, and salt. Mix well.

2. Beat the egg whites until stiff and fold into batter.

3. Spray waffle iron with cooking spray.

4. Using a 4-ounce measuring cup, pour batter into waffle iron.

5. Bake about 2–3 minutes, or until light golden brown.

6. Top with fruit or your favorite topping.

Breakfast Crepes

Here's another recipe the kids can be hands-on with in the kitchen.
And it's a wonderful Sunday brunch item.

INGREDIENTS | SERVES 8

1 cup all-purpose flour
2 eggs
½ cup low-fat milk
½ cup water
¼ teaspoon salt
2 tablespoons margarine, melted
1–2 tablespoons canola oil

Fillings for Breakfast Crepes

Berries and yogurt: Fill crepes with low-fat flavored or vanilla yogurt and fresh berries. Roll crepes and dust with powdered sugar. Dessert Crepes: Using above batter, spread crepes with low-fat frozen yogurt and sliced bananas. Roll crepes and dust with powdered sugar. This batter is so adaptable and delicious that you may fill the crepes with just about any combination of foods. Just fill, roll, and enjoy.

1. In a large mixing bowl, mix together the flour and the eggs.

2. Gradually add in the milk and water, stirring until smooth.

3. Add the salt and melted margarine. Beat until smooth.

4. Lightly oil a skillet and heat over low heat.

5. Pour the batter into the skillet, using approximately ¼ cup for each crepe.

6. Tilt pan in a circular motion, so that the batter coats the surface evenly.

7. Cook the crepe for about 2 minutes, until the bottom is light brown.

8. Loosen with a spatula; turn and cook the other side.

9. Fill as desired and serve.

Basil Vegetable Frittata

Substitute other favorite vegetables for the mushrooms if you like. If you use peppers or onions, pan-sauté them quickly first to ensure they're cooked through.

INGREDIENTS | SERVES 6

8 eggs
¾ cup whole milk
½ cup seeded and chopped tomato
6 ounces button mushrooms, sliced
2 tablespoons chopped basil
½ teaspoon salt
½ teaspoon ground black pepper
½ cup grated Parmesan cheese
Chopped fresh parsley, for garnish

1. Preheat oven to 375°F.

2. Combine the eggs and milk in a large bowl and whisk until well blended. Add the tomatoes, mushrooms, basil, salt, and pepper and stir to combine.

3. Lightly butter a 9-inch square nonstick baking pan. Pour the egg mixture into the prepared pan and top with the Parmesan cheese. Bake for 20–22 minutes, or until lightly browned and eggs are set. Allow to rest for 1–2 minutes and serve hot, garnished with parsley.

Spicy Breakfast Wrap

Choose your own level of salsa! Mild or hot, this is a fun and unique portable breakfast!

INGREDIENTS | SERVES 1

1–2 eggs
1 whole wheat tortilla
3 tablespoons salsa

1. Spray a small skillet with nonstick cooking spray.

2. Scramble the eggs in the pan.

3. Lay tortilla flat and place scrambled eggs down the center. Top eggs with salsa. Roll tortilla up and serve.

Talk about Quick and Easy!

With the protein of eggs, the tomato salsa for kick (and even a little bit of vitamin C and antioxidants), the fiber of the wrap or tortilla, and a glass of milk, mornings do not get any better than this. It takes moments to prepare and just a few minutes to eat, but the children will have a nutritious breakfast, which will absolutely improve their performance on that school day!

Brie and Asparagus Open-Faced Omelet

The rind on the Brie is edible, but is usually trimmed off and discarded.
Slightly freeze the cheese to make slicing easier.

INGREDIENTS | SERVES 2

4 large eggs

2 tablespoons freshly grated Parmesan cheese

1 tablespoon butter

1 tablespoon sour cream

¼ teaspoon ground nutmeg

½ teaspoon seasoned salt

½ teaspoon freshly cracked black pepper

½ cup of 1½-inch pieces asparagus, cooked and cooled

2 ounces Brie cheese, sliced

Parsley sprigs, for garnish

Egg Storage

Fresh eggs in their shells will last 3 weeks. Raw yolks/raw whites will last 2–3 days, and hard-cooked eggs will last 1 week.

1. Preheat broiler to medium. Oil a baking sheet.

2. In a large bowl, beat the eggs and Parmesan cheese.

3. Melt the butter in a medium-sized nonstick skillet over medium-high heat. Pour in half of the egg mixture and cook, without stirring, until just set. Transfer the omelet to the prepared baking sheet. Repeat with the remaining egg mixture.

4. Combine the sour cream, nutmeg, seasoned salt, and pepper in a small bowl and set aside.

5. Arrange the asparagus pieces on top of each omelet and top with the sliced Brie. Broil for 1 minute, until the cheese melts.

6. Place omelets on serving plates and garnish with the parsley sprigs. Serve hot, with nutmeg sour cream on the side.

Egg, Cheese, and Italian Sausage Pie

If you don't have a pie pan, you can use a medium-sized ovenproof skillet.
Use hot sausage and pepper jack cheese for a spicy wake-up call.

INGREDIENTS | SERVES 4

1 tablespoon butter

8 ounces Italian sausage (mild or hot, or a mixture)

8 eggs, beaten

2 tablespoons chopped fresh parsley

Salt, to taste

Freshly ground black pepper, to taste

¾ cup grated Cheddar cheese

Put It to the Test

To tell if an egg is old or fresh, place the egg in a bowl of salted water. If it sinks, it's fresh. Older eggs will float, as the air cell inside the shell expands with age.

1. Preheat oven to 350°F. Lightly oil a 9-inch pie pan or glass baking dish.

2. Heat the butter in a medium-sized nonstick skillet over medium heat. Add the sausage and cook until fully browned, about 7 minutes. Let cool slightly.

3. Press the sausage into the pie pan, spreading it in an even layer over the bottom.

4. Whisk eggs in medium bowl. Pour the eggs over the sausage and sprinkle with parsley, salt, and pepper. Bake for 7–8 minutes, or until the eggs are almost set. Remove from oven.

5. Sprinkle the cheese over the top of the eggs and return to the oven until the eggs are done and the cheese is melted, about 6–7 minutes. Serve hot.

Breakfast Kebabs

These kebabs can be assembled in advance and held at room temperature before broiling.
You can also add small slices of precooked sausage if desired.

INGREDIENTS | SERVES 4

4 skewers
12 strips bacon (not thick-sliced)
2 ounces Gruyère cheese
16 cherry tomatoes
16 button mushrooms
1 tablespoon vegetable oil
1 teaspoon tomato paste
1 teaspoon Worcestershire sauce
1 teaspoon Dijon mustard
1 teaspoon soy sauce
¼ teaspoon garlic salt
Freshly cracked black pepper, to taste

Brunch Buffet Tip

Use hollowed-out, colorful bell peppers as bowls for sauces. You can also use unsliced bread loaves to serve sauces; rounds work best. Use a sharp knife to cut out the center, insert a bowl, and fill with the sauce.

1. Clean and oil broiler rack. Preheat broiler to medium-high. If using wooden skewers, soak in warm water for about 15–20 minutes before using.

2. Cut the bacon slices in half, widthwise. Cut the cheese into 24 small chunks and wrap a piece of bacon around each.

3. Thread the bacon rolls, tomatoes, and mushrooms alternately onto the skewers, starting and ending with a bacon roll.

4. Mix together all the remaining ingredients in a small bowl. Brush the mixture over the kebabs.

5. Broil for 5–7 minutes, turning frequently and brushing with any extra sauce. Serve hot.

Fresh Fruit Kebabs with Vanilla Yogurt Sauce

These are easy to prepare in advance. It is best to use only the freshest, ripest fruits available.

INGREDIENTS | SERVES 4

4 skewers

1 cup diced cantaloupe (1-inch dice)

1 cup diced pineapple (1-inch dice)

1 cup strawberries

1 cup blueberries

¾ cup vanilla whole-milk yogurt

¼ cup heavy cream

Sugar substitute equal to 2–4 tablespoons granulated sugar (to taste)

½ teaspoon vanilla extract

1. On each skewer thread a piece of cantaloupe, a piece of pineapple, a strawberry, and 2 blueberries.

2. Whisk together the yogurt, heavy cream, sugar substitute, and vanilla extract in a small bowl. Pour into a serving dish. Serve the kebabs with the dipping sauce on the side.

CHAPTER 3

Lunch and Snacks

Taco Salad

You can use Spicy Vegetarian Chili (see Chapter 9) in place of the beef mixture and refried bean mixture. Top the salad with chopped tomato and chunky salsa, sour cream, or more tortilla chips.

INGREDIENTS | SERVES 8

1 pound ground beef

1 (1-ounce) package taco seasoning mix

2 tablespoons vegetable oil

1 small onion, chopped

1 (16-ounce) can seasoned refried beans

2 (10-ounce) bags mixed salad greens

3 cups blue corn tortilla chips

2 cups shredded Colby cheese

Tortilla Chips

You can make your own tortilla chips. Choose flavored or plain corn or flour tortillas and cut them into wedges using a pizza cutter. Heat 2 cups of oil in a large pan over medium-high heat and fry the tortilla wedges until crisp. Drain on paper towels, sprinkle with salt and seasonings, and serve.

1. In a large skillet, cook ground beef with taco seasoning mix according to package directions. Pour ground beef mixture into a large bowl.

2. In the same skillet, heat oil over medium heat. Cook onion, stirring frequently, until tender, about 5–6 minutes. Stir in refried beans and cook for 3–4 minutes longer, until hot. Combine refried bean mixture with ground beef mixture and set aside.

3. Place salad greens on plates and top with tortilla chips.

4. Spoon beef mixture over tortilla chips and top with shredded cheese. Serve immediately.

Steak Quesadillas

Serve these spicy little Tex-Mex sandwiches with more salsa, chopped tomato, sour cream, and guacamole, along with some fresh fruit.

INGREDIENTS | SERVES 4–6

2 cups sliced cooked Spicy Grilled Flank Steak (see Chapter 7)

½ cup salsa

1 (4-ounce) can diced green chilies, drained

2 cups shredded pepper jack cheese

12 (10-inch) flour tortillas

Guacamole

To make your own guacamole, combine 2 mashed avocados with ¼ cup mayonnaise, 2 tablespoons fresh lemon or lime juice, ½ teaspoon salt, a dash of cayenne pepper, a dash of hot sauce, and 1 chopped tomato. Blend well and put into a small bowl. Press plastic wrap onto the surface and refrigerate for 2–4 hours before serving.

1. Slice steak across the grain and combine in medium bowl with salsa and green chilies.

2. Place 6 tortillas on work surface and divide steak mixture among them. Top with cheese and remaining tortillas.

3. Heat griddle or skillet over medium-high heat. Cook quesadillas, pressing down with spatula and turning once, until tortillas begin to brown and cheese melts, about 4–7 minutes. Cut into quarters and serve immediately.

Fast Chicken Fajitas

Deli chicken and coleslaw mix take a lot of prep work out of this recipe. Instead of deli chicken, you can use stir-fry chicken strips—stir-fry the chicken strips with the lime juice and paprika until they turn white and are nearly cooked through. If you like, top each fajita with shredded cheese before rolling it up.

INGREDIENTS | SERVES 6

1 tablespoon vegetable oil
½ teaspoon chili powder
1 cup cooked deli chicken, shredded
1 tablespoon lime juice
1 cup packaged coleslaw mix
½ teaspoon salt
1 tablespoon apple juice
½ cup canned black beans, drained
6 tortilla wraps

Fantastic Fajitas

Originally conceived of as a creative way to add extra flavor to a tough cut of beef, fajitas are now one of the most popular items on Mexican restaurant menus. Traditionally, fajitas are made with skirt steak. In this recipe the beef is replaced with chicken from the delicatessen.

1. Heat the vegetable oil in a skillet over medium-high heat. Stir in the chili powder. Add the deli chicken and cook for a minute, stirring to heat through. Stir in the lime juice while cooking the chicken.

2. Add the packaged coleslaw mix. Stir in the salt. Cook, stirring frequently, until the packaged coleslaw mix is heated through (1–2 minutes). Splash with the apple juice while cooking.

3. Stir in the black beans. Cook briefly, stirring to mix everything together.

4. Lay a tortilla wrap in front of you. Spoon one-sixth of the chicken and bean mixture in the center of the tortilla wrap, taking care not to come too close to the edges. Fold in the left and right sides and roll up the wrap. Repeat with the remainder of the tortillas. Serve immediately.

Easy Enchiladas

Preparing enchiladas in the microwave instead of baking them in the oven substantially reduces the cooking time. To speed things up even further, use leftover cooked ground beef and reheat in the microwave.

INGREDIENTS | SERVES 4

1 cup ground beef
¼ teaspoon ground cumin
¼ teaspoon salt, or to taste
⅛ teaspoon black pepper, or to taste
8 corn tortillas
2 cups store-bought enchilada sauce
1 cup shredded Cheddar cheese

1. In a bowl, season the ground beef with the cumin, salt, and pepper, using your fingers to mix it in. Let the ground beef stand while you are preparing the tortillas and sauce.

2. Place the corn tortillas on a microwave-safe plate. Microwave on high heat for 30 seconds, and then for 10 seconds at a time until the tortillas look slightly dried out and are cooked. Dip each of the tortillas into the enchilada sauce, letting the excess sauce drip off.

3. Place the ground beef into a 1-quart microwave-safe casserole dish, using your fingers to crumble it in. Microwave on high heat for 2 minutes. Stir and cook for another 2–3 minutes, until the ground beef is cooked through. Remove from the microwave and drain off the fat. Stir in ½ cup leftover enchilada sauce and cook for another minute.

4. Lay a tortilla flat and spoon a portion of the meat and sauce mixture in the lower half of the tortilla. Roll up the tortilla and place in a shallow, microwave-safe 9" × 13" baking dish. Continue with the remainder of the tortillas. Spoon any leftover enchilada sauce on top. Sprinkle with the cheese.

5. Microwave on high heat for 5 minutes, or until the cheese is melted and everything is cooked through. Let stand for 5 minutes before serving.

Chicken Fried Rice

If you don't have leftover cooked chicken and rice, you can get some cooked chicken from your local deli and purchase cooked rice from any Chinese takeout place.

INGREDIENTS | SERVES 4

2 cooked Herbed Chicken Breasts (see Chapter 6)

2 tablespoons olive oil

2 cups cooked Jasmati rice

1 cup frozen sugar snap peas, thawed and drained

⅓ cup apricot jam

2 tablespoons soy sauce

¼ cup water

1. Remove cooked meat from chicken; discard skin and bones. Cut chicken into 1-inch pieces.

2. Heat olive oil in wok or heavy skillet. Add chicken and rice; stir-fry for 4–5 minutes until heated, stirring gently to separate rice grains.

3. Add peas, jam, soy sauce, and water and stir-fry for 4–5 minutes longer, until peas are hot and flavors are blended. Serve immediately.

Turkey Pizza

Pizza is fun to make at home. Use your family's favorite foods and flavors to create your own specialty. This one is a variation of the classic ham and pineapple pizza.

INGREDIENTS | SERVES 4

1 (12- or 14-inch) Boboli pizza crust

1 cup pizza sauce

4 cooked turkey cutlets

1 (8-ounce) can pineapple tidbits, drained

1½ cups shredded Swiss cheese

Pizza Crusts

There are lots of places to buy pizza crust. The deli department at your local grocery store has Boboli pizza crusts, focaccia, thin prebaked pizza crusts, and refrigerated pizza dough. You can even buy pizza dough from your local pizza parlor; roll it out, bake for a few minutes at 400°F, and then freeze for later use.

1. Preheat oven to 400°F. Place pizza crust on a large cookie sheet and spread with pizza sauce. Cut turkey cutlets into thin strips and arrange on pizza sauce along with well-drained pineapple tidbits. Sprinkle with cheese.

2. Bake pizza for 15–20 minutes, or until pizza is hot and cheese is melted and beginning to brown. Let stand for 5 minutes, and then serve.

Spicy Veggie Pizza

Boboli pizza crusts are available in any deli, and you can usually find plain pizza crusts there too. This easy pizza is delicious served with some deli fruit salad and cold milk.

INGREDIENTS | SERVES 4

2 cups marinated deli vegetables

1 (12- or 14-inch) Boboli pizza crust

1 (10-ounce) container garlic and herb cream cheese

1 cup shredded provolone cheese

½ cup grated Parmesan cheese

Make Your Own Pizza Crust

Make your own crust by combining 2 cups flour, 1 cup cornmeal, 3 tablespoons oil, 1 (0.75-ounce) package yeast, and 1⅓ cups water in a bowl. Knead thoroughly, let rise, punch down, divide in half, and roll out. Prebake the crust at 400°F for 8–10 minutes; then cool, wrap well, and freeze until ready to use.

1. Preheat oven to 400°F. Chop the marinated vegetables into smaller pieces and place in saucepan with the marinade. Bring to a simmer over medium heat; simmer for 3–4 minutes, until vegetables are tender. Drain thoroughly.

2. Place pizza crust on a cookie sheet and spread with the cream cheese. Arrange drained vegetables on top and sprinkle with provolone and Parmesan cheeses. Bake for 15–18 minutes, until crust is hot and crisp and cheese is melted and begins to brown.

Roast Beef Calzones

Calzones are a baked Italian sandwich, usually made with pizza dough.
This version, made with pie crusts, is more delicate and flaky.

INGREDIENTS | SERVES 6

1 (14-ounce) package refrigerated pie crusts

1 (7-ounce) can artichoke hearts, drained

2 cups chopped deli roast beef

1½ cups diced Swiss cheese

⅓ cup sour cream

1. Preheat oven to 400°F. Let pie crusts stand at room temperature while preparing filling.

2. Drain artichoke hearts, place on paper towels to drain further, and then cut into smaller pieces. In medium bowl, combine artichoke hearts, chopped beef, cheese, and sour cream and mix gently.

3. Place pie crusts on cookie sheet, placing the edges in the center of the cookie sheet, about 1 inch apart, and letting the excess hang beyond the cookie sheet. Divide filling between pie crusts, placing on one half of each crust and leaving a 1-inch border. Fold the unfilled half of the pie crust (the part hanging beyond the cookie sheet) over the filling to form a half-moon shape. Press edges with a fork to firmly seal. Cut decorative shapes out of the top of each crust. Discard excess crust.

4. Bake for 18–24 minutes, until crust is golden brown and crisp and filling is hot. Let stand for 5 minutes, and then cut into wedges to serve.

Asian Beef Rolls

*This cold entrée wraps tender roast beef around crunchy
coleslaw mix seasoned with Asian ingredients. Yum!*

INGREDIENTS | SERVES 6

3 tablespoons hoisin sauce
¼ cup plum sauce
1½ cups coleslaw mix
¼ cup chopped green onion
6 slices cooked deli roast beef

Menu Suggestion

These spicy and crunchy rolls are delicious
paired with cold pea soup and Pumpkin
Bread (see Chapter 2) for lunch on the
porch on a hot summer day.

1. In medium bowl, combine hoisin sauce and plum sauce and mix well. Stir in coleslaw mix and green onion and mix gently.

2. Place roast beef slices on work surface and divide coleslaw mixture among them. Roll up beef slices, enclosing filling. Serve immediately, or cover and refrigerate up to 8 hours before serving.

Hummus

*Roasting garlic usually takes about 35–40 minutes in a hot oven. But you can sauté the cloves in oil
on the stovetop for just about 10 minutes. The cloves will become sweet and nutty-tasting.*

INGREDIENTS | YIELDS 2 CUPS

4 cloves garlic
2 tablespoons olive oil
1 (15-ounce) can garbanzo beans,
drained
¼ cup tahini
2 tablespoons lemon juice
¼ cup sour cream
½ teaspoon salt
⅛ teaspoon crushed red pepper flakes

About Tahini

True hummus is made with tahini, which is a
peanut butter–like paste made of ground
sesame seeds. It adds a rich flavor and
smooth, creamy texture to any recipe. You
can make hummus without it, but do try it
with tahini at least once.

1. Peel garlic cloves but leave whole. Place in a small heavy skillet along with olive oil over medium heat. Cook the garlic until it turns light brown, stirring frequently, for about 5–8 minutes; watch carefully. Remove from heat and let cool for 10 minutes.

2. Combine the garlic and oil with all remaining ingredients in a blender or food processor and blend or process until smooth. Spread on serving plate, drizzle with a bit more olive oil, and serve immediately with pita chips.

Crab Cakes

Crab cakes are a wonderful light lunch. These little cakes are creamy and crunchy.
Serve them with more of the Dijon mustard/mayonnaise combo, and a few lemon wedges on the side.

INGREDIENTS | SERVES 8

1 egg

3 tablespoons Dijon mustard and mayonnaise combination (1½ tablespoons mustard and 1½ tablespoons mayonnaise mixed, or adjust proportions to taste)

½ teaspoon salt

½ teaspoon Old Bay seasoning

⅛ teaspoon white pepper

8 round buttery crackers, crushed

1 pound lump crabmeat, picked over

4 tablespoons olive oil

Using Canned Crabmeat

You can substitute canned crabmeat for the lump crabmeat. Two 8-ounce cans, well drained, will equal about a pound of lump crabmeat. Taste a bit of the crabmeat; if it tastes salty, rinse it briefly under cold water and drain well again before using in the recipe.

1. In medium bowl, combine egg, mustard/mayonnaise combo, salt, Old Bay seasoning, pepper, and cracker crumbs; mix well. Let stand for 5 minutes.

2. Meanwhile, carefully pick over the crabmeat, removing any cartilage or bits of shell. Add crabmeat to cracker-crumb mixture and mix gently but thoroughly.

3. Using a ¼-cup measure, scoop out some crab mixture and press into a small cake on waxed paper. When crab cakes are all formed, place in freezer for 5 minutes.

4. Heat olive oil in nonstick skillet and sauté crab cakes, turning once, until they are golden brown, about 3–4 minutes per side. Serve immediately.

Southwest Potato Salad

If you like your food extra spicy, use more chili powder or add more jalapeño peppers.
If you're really brave, try habanero peppers!

INGREDIENTS | SERVES 8

1 quart deli potato salad

1 tablespoon chili powder

2 red bell peppers, chopped

1 pint cherry or grape tomatoes

1 jalapeño pepper, minced

2 cups canned corn, drained

Place potato salad in serving bowl and sprinkle evenly with chili powder. Add remaining ingredients and gently stir to mix thoroughly. Serve immediately, or cover and chill for 1–2 hours to blend flavors.

Dress Up Potato Salad

It's easy to dress up plain potato salad. To make a curried potato salad, mix curry powder with chutney and stir into potato salad along with sliced green onions and sliced celery. For an all-American potato salad, add grape tomatoes, some chopped dill pickles, and some yellow mustard.

Shrimp-Filled Avocados

For a more attractive presentation, sprinkle a bit of extra lime juice on the avocados to prevent discoloration, and serve the shrimp-stuffed avocados on a bed of lettuce leaves.

INGREDIENTS | SERVES 4

2 cups cooked shrimp

1 cup drained pineapple bits

2 tablespoons reserved pineapple juice

1 tablespoon lime juice

2 tablespoons natural plain yogurt

2 green onions, finely chopped

½ teaspoon crushed red pepper, or to taste

Salt, to taste

4 avocados, peeled

1. In a large bowl, combine the shrimp, pineapple, reserved pineapple juice, lime juice, yogurt, green onions, crushed red pepper, and salt. Stir to mix well.

2. Cut the avocados in half lengthwise, removing the pit in the middle.

3. Fill the avocados with the shrimp mixture and serve.

Amazing Avocados

Its buttery flesh leads many people to mistake the avocado for a vegetable, but it is actually a type of fruit. Avocado leads all other fruits in protein content, and is a good source of vitamin E. An avocado filled with shellfish, or cottage or ricotta cheese, makes a quick and healthy midday meal. Just don't get carried away—a single avocado has more than 300 calories.

Greek Pita Pockets with Tzatziki

A popular Greek dip, tzatziki also makes a satisfying sandwich filling.
To turn this recipe into an appetizer, simply cut each pita round into eight equal
wedges and bake at 250°F until crisp. Spread the dip on the pita wedges.

INGREDIENTS | SERVES 8

1 English cucumber
1½ teaspoons virgin olive oil
1½ teaspoons lemon juice
1 cup plain low-fat yogurt
2 tablespoons chopped red onion
½ teaspoon garlic salt
Freshly ground black pepper, to taste
8 pita wraps

Choosing Olive Oil

Virgin olive oils are the best choice in recipes where the dressing isn't being heated, such as in this recipe. Either the virgin or extra-virgin variety of olive oil can be used, although extra-virgin olive oil has less acidity and a better flavor. Pure olive oil (also simply called olive oil) has a higher smoke point than virgin oils—use it in stir-fries or whenever the oil is going to be heated.

1. Peel and grate the cucumber until you have ½ cup. Thinly slice the remainder of the cucumber and set aside.

2. In a small bowl, stir the olive oil and lemon juice into the yogurt. Stir in the chopped red onion, garlic salt, grated cucumber. Taste and season with pepper.

3. Lay out a pita wrap in front of you. Spread up to 2 tablespoons tzatziki over the inside of the wrap. Lay a few cucumber slices on top and roll up the wrap.

4. Continue with the remainder of the pita wraps.

Easy Skillet Zucchini Quiche

Removing the crust from a standard quiche recipe substantially reduces the time it takes to make. On days when you do have a bit more time, feel free to bake the quiche instead of broiling it—after combining the ingredients in the bowl, bake at 325°F for 30 minutes, or until the quiche has set.

INGREDIENTS | SERVES 4

4 eggs
½ teaspoon salt, or to taste
Black pepper, to taste
¼ teaspoon dried oregano, or to taste
1 teaspoon onion powder
2 ounces canned sliced mushrooms
1 tomato, diced
½ cup grated Swiss cheese
¼ cup grated mild Cheddar cheese
1 tablespoon margarine
1½ cups chopped zucchini, fresh or frozen

1. Preheat the broiler.

2. In a medium bowl, lightly beat the eggs with the salt, pepper, dried oregano, and onion powder. Stir in the mushrooms, tomato, and cheeses.

3. Melt the margarine in a heavy skillet over medium heat. Add the chopped zucchini and sauté for 2–3 minutes, until the zucchini turns dark green.

4. Pour the egg and cheese mixture into the skillet, stirring to mix it in with the zucchini. Cook for 7–8 minutes, until the cheese is melted and the quiche is cooked through but still moist on top.

5. Place the skillet under the broiler. Cook until the top has set but has not yet browned. Serve immediately.

Indonesian-Style Potato Salad

The Indonesian version of potato salad, gado gado salad, is a popular restaurant dish.
This simplified version is perfect for busy weekdays during the summer months.

INGREDIENTS | SERVES 3

½ cup coconut milk

½ cup peanut butter

2 tablespoons lime juice

1 tablespoon soy sauce

1 tablespoon fish sauce

1 garlic clove, minced

½ teaspoon red pepper flakes, or to taste

2 leftover cooked potatoes, cut into chunks

3½ cups packaged salad greens

3 leftover hard-boiled eggs, peeled and sliced

1. In a small saucepan, heat the coconut milk. Stir in the peanut butter, lime juice, soy sauce, fish sauce, garlic, and red pepper flakes.

2. Heat, stirring occasionally, until the peanut butter is melted and the ingredients combine.

3. While the sauce is heating, assemble the salad ingredients on a large serving platter, with the potatoes on the outside, the greens on the inside, and the hard-boiled eggs on top.

4. Pour the peanut sauce over the salad. Serve immediately.

Make-Ahead Gado Gado Salad

If you're planning to prepare a potato salad for a picnic or other outdoor gathering, you may want to do as much work as possible ahead of time. In the case of this salad, the hard-boiled eggs can be prepared up to 5 days ahead of time, while the peanut sauce can be made up to 3 days ahead of time. Shell the eggs, assemble the salad, and garnish with the peanut sauce just before serving (thin the sauce with a bit of water if needed).

Veggie-Loaded Salad Rolls

Feel free to use Asian rice paper wrappers instead of tortilla wrappers to make the salad rolls if desired. Thai basil leaves can be found in the produce section of many supermarkets, or you can use regular basil.

INGREDIENTS | SERVES 8

⅓ cup soy sauce

1 tablespoon white vinegar

1 tablespoon granulated sugar

1 teaspoon bottled minced garlic

1 tablespoon bottled chopped jalapeño peppers

1½ cups packaged salad greens

1 cup cooked shrimp

¼ cup chopped fresh Thai basil leaves

8 vegetable-flavored tortilla wrappers

1. In a small bowl, stir together the soy sauce, vinegar, sugar, garlic, and jalapeño peppers.

2. In a separate bowl, stir together the salad greens, cooked shrimp, and basil leaves.

3. Lay a tortilla wrapper on a cutting board in front of you. Place about ¼ cup of the shrimp and salad mix on the bottom half of the wrapper, being careful not to come too close to the edges.

4. Roll up the wrapper like a taco, tucking in the sides. Continue filling and rolling up the remainder of the wrappers.

5. Serve the rolls cold with the soy dipping sauce.

No-Cook Spring Rolls

These rolls are incredibly easy to make—the secret is rice paper wrappers, which only need to be briefly dipped in warm water before using. You'll find them in the refrigerated section of many local supermarkets.

INGREDIENTS | SERVES 8

8 rice paper wrappers
2 cups packaged coleslaw mix
¼ cup hoisin sauce
1 teaspoon lime juice
1½ tablespoons water
⅛ teaspoon garlic powder, or to taste
¼ teaspoon red pepper flakes, or to taste
1 tablespoon chopped peanuts

Substitutes for Rice Paper Wrappers

The beauty of rice paper wrappers is that once the wrapper is softened in water, it can be filled and served without any further cooking. While spring roll wrappers or even phyllo dough can be used as a substitute for rice paper wrappers, the rolls will then need to be fried after they are filled. If you're looking for a quick and easy no-cook substitute for rice paper wrappers, one option is to use a tortilla wrapper—try using one of the flavored wraps, such as spinach or roasted red pepper.

1. Carefully dip each rice paper wrapper in a small bowl filled with warm water to moisten (about 20 seconds).

2. Lay the wrapper on a cutting board in front of you. Place about ¼ cup of the packaged coleslaw mix on the bottom half of the wrapper, being careful not to come too close to the edges.

3. Roll up the wrapper like a taco, tucking in the sides. Continue filling and rolling up the remainder of the rice paper wrappers.

4. In a small bowl, stir together the hoisin sauce, lime juice, water, garlic powder, and red pepper flakes. Garnish the dip with the chopped peanuts.

5. Serve the rolls cold with the hoisin dip.

Basic Guacamole

Salsa takes the work out of dicing tomatoes, while bottled jalapeño peppers replace fresh chili peppers in this simple guacamole recipe. If you wish, you can increase the heat by mixing in 1 teaspoon of chili powder.

INGREDIENTS | SERVES 4

3 avocados
⅔ cup salsa
1 tablespoon bottled chopped jalapeño peppers
2 tablespoons finely chopped cilantro, or to taste
1 tablespoon lemon juice
1 (6-ounce) bag tortilla chips

1. Peel the avocados. With a knife, cut the avocados in half and remove the round pit in the middle. Place the pitted avocados in a medium bowl and mash with a fork or potato masher.

2. In a medium bowl, stir together the remaining ingredients except for the chips. Add the mashed avocado, stirring to mix it in. If the guacamole is too chunky, mash a bit more.

3. Serve the guacamole with tortilla chips.

Peanut Butter and Banana Wrap

Prepare this quick and easy wrap first thing in the morning. If prepared the night before, it is going to be soggy!

INGREDIENTS | SERVES 1

1 whole wheat wrap
2 tablespoons peanut butter
2 teaspoons honey
Small ripe banana

A High-Energy Way to Start the Day

A whole wheat wrap, peanut butter, and banana hits all of those necessary groups of food first thing in the morning. Those first few classes of the day will have students' ultimate concentration! Whole wheat bread or a whole wheat roll can always be interchanged with the wrap.

1. Spread peanut butter and honey onto wrap.

2. Mash banana. Spread onto wrap.

3. Pull up one side of the wrap about ⅓ of the way and fold over.

4. Wrap both sides in, and close the top. Serve immediately.

Soft Tacos with Spicy Chicken Breast

Chopping the vegetables is what takes time for this recipe.
Use precut veggies from the salad bar where possible as a timesaver.

INGREDIENTS | SERVES 2

2 (6-ounce) skinless, boneless chicken breast halves

¼ teaspoon garlic salt, or to taste

¼ teaspoon cayenne pepper, or to taste

1 tablespoon vegetable oil

¾ cup salsa, divided

1 tablespoon chopped cilantro, plus extra for garnish

2 (8-inch) tortillas

¼ cup shredded pepper jack cheese

¼ cup seeded and diced tomato

½ cup shredded romaine lettuce leaves

⅓ cup diced avocado

¼ cup sour cream

How Much Spice Is Spicy?

The definition of spicy is a very personal preference. When preparing and serving spicy dishes, it's best to prepare the dish at a moderate spiciness and serve salsas and hot sauces on the side.

1. Rinse the chicken under cold, running water and pat dry with paper towels. Cut the chicken across the grain into ½-inch strips. Season with garlic salt and cayenne.

2. Heat the oil in a medium-sized nonstick skillet over medium-high heat. Cook the chicken until almost done, about 5 minutes, stirring frequently. Add ¼ cup of the salsa and stir to combine. Bring to a simmer and finish cooking the chicken, about 2–3 minutes. Remove from heat and stir in the cilantro.

3. To serve, place each tortilla on a serving plate. Equally divide the chicken between the tortillas. Top with equal amounts of cheese, tomato, lettuce, and avocado. Serve the remaining salsa and the sour cream on the side. Garnish with cilantro leaves.

CHAPTER 4

Sandwiches and Salads

Chicken Tortellini Salad

Most delis have a selection of prepared salads. Serve this gorgeous salad on some baby spinach leaves along with iced tea and bakery breadsticks.

INGREDIENTS | SERVES 4–6

1 quart deli tortellini salad
2 cups chopped deli chicken
1 red bell pepper, chopped
1 cup cubed Havarti cheese
½ cup mayonnaise

In large bowl, combine all ingredients and toss gently to coat. Serve immediately, or cover and refrigerate up to 24 hours.

Salad Inspirations

Take some time to browse through your supermarket to find ideas for salads. In the produce section you'll find salad kits and lots of refrigerated dressings to inspire you. Many companies make salad kits that are placed in the meat aisle, and some are in the grocery aisle near the bottled salad dressings.

Monte Cristo Sandwiches

Find fish batter mix near the fish in the supermarket's meat aisle. It makes a wonderful crispy coating on these delicious sandwiches.

INGREDIENTS | SERVES 4

¼ pound thinly sliced deli ham
¼ pound thinly sliced deli turkey
¼ pound thinly sliced deli Colby cheese
8 slices whole grain bread
1 cup fish batter mix
⅓ cup oil

1. Make sandwiches using ham, turkey, cheese, and bread. In shallow bowl, prepare batter mix as directed on package.

2. Pour oil into heavy skillet and heat over medium heat until a drop of water sizzles and evaporates. Dip sandwiches into batter mixture and immediately place in oil in skillet. Cook over medium heat, turning once, until bread is golden brown and cheese is melted, about 3–5 minutes per side.

3. Cut sandwiches in half and serve immediately.

Monte Cristo Sandwich Dips

Serve these dips with Monte Cristo Sandwiches or any grilled sandwich. For a sweet dip, combine ½ cup sour cream with ¼ cup raspberry jam and mix well. For a spicy dip, combine ½ cup mayonnaise with 2 tablespoons honey Dijon mustard and a teaspoon of chili sauce and blend well.

Tuna Melts

Tartar sauce is made of mayonnaise, pickles, and seasonings. It is delicious paired with mild canned tuna and Swiss cheese in these quick and easy sandwiches.

INGREDIENTS | SERVES 4

4 pita breads, unsplit

4 slices Swiss cheese

1 avocado

1 (6-ounce) can tuna, drained

½ cup tartar sauce

¾ cup shredded Swiss cheese, divided

½ teaspoon dried dill weed

Sandwich Melts

Melts are open-faced sandwiches, or sandwiches without a "lid," that are usually grilled, baked, or broiled to heat the filling and melt the cheese. Serve them with a knife and fork, and with a simple fruit salad or green salad for a hearty, quick lunch or dinner.

1. Preheat oven to 400°F. Toast pita breads in oven until crisp, about 5 minutes. Remove from oven and top each one with a slice of Swiss cheese.

2. Peel avocado and mash slightly, leaving some chunks. Spread this on top of the Swiss cheese. In small bowl, combine tuna and tartar sauce with ¼ cup shredded Swiss cheese. Spread on top of avocado.

3. Sprinkle sandwiches with remaining shredded Swiss cheese and the dill weed. Bake for 7–11 minutes, until cheese melts. Serve immediately.

Bacon Crisp Sandwiches

This unusual way of cooking bacon makes these sandwiches simply superb. Be sure the tomatoes are ripe and juicy for best results. You could also add some fresh lettuce leaves or baby spinach.

INGREDIENTS | SERVES 4

8 slices bacon
¾ cup grated Parmesan cheese, divided
½ teaspoon dried thyme leaves
¼ cup mayonnaise
4 hoagie buns, sliced
2 tomatoes, thickly sliced

1. Dip bacon slices in ½ cup Parmesan cheese and press to coat. Place 4 slices of the coated bacon on microwave-safe paper towels in a 12" × 8" microwave-safe baking dish. Cover with another sheet of microwave-safe paper towels. Microwave on high for 3–4 minutes or until bacon is light golden brown. Repeat with remaining bacon slices.

2. Meanwhile, in a small bowl, combine thyme, mayonnaise, and remaining ¼ cup Parmesan cheese and spread on cut sides of hoagie buns. Toast in toaster oven or under broiler until cheese mixture bubbles.

3. Make sandwiches with the cooked bacon, tomatoes, and toasted buns and serve immediately.

Instant Mashed Potato Salad

For a more tart flavor, feel free to increase the amount of white wine vinegar to 1 tablespoon.

INGREDIENTS | SERVES 4

4 cups boiling water
8 ounces instant flavored mashed potatoes
⅔ cup mayonnaise
3 tablespoons sour cream
2 teaspoons white wine vinegar
1 teaspoon dried dill
4 hard-boiled eggs, peeled, chopped
2 ribs celery, thinly sliced

1. Pour the boiling water into a large bowl. Add the instant flavored mashed potatoes, stirring with a fork to make sure they are completely covered. Cover and let sit for 5 minutes while preparing the mayonnaise dressing.

2. In a medium bowl, stir together the mayonnaise, sour cream, white wine vinegar, and dried dill.

3. In a large salad bowl, combine the mashed potatoes with the mayonnaise dressing, chopped eggs, and celery.

4. Chill until ready to serve.

Classic Greek Salad

For an extra touch, cut a garlic clove in half and rub it over the salad bowl.
You can use Greek oregano if it is available.

INGREDIENTS | SERVES 4

4 romaine lettuce leaves, washed, drained, and torn

½ red onion, peeled, cut into thin rings

12 cherry tomatoes, cut in half

1 English cucumber, thinly sliced

1 green bell pepper, seeded, cut into chunks

3 tablespoons extra-virgin olive oil

2 tablespoons red wine vinegar

1 teaspoon granulated sugar

¼ teaspoon black pepper

½ teaspoon sea salt

½ teaspoon bottled minced garlic

¼ teaspoon dried oregano, or to taste

1 cup crumbled feta cheese

12 whole olives, chopped and pitted

1. In a large salad bowl, combine the lettuce, red onion, tomatoes, cucumber, and bell pepper.

2. In a small bowl, whisk together the olive oil, red wine vinegar, sugar, pepper, sea salt, garlic, and oregano.

3. Drizzle the olive oil dressing over the salad.

4. Sprinkle the crumbled feta on top.

5. Add the olives. Serve immediately.

Greek Salad

A staple on Greek restaurant menus around the world, traditional Greek salad (horiatiki) is made with tomatoes, cucumbers, Greek oregano, and an olive oil dressing. Although they are popular additions, feta cheese and plump kalamata olives are optional.

Tropical Fruit Salad with Pecans

A rich source of vitamin C and several B vitamins, papayas are available year-round in many supermarkets. Canned lychees can be found in the canned fruit section, or at ethnic supermarkets.

INGREDIENTS | SERVES 4

2 papayas

¼ cup tropical fruit punch

1 teaspoon granulated sugar

1 cup drained canned pineapple chunks

1 cup drained canned lychees

2 bananas, peeled, thinly sliced

½ cup pecan pieces

How to Pick a Papaya

When choosing a papaya, look for one that is neither too firm nor too soft, but yields to gentle pressure. The skin should be smooth and firm, and the color mainly yellow. Avoid papayas that have a wrinkled skin or a strong smell.

1. Cut the papayas in half and use a spoon to remove the seeds. Remove the peel from each half of the papaya with a paring knife. Lay the papayas flat, scooped side downward, and cut crosswise into thin strips.

2. In a small bowl, stir together the fruit punch and sugar.

3. Combine the fruit in a large salad bowl.

4. Sprinkle the juice and sugar mixture over the top and toss gently. Garnish with the pecans.

5. Serve immediately, or cover and chill until ready to serve.

Mandarin Orange Salad

The sweet taste of mandarin oranges adds something extra to a plain cottage cheese salad. For a special touch, top the salad with walnut halves or candied (sugared) walnuts.

INGREDIENTS | SERVES 4

¼ teaspoon black pepper

¼ teaspoon salt

1 cup low-fat cottage cheese

¼ cup reserved mandarin orange juice

1 teaspoon granulated sugar

1 head romaine lettuce leaves, washed, drained, torn

2 green onions, finely chopped

½ medium red onion, peeled and chopped

2 (10-ounce) cans mandarin oranges, drained

1. In a medium bowl, stir the pepper and salt into the cottage cheese. Stir in the mandarin orange juice and sugar.

2. Put the torn romaine lettuce leaves in a salad bowl. Toss with the onions.

3. Add the cottage cheese and the mandarin oranges on top.

4. Serve immediately, or chill until ready to serve.

Make-Ahead Salads

Many of the vegetables found in a typical salad, including lettuce, can be prepared ahead of time. Wrap the cut vegetables in paper towels and store in a resealable plastic bag in the crisper section of your refrigerator until ready to use.

Chicken and Strawberry Salad

A simple yogurt dressing jazzes up this salad made with fresh strawberries and leftover chicken.

INGREDIENTS | SERVES 4

2 leftover cooked chicken breasts
1¼ teaspoons Dijon mustard
½ teaspoon salt
⅛ teaspoon black pepper
1 cup vanilla yogurt
1 pint strawberries, washed, hulled
4 cups packaged salad greens

1. Cut the chicken breasts into thin strips.

2. In a medium bowl, stir the mustard, salt, and pepper into the yogurt.

3. Stir in the chicken and strawberries.

4. Arrange the greens in a salad bowl. Spoon the yogurt, fruit, and chicken mixture over the greens.

5. Serve the salad immediately, or cover and chill until ready to serve.

Delicious Dijon Mustard

Originating in the Dijon region in southeastern France, Dijon mustard gets its sharp taste from brown or black mustard seeds. Although mustard has been cultivated in France since ancient times, Dijon mustard was invented in the mid-1800s by Jean Naigeon, who came up with the idea of replacing the vinegar used to make mustard with verjuice, the sour juice from unripe grapes. Today, Dijon-style mustard is produced throughout the world.

Asian Chicken Noodle Salad

This is a California classic—chow mein noodles, mandarin oranges, and salad vegetables, all topped with a tart vinegar and sesame oil dressing.

INGREDIENTS | SERVES 4

1 pound cooked chicken breast meat

3 tablespoons red wine vinegar

1 tablespoon olive oil

2 tablespoons soy sauce

2 tablespoons Asian sesame oil

1 teaspoon granulated sugar

1 head romaine lettuce, washed, drained, torn

4 green onions, finely chopped

1 (11-ounce) can mandarin oranges, drained

1 cup chow mein noodles

1. Cut the chicken into thin strips.

2. In a small bowl, whisk the red wine vinegar, olive oil, soy sauce, sesame oil, and sugar.

3. Place the salad dressing in the bottom of a large salad bowl. Stir in the romaine lettuce, green onions, and chicken strips.

4. Add the mandarin oranges and the chow mein noodles on top. Serve immediately.

Salad Basics

Always make sure lettuce is drained thoroughly—wet, soggy lettuce can affect the salad's flavor. Shred the lettuce leaves instead of cutting them with a knife. Unless the recipe states otherwise, if preparing a salad ahead of time, add the dressing just before serving. Toss the salad gently with the dressing, taking care not to overstir.

Basic Spinach Salad

*Using low-fat yogurt provides a light alternative to mayonnaise in this easy recipe.
Both the salad and the dressing can be prepared ahead of time and refrigerated,
but don't toss the salad with the dressing until you're ready to serve.*

INGREDIENTS | SERVES 6

4 cups packed fresh spinach leaves

¾ cup plain low-fat yogurt

1 teaspoon Dijon mustard

1 teaspoon dried dill

½ teaspoon salt

⅛ teaspoon black pepper, or to taste

1 cup sliced fresh mushrooms

2 Roasted Red Peppers (see Chapter 10), chopped

½ cup bacon bits

1. Wash the spinach leaves and drain in a colander or salad spinner.

2. In a medium bowl, stir together the yogurt, mustard, dill, salt, and pepper.

3. Combine the spinach leaves, mushrooms, chopped peppers, and bacon bits in a salad bowl.

4. Toss the vegetables with the yogurt dressing. Serve.

Caesar Turkey Salad

*Ground turkey turns a standard Caesar salad into a high-protein meal.
To increase the health benefits, replace the bacon bits with chopped nuts.*

INGREDIENTS | SERVES 3

2 cups ground turkey

¼ teaspoon salt

¼ teaspoon black pepper

1 teaspoon bottled minced garlic

1 head romaine lettuce, washed, drained, torn

2 cups croutons

⅓ cup bacon bits

¾ cup Caesar salad dressing

¼ cup Parmesan cheese

1. Brown the turkey in a skillet over medium-high heat.

2. Sprinkle the salt and pepper over the turkey. Stir in the minced garlic.

3. Continue cooking the turkey until it is cooked through and there is no pinkness (about 10 minutes).

4. While the turkey is cooking, in a salad bowl combine the romaine lettuce leaves, croutons, and bacon bits.

5. Drain the turkey and add it to the salad. Toss the salad with the Caesar dressing. Sprinkle the cheese on top and serve.

Three-Bean Salad

You can dress up this salad by serving it on a bed of romaine lettuce leaves.

INGREDIENTS | SERVES 6

¼ cup olive oil

⅓ cup white wine vinegar

1 teaspoon Dijon mustard

½ teaspoon salt, or to taste

⅛ teaspoon black pepper, or to taste

1 teaspoon minced onion

2 cups drained, rinsed canned green beans

1 (15-ounce) can kidney beans, drained, rinsed

1 (15-ounce) can yellow beans, drained, rinsed

1. In a small bowl, whisk together the olive oil, white wine vinegar, Dijon mustard, salt, pepper, and minced onion.

2. Place all the beans in a salad bowl and toss gently with the dressing.

3. Serve the salad immediately, or cover and chill until ready to serve.

Bean Salad Basics

Beans are an excellent choice for salads, as they easily absorb the dressing. When using canned beans, always drain and rinse them to remove any "tinny" taste. Rinsing the beans also removes excess sodium.

Colorful Pasta Salad

Fusilli vegetable pasta adds color and flavor to this simple salad.
To speed up the preparation time even further, use leftover cooked pasta.

INGREDIENTS | SERVES 4

Water to cook pasta, as needed

3 cups fusilli vegetable pasta

½ cup low-fat mayonnaise

½ cup plain yogurt

1 tablespoon Dijon honey mustard

1 cup green seedless grapes

1. Bring a large saucepan with the water to a boil. Cook the pasta according to the package directions, or until it is tender but still firm. Drain and allow to cool.

2. In a medium mixing bowl, stir together the mayonnaise, yogurt, and honey mustard.

3. Put the cooked pasta and grapes in a large salad bowl.

4. Toss gently with the yogurt and mayonnaise dressing. Serve.

Spicy Mexican Potato Salad

This quick and easy potato salad is perfect for a romantic picnic for two.
Feel free to adjust the amount of jalapeño peppers according to your own taste.

INGREDIENTS | SERVES 2

2 medium red potatoes

½ medium tomato, seeded and chopped

½ red onion, chopped

½ cup drained canned Mexican-style corn

1 tablespoon bottled chopped jalapeño peppers

¼ cup Orange-Cilantro Marinade (see Orange-Cilantro Chicken in Chapter 6)

What Makes a Dish Microwave-Safe?

The main material that makes a dish unsuitable for microwaving is metal. During cooking, microwaves bounce off the metal instead of harmlessly passing through. This causes sparks that may damage the oven or blacken the dish. Today, most microwave-safe dishware is clearly marked.

1. Wash the potatoes, peel if desired, and cut into chunks. Place the potatoes in a large, microwave-safe bowl with enough water to cover. Cover the dish with microwave-safe plastic wrap. Microwave the potatoes on high heat for 8 minutes, give the bowl a quarter turn, and then continue cooking for 1 minute at a time until the potatoes are fork-tender (total cooking time should be about 10 minutes). Drain.

2. While the potatoes are cooking, prepare the vegetables: seed and chop the tomato and chop the onion.

3. Combine the potatoes and other vegetables (including the corn and chopped peppers) in a large salad bowl.

4. Whisk the Orange-Cilantro Marinade. Add it to the salad and toss to mix thoroughly. Serve immediately.

Swiss Cheese and Ham Sandwich

Adding a spice or combination of spices is a great way to create your own
gourmet mayonnaise. In addition to cayenne pepper, good choices include curry powder,
prepared Italian pesto sauce, or even sweet Thai chili sauce.

INGREDIENTS | SERVES 1

1½ tablespoons mayonnaise

¼ teaspoon cayenne pepper, or to taste

2 slices rye bread

2 slices processed Swiss cheese

2 teaspoons mustard

1 slice cooked ham

½ medium tomato, thinly sliced

1. In a small bowl, combine the mayonnaise and cayenne pepper.

2. Spread the mayonnaise on the inside of one slice of bread and place the Swiss cheese on top.

3. Spread the mustard on the inside of the other slice of bread and add the sliced ham. Add the sliced tomato. Close up the sandwich.

Hot and Spicy Cucumber Sandwich

*Paprika adds extra heat to the traditional cucumber sandwich,
while cream cheese turns it from an afternoon snack into a nutritious midday meal.*

INGREDIENTS | SERVES 2

1½ teaspoons lemon juice
4 tablespoons cream cheese, softened
¼ teaspoon paprika, or to taste
1½ teaspoons chopped red onion
4 slices bread
4 teaspoons margarine, or as needed
½ medium cucumber, thinly sliced

1. In a small bowl, stir the lemon juice into the cream cheese. Stir in the paprika and chopped red onion.

2. Lay two slices of bread out in front of you. Spread 2 teaspoons of margarine on the inside of one slice of bread. Lay out half of the cucumber slices on top.

3. Spread half the cream cheese mixture on the inside of the other slice of bread.

4. Close up the sandwich. Cut in half or quarters as desired.

5. Repeat with the remaining two slices of bread.

Grilled Chicken Sandwich

*For a fancier sandwich, try replacing the margarine and mayonnaise with Italian pesto.
Instead of broiling, the chicken breast can also be cooked on the grill.*

INGREDIENTS | SERVES 1

1 boneless, skinless chicken breast half
¼ teaspoon salt
¼ teaspoon black or white pepper
2 slices crusty French or Italian bread
2 teaspoons margarine
1 tablespoon low-fat mayonnaise
½ medium tomato, thinly sliced

1. Preheat the broiler.

2. Rinse the chicken breast under running water and pat dry. Rub the salt and pepper over the chicken to season.

3. To broil the chicken, place it on a broiling rack sprayed with nonstick cooking spray. Broil the chicken on high heat, 9 inches from the heat source, for about 7–8 minutes, or until cooked through.

4. Lay out the bread in front of you. Spread the margarine over the inside of one slice of bread and the mayonnaise over the inside of the other.

5. Add the sliced tomato on the slice with mayonnaise. Add the broiled chicken on the other side. Close up the sandwich.

Marinated Vegetable Salad

This simple salad requires little preparation and has a (comparatively) short marinating time. It makes a nice salad, or you could serve it as a side dish in place of cooked vegetables or over cooked pasta.

INGREDIENTS | SERVES 2

⅓ cup olive oil
3 tablespoons apple cider vinegar
1 tablespoon chopped fresh basil
¼ teaspoon salt
⅛ teaspoon black pepper, or to taste
2 medium cucumbers, thinly sliced
2 tomatoes, chopped into chunks
½ red onion, peeled, sliced

1. In a small bowl, whisk together the olive oil, apple cider vinegar, chopped basil, salt, and pepper.

2. Place the vegetables in a salad bowl and gently toss with the vinegar dressing.

3. Cover the salad and chill for 1 hour. Stir again gently before serving.

Caprese Salad

When the children are ready to take a reprieve from the lettuce salads, this is a great way to get lots of necessary vitamins, calcium, and healthy fats.

INGREDIENTS | SERVES 4–6

3–4 large ripe tomatoes
1 pound fresh part-skim mozzarella
¼ cup olive oil
8–10 fresh basil leaves, chopped
Salt and pepper to taste

Get the Calcium in Any Way You Can!

Encouraging your child to consume dairy products—in any way, shape, or form—is non-negotiable. Calcium is the supreme nutrient for your children to consume in order to achieve their optimum growth, especially their height. The less-absorbed calcium comes from certain vegetables, such as spinach, broccoli, kale, and asparagus. Stick with the dairy sources of low-fat milk, low-fat chocolate milk (low-sugar when possible), low-fat yogurts, low-fat cheeses, and cottage cheese.

1. Slice the tomatoes ½-inch thick.

2. Slice the mozzarella cheese into ¼-inch slices.

3. Arrange 2–3 slices of tomato and 2–3 slices of cheese on a small plate, alternating slices.

4. Drizzle olive oil on top.

5. Sprinkle on the chopped basil leaves. Season with salt and pepper as desired.

6. For best flavor, refrigerate for 30 minutes prior to serving.

Sirloin Steak Salad

Increase the amount of steak if you have larger appetites at the table.
Use a stovetop grill pan for the steak and vegetables for great results.

INGREDIENTS | SERVES 2

2 teaspoons olive oil

8 ounces top sirloin, 1-inch thick

Salt and freshly cracked black pepper, to taste

¼ cup sliced scallions (2-inch pieces)

½ cup red pepper strips (about ¼-inch strips)

1 tablespoon soy sauce

1 tablespoon red wine vinegar

1 teaspoon sesame oil

1 teaspoon minced fresh ginger

¼ teaspoon kosher salt

4 cups salad greens, rinsed and dried

1. Heat the oil in a large nonstick skillet over medium-high heat. Season the steak with salt and pepper.

2. Place the meat, scallions, and red peppers in the hot skillet and cook until the vegetables begin to brown and the steak is medium-rare, about 10 minutes total, turning the steak once and stirring the vegetables occasionally. Transfer the cooked meat and vegetables to a plate and tent with tinfoil to keep warm. Let the meat rest for 5 minutes to allow the juices to reabsorb.

3. Combine the soy sauce, vinegar, sesame oil, ginger, and kosher salt in a salad bowl and whisk to combine. Add the greens and toss with the dressing. Divide between 2 large dinner plates.

4. Slice the meat against the grain into very thin slices. Fan the meat over the salad greens and arrange the cooked scallions and peppers alongside the meat. Serve immediately.

Spinach Salad with Shrimp and Roasted Pepper Vinaigrette

It's important to use spinach leaves in this salad.
Normal salad greens won't stand up to the warm vinaigrette dressing.

INGREDIENTS | SERVES 4

¾ cup sliced almonds

9 ounces (about 8 lightly packed cups) baby spinach

5 tablespoons extra-virgin olive oil, divided

1 pound medium-sized shrimp, peeled and deveined (tail optional)

Salt, to taste

4 ounces jarred roasted red peppers, drained and cut into thin strips (about ½ cup)

¼ cup thinly sliced shallots

¼ teaspoon salt

⅛ teaspoon ground black pepper

1½ tablespoons sherry vinegar

Bag It

There are many convenience packages of salad greens available in the produce section of your grocer. Take a minute to read the labels, because many of the newer greens additions are actually "kits" that contain everything to make the salad, including hidden carbs.

1. Toast the almonds in a large nonstick skillet over medium heat until lightly browned, about 3 minutes. Shake the pan frequently and turn the almonds to prevent scorching. Place the spinach in a serving bowl and sprinkle the almonds on top.

2. In a large skillet over medium-high heat, add 2 tablespoons of the oil, add the shrimp, and cook until just starting to turn pink, about 1½ minutes. Turn the shrimp over and cook through (the center will be opaque), about 45 seconds. Transfer the shrimp to a plate, season with salt, and set aside.

3. Lower the heat to medium and add the remaining 3 tablespoons oil, the red peppers, shallots, ¼ teaspoon salt, and pepper. Cook until the shallots soften, about 2 minutes. Remove from heat and whisk in the vinegar.

4. Pour the warm dressing over the spinach and toss. Divide the spinach salad among 4 plates and arrange the shrimp on top. Serve immediately.

Garlic Ranch-Style Dressing

This is a rich and creamy treat that is great on greens or drizzled over grilled fish or chicken.

INGREDIENTS | SERVES 6

2 teaspoons minced garlic

2 teaspoons garlic powder

½ cup mayonnaise

½ cup sour cream

3 teaspoons Dijon mustard

3 tablespoons freshly squeezed lemon juice

¼ teaspoon seasoned salt

Freshly cracked black pepper, to taste

Combine all the ingredients in a small nonreactive bowl and whisk to combine. Refrigerate, up to 4 days, until ready to use.

Homemade vs. Store-Bought

There are a number of delicious dressings in the refrigerated section of your local supermarket, but homemade dressings are still better—both in taste and nutrition. The other advantage of homemade dressings is that you can customize them to your own taste.

Cilantro and Red Onion Dressing

A great dressing for a summer salad that can include any fruits such as strawberries or mandarin oranges.

INGREDIENTS | SERVES 6

2 tablespoons finely chopped red onion

½ teaspoon ground ginger

3 tablespoons slivered almonds

1 tablespoon sesame seeds

1 teaspoon anise seeds

3 tablespoons chopped fresh cilantro

¼ teaspoon paprika

2 tablespoons white wine vinegar

3 tablespoons freshly squeezed lemon juice

½ cup extra-virgin olive oil

¼ teaspoon seasoned salt

Combine all the ingredients in a medium-sized nonreactive bowl and whisk to combine. Taste and adjust seasoning as desired. Remix just before serving. Refrigerate any unused portion and bring to room temperature before serving.

Creamy Asian Dressing

You can use this as a dressing for chicken salad and add a small amount of water chestnuts, sprouts, and scallions for added crunch.

INGREDIENTS | SERVES 6

¾ cup mayonnaise

¼ cup sour cream

2 tablespoons tamari

1 teaspoon minced garlic

2 tablespoons rice wine

1 teaspoon honey

¼ cup thinly sliced scallion

Freshly cracked black pepper, to taste

Combine all the ingredients in a nonreactive bowl and whisk until well blended. Taste and adjust seasoning as desired. Refrigerate until ready to use.

CHAPTER 5

Soups and Stews

Tomato Bisque

A bisque is a rich soup that combines vegetables, stock, and milk or cream.
Serve for lunch with some chewy breadsticks and a mixed fruit salad.

INGREDIENTS | SERVES 6

1 tablespoon olive oil

1 onion, finely chopped

1 (10-ounce) container refrigerated Alfredo sauce

1½ cups chicken or vegetable broth

1½ cups whole milk

2 (14-ounce) cans diced tomatoes, undrained

½ teaspoon dried basil leaves

¼ teaspoon dried marjoram leaves

Alfredo Sauce

Alfredo sauce is basically a white sauce, usually with some cheese added. You can find it in the refrigerated dairy section of your supermarket. It can also be found on the pasta aisle. In addition to Alfredo sauce, four-cheese sauce, Cheddar pasta sauce, and roasted garlic Parmesan pasta sauce are available.

1. In a heavy saucepan, heat olive oil over medium heat and add onion. Cook and stir until onion is tender, about 4 minutes.

2. Add Alfredo sauce and broth; cook and stir with wire whisk until mixture is smooth. Add milk and stir; cook over medium heat for 2–3 minutes.

3. Meanwhile, purée undrained tomatoes in food processor or blender until smooth. Add to saucepan along with basil and marjoram leaves.

4. Heat soup over medium heat, stirring frequently, until mixture just comes to a simmer. Serve immediately.

Super-Quick Beef Vegetable Stew

There are so many types of fully prepared meat entrées in your grocery store;
browse the selection and stock up!

INGREDIENTS | SERVES 6

3 tablespoons olive oil

1 onion, chopped

3 cloves garlic, minced

1 (16-ounce) package prepared roast beef in gravy

1 (16-ounce) package frozen mixed vegetables

1 (10-ounce) can cream of mushroom soup

2 cups water

½ teaspoon dried thyme leaves

1. In a heavy large saucepan, heat olive oil over medium heat. Add onion and garlic; cook and stir until tender, 4–5 minutes. Meanwhile, cut the cooked roast beef into 1-inch chunks. Add to saucepan along with gravy, frozen mixed vegetables, soup, water, and thyme leaves.

2. Cook over medium-high heat until soup comes to a boil, about 7–9 minutes. Reduce heat to low and simmer for 6–7 minutes longer, until vegetables and beef are hot and tender. Serve immediately.

Soup or Stew?

The difference between soup and stew is the thickness of the liquid. Soups are generally thin, sometimes made with just broth or stock. Stews have ingredients that thicken the liquid, including potatoes, flour, cornstarch, or puréed vegetables. You can make any soup into a stew by adding some cornstarch dissolved in water.

Tortellini Soup

This rich soup is full of flavor. Serve it with some water crackers, a chopped vegetable salad, and melon slices.

INGREDIENTS | SERVES 6–8

1 pound sweet Italian bulk sausage

1 (8-ounce) package sliced mushrooms

4 cloves garlic, minced

3 (14-ounce) cans beef broth

1½ cups water

1 teaspoon dried Italian seasoning

⅛ teaspoon pepper

1 (24-ounce) package frozen cheese tortellini

1. In large saucepan over medium heat, brown sausage with mushrooms and garlic, stirring to break up sausage. When sausage is cooked, drain thoroughly.

2. Add broth, water, Italian seasoning, and pepper to saucepan and bring to a boil over high heat. Reduce heat to low and simmer for 8–10 minutes.

3. Stir in frozen tortellini and cook, stirring frequently, over medium-high heat for 6–8 minutes or until tortellini are hot and tender. Serve immediately.

Frozen or Refrigerated Tortellini?

Refrigerated, or fresh, tortellini is found in the dairy aisle of the regular grocery store. It is generally more expensive than the frozen, and package sizes are smaller. Frozen tortellini and tortelloni take a bit longer to cook. Choose your favorite and stock up.

Chicken Corn Chowder

Open four packages and grate some cheese, and you'll have a hearty,
hot soup on the table in about 15 minutes. Serve with some crackers and fresh fruit.

INGREDIENTS | SERVES 6

1 (26-ounce) jar double Cheddar pasta sauce

2 (14-ounce) cans chicken broth

2 (15-ounce) cans corn, drained

2 (9-ounce) packages frozen cooked Southwest-style chicken strips

½ teaspoon dried Italian seasoning

2 cups shredded sharp Cheddar cheese

1. In large saucepan, combine all ingredients, except cheese, and bring to a boil over medium-high heat. Reduce heat to low, cover, and simmer for 6–8 minutes, until chicken is hot.

2. Stir in Cheddar cheese, remove from heat, and let stand, covered, for 3–4 minutes. Stir thoroughly and serve.

Frozen Precooked Chicken

There are lots of varieties of frozen precooked chicken in your supermarket's meat aisle. You can find cooked grilled chicken, chicken strips, and chopped chicken in flavors that range from Southwest to plain grilled. Some varieties come with a sauce; be sure to read the label to make sure you're getting what you want.

French Onion Soup

Because the onions need to sauté for a fairly long time to develop caramelization, this recipe starts with frozen chopped onions. You can chop fresh onions, but the recipe will take longer than 30 minutes.

INGREDIENTS | SERVES 6

2 tablespoons olive oil

2 tablespoons butter

2 (10-ounce) packages frozen chopped onions

2 tablespoons flour

2 (16-ounce) boxes beef stock

6 slices French bread

¼ cup butter, softened

1½ cups shredded Gruyère cheese

Boxed Stocks

If your grocery store carries boxed stocks, buy them. These stocks tend to be richer and less salty than canned stocks. If you don't use all of the stock, these boxes come with a flip-top lid so you can close the box and store it in the refrigerator for a couple of weeks.

1. In large saucepan, combine olive oil and 2 tablespoons butter over medium heat until butter is foamy. Add onions; cook over medium heat for 10–12 minutes, stirring frequently, until onions brown around edges. Sprinkle flour over onions; cook and stir for 2–3 minutes.

2. Stir in stock, bring to a simmer, and cook for 10 minutes.

3. Meanwhile, spread French bread slices with ¼ cup butter. In toaster oven, toast the bread until browned and crisp. Sprinkle with cheese and toast for 2–4 minutes, until cheese melts. Divide soup among soup bowls and float the toasted cheese bread on top. Serve immediately.

Pressure Cooker Beef Stew

This stew tastes like it simmered for hours on your stove, but the pressure cooker makes quick work of the recipe. Serve with some crusty bread to soak up the wonderful sauce.

INGREDIENTS | SERVES 8

2 pounds bottom-round steak

3 tablespoons flour

½ teaspoon garlic salt

⅛ teaspoon pepper

3 tablespoons olive oil

3 russet potatoes, cubed

1 (16-ounce) package baby carrots

½ teaspoon dried thyme leaves

½ teaspoon dried oregano leaves

4 cups beef stock, heated

1 (14-ounce) can diced tomatoes with garlic, undrained

1. Cut steak into 1-inch cubes. Sprinkle meat with flour, garlic salt, and pepper and toss to coat. Heat oil in the pressure cooker and brown the coated beef, stirring frequently, about 5–7 minutes. Add remaining ingredients and lock the lid. Bring up to high pressure and cook for 20 minutes.

2. Release pressure using quick-release method and stir stew. Serve immediately.

Potato Soup

This creamy and rich soup uses two kinds of potatoes—
scalloped and hash brown—for a nice depth of flavor.

INGREDIENTS | SERVES 6

4 slices bacon

1 onion, chopped

1 (5-ounce) package cheese-flavored
scalloped potato mix

3 cups water

1 (15-ounce) can evaporated milk

2 cups frozen hash brown potatoes

½ teaspoon dried dill weed

⅛ teaspoon white pepper

1. In heavy saucepan, cook bacon until crisp. Remove bacon, drain on paper towels, crumble, and set aside.

2. Cook onion in bacon drippings until tender, about 5 minutes. Add potato mix and seasoning packet from potato mix, along with remaining ingredients. Bring to a boil and simmer for 17–20 minutes, until potatoes are tender. If desired, purée using an immersion blender. Sprinkle with bacon and serve.

Precooked Bacon?

When recipes call for crumbled bacon, you can use the precooked version. But if the recipe calls for cooking the bacon and using the bacon fat to sauté other ingredients, you must used uncooked bacon. Or you can use the precooked bacon and use butter or olive oil as a substitute for the bacon fat.

Two-Bean Chili

This vegetarian chili can be varied so many ways. Add more beans, salsa, cooked ground beef or pork sausage, jalapeño peppers, or tomato sauce.

INGREDIENTS | SERVES 4

2 tablespoons olive oil

1 onion, chopped

1 (1.25-ounce) package taco seasoning mix

1 (15-ounce) can kidney beans, drained

1 (15-ounce) can black beans, drained

2 (14-ounce) cans diced tomatoes with green chilies, undrained

1 cup water

1. In heavy saucepan over medium heat, add olive oil and sauté onion until tender, about 4–5 minutes. Sprinkle taco seasoning mix over onions; cook and stir for 1 minute.

2. Add drained but not rinsed beans, tomatoes, and water. Bring to a simmer; cook for 10–12 minutes, until thickened and blended. Serve immediately.

Taco Seasoning Mix

You can make your own taco seasoning mix by combining 2 tablespoons chili powder, 2 teaspoons onion powder, 2 tablespoons cornstarch, 1 teaspoon dried oregano, 1 teaspoon dried red pepper flakes, 2 teaspoons salt, and ½ teaspoon cumin. Blend well and store in a cool, dry place: 2 tablespoons equals one envelope mix.

Bean and Bacon Soup

This simple soup is great for kids' lunchboxes. Pack into an insulated thermos and provide some cheese crackers, baby carrots, and shredded Cheddar cheese for topping the soup.

INGREDIENTS | SERVES 4–6

1 (8-ounce) package bacon

1 onion, chopped

1 (14-ounce) can diced tomatoes, undrained

2 (15-ounce) cans pinto beans, drained

2 cups chicken broth

1. In large saucepan, cook bacon until crisp. Drain bacon on paper towels, crumble, and set aside.

2. Drain off all but 2 tablespoons bacon drippings. Cook onion in drippings over medium heat for 3–4 minutes. Add remaining ingredients and bring to a simmer. Simmer for 10–12 minutes; then use a potato masher to mash some of the beans.

3. Add reserved bacon, stir, and simmer for 5 minutes longer. Serve immediately, or pour into warmed insulated thermoses and store up to 6 hours.

Egg Drop Soup

Because this soup is so simple, it demands the best chicken stock. Try to find the boxed chicken stock at your grocery store, or order it online. You can also make your own stock.

INGREDIENTS | SERVES 4

5 cups chicken broth

1 cup shredded carrots

½ cup grated onion

2 eggs

1 egg yolk

Make Your Own Chicken Stock

This recipe takes some time, but you can freeze it and it will add lots of flavor to your recipes. Cover 1 stewing chicken, some chopped onion, carrots, 1 bay leaf, some parsley, and celery with water and simmer for 3–4 hours. Strain broth, cool, pour into ice cube trays, and freeze; then package the cubes in freezer bags.

1. In heavy saucepan, combine chicken broth, carrots, and onion. Bring to a simmer; cook for 3–5 minutes, until vegetables are tender.

2. Meanwhile, in small bowl, place eggs and egg yolk; carefully remove the chalazae (the white ropy strand that connects the egg white and the yolk). Beat eggs and egg yolk with a fork until smooth; do not overbeat.

3. Remove the saucepan from the heat. Using a fork, drizzle the egg mixture into the soup. When all the egg is added, stir the soup for 30 seconds; then serve immediately.

Easy Coconut Soup

Toasted coconut enhances the appearance and flavor of this simple soup.

INGREDIENTS | SERVES 4

¼ cup unsweetened coconut flakes

1 cup whole milk

1 cup coconut milk

1 cup water

⅓ cup light cream

⅛ teaspoon ground cinnamon

3 tablespoons granulated sugar

¼ teaspoon salt, or to taste

1. Preheat oven to 325°F. Spread out the coconut flakes on a baking sheet.

2. In a medium saucepan, bring the milk, coconut milk, water, and light cream to a boil.

3. While waiting for the soup to boil, place the coconut flakes in the oven. Toast for 5 minutes, or until they turn a light brown and are fragrant.

4. When the soup comes to a boil, stir in the cinnamon, sugar, and salt. Turn the heat down to medium-low, cover, and simmer for 5 minutes.

5. To serve, garnish the soup with the toasted coconut.

Frozen Garden Vegetable Soup

Frozen vegetables take the work out of peeling and chopping fresh vegetables in this quick and easy recipe. While the soup doesn't take long to make, if you want to speed up the cooking time even more, cook the frozen vegetables in the microwave while sautéing the onion.

INGREDIENTS | SERVES 4

2 teaspoons olive oil

1 teaspoon minced garlic

1 onion, peeled, chopped

1 teaspoon dried parsley

2 cups frozen vegetables

2 cups low-sodium beef broth

1 cup water

¼ teaspoon salt

Black pepper, to taste

½ teaspoon Tabasco sauce

1. In a medium saucepan, heat the olive oil over medium-high heat. Add the garlic and onion. Sprinkle the dried parsley over the onion. Sauté for about 4 minutes, until the onion is softened.

2. Add the frozen vegetables. Cook for about 4–5 minutes, until they are thawed and heated through, using a rubber spatula to break them up while cooking.

3. Add the beef broth and water. Bring to a boil (this takes about 4 minutes).

4. Stir in the salt, pepper, and Tabasco sauce.

5. Turn down the heat and simmer for 3–4 minutes. Serve immediately.

New England Clam Chowder

Traditionally, New England's take on clam chowder is served with hexagon-shaped oyster crackers. For a special touch, sprinkle ¼ cup of bacon bits over the soup.

INGREDIENTS | SERVES 4

1 cup frozen corn
1 tablespoon margarine
¼ cup chopped onion
½ cup clam juice
1½ cups whole milk
1 cup cream
1 teaspoon dried parsley
¼ teaspoon paprika, or to taste
¾ teaspoon salt
½ teaspoon black pepper
1½ cups canned chopped clams

Soup Facts

A bisque is a creamy soup made with shellfish, while chowder is a heartier soup with fish or shellfish and vegetables in a milk-based broth. A Southern specialty, gumbo is a thick soup made with meat or seafood, served over rice.

1. Place the frozen corn in a microwave-safe bowl. Cover with microwave-safe plastic wrap, leaving one corner open to vent steam. Microwave on high heat for 2 minutes and then for 30 seconds at a time until cooked, stirring each time (total cooking time should be about 3 minutes).

2. Heat the margarine over medium-high heat in a medium-sized sauté pan. Add the onion. Sauté for 4–5 minutes, until the onion is softened.

3. Add the clam juice, milk, cream, dried parsley, paprika, salt, and pepper. Bring to a boil.

4. Stir in the cooked corn. Return to a boil.

5. Turn down the heat, cover, and simmer for 3 minutes. Add the clams and cook for 2 more minutes. Serve hot.

Chicken and Corn Soup

Cayenne pepper adds a bit of spice to this nourishing chicken and vegetable soup. You can replace the frozen corn with your favorite type of corn in this recipe, including canned cream corn.

INGREDIENTS | SERVES 4

2 teaspoons olive oil

2 shallots, peeled, chopped

5 cups chicken broth

2 cups frozen corn

½ teaspoon salt

⅛ teaspoon cayenne pepper

1 teaspoon ground cumin

1 leftover chicken breast, shredded

¼ cup chopped fresh parsley

1. Heat the olive oil in a saucepan over medium heat. Add the shallots and sauté until softened, about 2 minutes.

2. Add the chicken broth. Bring to a boil.

3. Add the frozen corn. Return to a boil.

4. Stir in the salt, cayenne pepper, and cumin.

5. Add the shredded chicken pieces. Stir in the fresh parsley. Simmer for a minute and serve hot.

Minestrone

Minestrone—literally, big soup—is one of Italy's signature dishes. Every region has its own special way of preparing this popular vegetable soup.

INGREDIENTS | SERVES 6

5 cups water

2 (2-ounce) packages instant onion soup mix

1 zucchini, cubed

12 baby carrots

1 cup drained canned white beans

1 cup drained canned green beans

1 cup elbow macaroni

1 (28-ounce) can plum tomatoes

1 teaspoon dried parsley

1 teaspoon dried oregano

½ teaspoon salt, or to taste

¼ teaspoon black pepper, or to taste

⅓ cup grated Parmesan cheese

1. In a large saucepan over medium-high heat, bring the water to a boil. Stir in the onion soup mix.

2. Add the zucchini, carrots, white and green beans, and macaroni. Return to a boil.

3. Add the tomatoes with their juice. Return to a boil.

4. Stir in parsley, oregano, salt, and pepper.

5. Turn the heat down to medium-low, cover, and simmer for 10 minutes or until the zucchini is tender and the elbow macaroni is cooked. Pour the soup into serving bowls and garnish with the Parmesan cheese.

Turning Sauce into Soup

Your favorite pasta sauce can easily be transformed into a flavorful soup. For example, when preparing tomato sauce, reserve 1 cup of the sauce. To make the soup, simply combine the reserved sauce with 2½–3 cups of canned or packaged beef broth. Bring to a boil and simmer for 5 minutes to allow the flavors to blend.

Chicken Noodle Soup

*Don't have leftover chicken on hand? This recipe uses canned chicken,
a quick and easy alternative that is very economical.*

INGREDIENTS | SERVES 4

3 cups water

1 (3-ounce) package chicken-flavored ramen noodles

1 cup frozen peas

1 cup canned chicken

1 tablespoon soy sauce

¼ teaspoon red pepper flakes

1. Bring the water to a boil in a large saucepan over medium-high heat. Add the ramen noodles and the contents of the flavor packet. Return to a boil, stirring.

2. Add the frozen peas. Return to a boil, reduce the heat, and simmer 2–3 minutes, until the peas are cooked.

3. Add the canned chicken. Stir in the soy sauce and red pepper flakes.

4. Return to a boil; then reduce the heat and simmer for 5 more minutes. Serve hot.

Wonton Soup

*Don't have time to fill and wrap wontons to make authentic wonton soup?
This recipe takes the ingredients normally used to make the wontons and combines
them with Chinese vegetables in a seasoned broth.*

INGREDIENTS | SERVES 4

5 cups chicken broth

½ pound leftover cooked ground pork

18 wonton wrappers

½ cup canned bamboo shoots

½ cup canned sliced water chestnuts

¼ teaspoon salt

½ teaspoon granulated sugar

⅛ teaspoon white pepper, or to taste

2 green onions, chopped

1 tablespoon oyster sauce

1. In a large saucepan, bring the chicken broth to a boil over medium-high heat.

2. Add the ground pork, breaking it up with a spatula.

3. Add the wonton wrappers, bamboo shoots, and water chestnuts. Return to a boil.

4. Stir in the salt, sugar, white pepper, and green onions. Stir in the oyster sauce.

5. Turn the heat down slightly and simmer for 5 minutes to soften the wonton wrappers and combine all the flavors. Serve hot.

Beef Burgundy Stew

Don't have leftover beef on hand? Brown 1 pound of cubed stewing beef over medium-high heat until nearly cooked through. This will add 5–10 minutes to the cooking time.

INGREDIENTS | SERVES 2

1 tablespoon vegetable oil
2 baby onions, cut in half
4 ounces sliced fresh mushrooms
1 zucchini, thinly sliced
¼ teaspoon dried oregano
2 cups leftover cooked beef, cubed
¼ cup burgundy
½ cup beef broth
1 tablespoon tomato paste
1 tablespoon Worcestershire sauce
⅛ teaspoon black pepper

1. Heat the oil in a skillet on medium heat. Add the onions, mushrooms, and zucchini. Stir in the dried oregano. Sauté for about 5 minutes, until the vegetables are softened.

2. Add the beef. Cook for 2–3 minutes to heat through.

3. Add the burgundy and beef broth. Stir in the tomato paste and Worcestershire sauce. Bring to a boil.

4. Stir in the pepper. Turn down the heat and simmer for about 5 minutes. Serve hot.

Cream of Carrot Soup

Carrots, in any form, along with all fruits and vegetables that are orange in color, are an incredible source of antioxidants and phytochemicals—cancer-fighting, heart-healthy nutrients. Incorporate them daily into your family's diet.

INGREDIENTS | SERVES 4–6

8 large carrots, scraped and thinly sliced
2 celery stalks, chopped finely
3 cups chicken or vegetable stock
Salt and pepper to taste
1 small bay leaf
1 egg yolk, beaten
¼ cup heavy whipping cream
½ cup 2% reduced fat milk

Phytochemicals

Over the past ten years or so, phytochemicals have been found to have an impact similar to antioxidants: protecting our cells from damage, reducing the risk of developing certain types of cancer, and helping to reduce osteoporosis. Sneak these foods in whenever you can. Phytochemicals can be found in foods such as tomatoes, carrots, broccoli, soy products, beans, and fruits such as blueberries, cranberries, and cherries.

1. In a large saucepan, combine carrots, celery, stock, salt and pepper, and bay leaf.

2. Bring to a boil and then simmer until carrots are tender, about 10–20 minutes.

3. Discard bay leaf. Pour soup mixture into a blender or food processor and purée until smooth. Return to saucepan and bring to a boil.

4. In a medium bowl combine beaten egg, cream, and milk. Mix a little of the soup with the egg/milk mixture, and then add that mixture to the soup.

5. Stir and bring to a boil for 1 minute. Serve hot or cold.

Sweet Strawberry Soup

A very refreshing cold soup—substitute low-fat yogurt for sour cream for a higher-protein dish; if the white wine doesn't appeal to you, consider light cranberry juice.

INGREDIENTS | SERVES 6

1 pint strawberries, fresh or frozen
1 cup low-fat sour cream
1 cup low-fat milk
¼ cup sugar
1 teaspoon vanilla extract
2 tablespoons white wine

1. Process berries in a blender or food processor until puréed.

2. Add sour cream, milk, sugar, vanilla, and white wine and pulse until well blended.

3. Chill before serving.

Chilled Soups—an Unusual Appetizer or Dessert

Delicious and different, offer cold soups to your children, and to guests. They not only offer a beautiful presentation, but are usually stocked with great nutrients, depending on the fruit or vegetable you make the soup with. Berries and mangos are full of antioxidants and vitamin C. Cold squash or pumpkin soup is a wonderful addition to any meal.

Creamy Broccoli Soup

Everyone's favorite! Creamy broccoli soup topped with Cheddar—served hot.
Pair this with a light, crispy salad and you have a great weekend luncheon menu.

INGREDIENTS | SERVES 4

1½ pounds broccoli

¾ cup chopped celery

½ cup chopped yellow onion

½ teaspoon salt, or to taste

2 tablespoons butter

2 tablespoons all-purpose flour

2½ cups chicken stock

⅛ teaspoon freshly grated nutmeg

¼ teaspoon freshly cracked pepper, or to taste

½ cup heavy cream, at room temperature

½ cup shredded Cheddar cheese, for garnish

Soup Garnishes

The more complex the soup, the simpler the garnish should be. For hot soups, you can use chopped fresh herbs, minced scallions, a dollop of sour cream, or grated Parmesan.

1. Trim the woody stalks from the broccoli and chop the remaining tender stems and tops into medium dice.

2. Combine the broccoli, celery, and onions in a medium-sized saucepan. Add just enough water to cover the vegetables, and salt generously. Bring to a boil and cook until the vegetables are tender, but not mushy, about 8 minutes.

3. Use a slotted spoon to transfer the vegetables to a food processor fitted with a metal blade (or a blender). Process until smooth, adding a few tablespoons of the cooking liquid if needed.

4. Melt the butter in a medium-sized saucepan over medium heat. Add the flour and whisk until smooth. Cook until smooth and bubbly, about 4 minutes.

5. Slowly add the chicken stock, whisking constantly. Bring to a simmer and cook for 2 minutes until thick.

6. Stir in the broccoli purée, the nutmeg, pepper, and salt to taste; bring to a simmer and cook to allow the flavors to blend, about 5 minutes.

7. Slowly pour in the cream, whisking to blend. Heat through but do not boil. Taste and adjust seasoning as desired. To serve, ladle soup into bowls and top with shredded cheese. Serve hot.

Beef Stroganoff Soup

Make sure the pan is really hot when you sear the meat to ensure it stays tender and the flavorful juices stay inside the meat.

INGREDIENTS | SERVES 6

2 pounds top sirloin steak, trimmed of visible fat and cut into ½-inch cubes

½ teaspoon salt

¼ teaspoon freshly ground black pepper

4 tablespoons all-purpose flour

4 tablespoons butter

1 tablespoon olive oil

½ cup sliced yellow onion

3 cups sliced mushrooms

2 tablespoons minced garlic

¼ cup dry white wine

2 cups beef stock

2 tablespoons chopped parsley, plus extra for garnish

2 teaspoons Worcestershire sauce

½ cup sour cream

Flavor Enhancer

You can use bouillon cubes to enhance the flavors of savory soups. Be careful when salting, as the bouillon cubes already contain quite a bit of salt.

1. Pat the meat dry with paper towels and season with salt and pepper. Place the flour in a shallow bowl. Dredge the meat in the flour, shaking off excess. Reserve remaining flour.

2. Melt the butter in a large nonstick skillet over high heat until bubbling. Add the meat and brown on all sides, stirring occasionally to cook evenly, about 6 minutes. Use a slotted spoon to transfer the meat to a plate and tent with tinfoil to keep warm.

3. Heat the oil in a saucepan over medium-high heat and add the onions, mushrooms, and garlic. Cook until soft, about 6 minutes, stirring occasionally.

4. Sprinkle the reserved flour over the vegetables. Cook and stir until thick. Add the white wine and cook until thick and reduced, about 4 minutes. Add the stock, parsley, and Worcestershire; bring to a simmer and cook until somewhat reduced, about 6 minutes.

5. Add the meat and any accumulated juices and simmer, uncovered, for 10 minutes. To serve, stir in the sour cream and heat through. Serve hot in warm shallow bowls.

Cheddar Cheese Soup

Use a quality aged Cheddar for a rich, creamy taste.
Using a sharp Cheddar will increase the intensity of this dish.

INGREDIENTS | SERVES 4

2 tablespoons butter
¼ cup chopped yellow onion
½ cup chopped celery
2 tablespoons all-purpose flour
½ teaspoon ground cayenne pepper
¼ teaspoon dry mustard
½ tablespoon Worcestershire sauce
1 cup whole milk
1½ cups chicken stock
2 cups shredded Cheddar cheese
Seasoned salt, to taste
Freshly cracked black pepper
Paprika, for garnish

1. Melt the butter in a medium-sized saucepan and sauté the onion and celery until tender, about 4 minutes. Add the flour, cayenne pepper, mustard, and Worcestershire and stir to combine.

2. Add the milk and chicken stock and bring to a boil. Cook for 1 minute, stirring constantly. Reduce heat to low, add the cheese, and stir occasionally just until the cheese is melted.

3. Add seasoned salt and pepper to taste. To serve, ladle hot soup into small decorative cups and sprinkle with paprika.

CHAPTER 6

Chicken and Turkey

Herbed Chicken Breasts

*Serve these well-flavored, tender chicken breasts with a rice pilaf,
a spinach salad, and some oatmeal cookies for dessert.*

INGREDIENTS | SERVES 8

2 tablespoons olive oil

2 tablespoons butter

2 cloves garlic, cut in half

¼ cup lemon juice

2 tablespoons chopped flat-leaf parsley

½ teaspoon dried thyme leaves

½ teaspoon salt

⅛ teaspoon white pepper

8 chicken breasts with skin

Chicken Breasts: Boned or Not?

Chicken breasts are sold boneless and skinless, and with bone in and skin on. The one you choose depends on what you're cooking. The skin and bone do add more flavor, so in simple broiled recipes, bone-in chicken is a good choice. When you want cubed chicken for stir-fries and sandwiches, boneless, skinless breasts are better.

1. In a small saucepan, combine olive oil, butter, and garlic over medium heat. Cook and stir until garlic sizzles, about 3 minutes; then remove garlic and discard.

2. Add lemon juice, herbs, and salt and pepper to oil and butter in pan; stir and remove from heat. Let cool for 5–10 minutes. Preheat broiler.

3. Loosen chicken skin from the flesh and pour a tablespoon of the lemon-herb mixture between the skin and flesh. Smooth skin back over flesh.

4. Place chicken pieces, skin-side down, on broiler pan. Brush with lemon mixture. Broil chicken, 4–6 inches from heat source, for 7–8 minutes, brushing often with the lemon mixture. Turn chicken and broil 6–9 minutes longer, brushing frequently with lemon mixture, until chicken is thoroughly cooked. Discard any remaining lemon mixture. Serve immediately.

Parmesan Chicken

This simple recipe demands the highest quality ingredients.
Serve it with some hot cooked couscous, bakery rolls, and melon wedges.

INGREDIENTS | SERVES 6

6 boneless, skinless chicken breasts
¼ cup lemon juice
1 teaspoon salt
⅛ teaspoon pepper
½ teaspoon dried thyme leaves
¼ cup unsalted butter
½ cup grated Parmesan cheese

1. Cut chicken breasts into 1-inch pieces. Sprinkle with lemon juice, salt, pepper, and thyme leaves. Let stand at room temperature for 10 minutes.

2. Melt butter in a heavy saucepan over medium heat. Sauté chicken until thoroughly cooked, about 5–6 minutes, stirring frequently. Sprinkle cheese over chicken, turn off heat, cover pan, and let stand for 2–3 minutes to melt cheese. Serve over hot cooked couscous.

Herb-Crusted Chicken Breasts

Soaking chicken in buttermilk, even if just for a few minutes, makes it tender and juicy.
You can use white or whole wheat bread in this easy and delicious recipe.

INGREDIENTS | SERVES 6

1 cup buttermilk

1 teaspoon salt

⅛ teaspoon cayenne pepper

6 boneless, skinless chicken breasts

3 slices bread

½ teaspoon dried thyme leaves

½ teaspoon dried basil leaves

½ teaspoon dried tarragon

½ cup grated Parmesan cheese

⅓ cup olive oil

1. Heat oven to 375°F. In large bowl, combine buttermilk with salt and cayenne pepper and mix well. Add chicken breasts, turn to coat, and set aside.

2. Place bread on cookie sheet and bake at 375°F until crisp, about 5–7 minutes. Remove from oven and break into pieces. Place in blender or food processor; blend or process until crumbs are fine. Pour crumbs onto large plate and add herbs and cheese; mix well.

3. Remove chicken from buttermilk mixture and roll in crumb mixture to coat. Set on wire rack. In a heavy skillet, heat olive oil over medium heat. Add chicken, two pieces at a time, and cook for 2–3 minutes on each side until browned. Remove to cookie sheet. Repeat to brown remaining chicken. Bake chicken at 375°F for 12–14 minutes or until thoroughly cooked. Serve immediately.

Spicy Chicken Tenders with Creamy Dip

This recipe is reminiscent of Buffalo Chicken Wings, a spicy appetizer that combines chicken with a creamy blue cheese dip.

INGREDIENTS | SERVES 4–6

1½ pounds chicken tenders

1 teaspoon cayenne pepper

1 tablespoon hot pepper sauce

1 egg, beaten

½ teaspoon salt

1 cup dry bread crumbs

1 cup creamy blue cheese salad dressing

½ cup chopped celery

¼ cup olive oil

Chicken Tenders

Chicken tenderloin is part of the breast; it is a small, thin muscle underneath, next to the bone. Chicken tenders can be made from the tenderloin or just cut from any part of the breast. They cook very quickly and are great for children because their shape makes them easy to pick up, dunk, and eat.

1. Spread chicken tenders onto waxed paper. On shallow plate, combine cayenne pepper, hot pepper sauce, egg, and salt and mix well.

2. Place bread crumbs on another plate. Dip chicken tenders, two at a time, into egg mixture and then into bread crumbs to coat. Place on wire rack while coating remaining tenders.

3. In small bowl, combine salad dressing and celery; cover and chill until ready to serve. Heat olive oil in heavy skillet over medium heat. Fry chicken tenders, 4 or 5 at a time, for 6–9 minutes, turning once, until brown and crisp on the outside and fully cooked. Drain on paper towels as they are finished. Serve hot with the celery dip.

Turkey and Bean Stir-Fry

Serve this quick and easy stir-fry over hot cooked rice, along with a green salad and brownies for dessert.

INGREDIENTS | SERVES 4–6

1 pound boneless, skinless turkey thighs

3 tablespoons flour

1 teaspoon garlic salt

⅛ teaspoon white pepper

2 tablespoons olive oil

2 cups frozen green beans, thawed and drained

1 cup frozen soybeans, thawed and drained

1 cup chicken stock

2 tablespoons cornstarch

1. Cut turkey into 1-inch pieces. On shallow plate, combine flour, garlic salt, and pepper and mix well. Add turkey pieces and toss to coat.

2. In large skillet or wok, heat olive oil over medium-high heat. Add turkey; stir-fry for 4–5 minutes, until browned. Add beans and soybeans; stir-fry for 3–6 minutes longer, until hot.

3. In small bowl, combine chicken stock with cornstarch and mix with wire whisk. Add stock mixture to turkey mixture; cook and stir over medium-high heat, until liquid bubbles and thickens. Serve immediately.

Thawing Frozen Vegetables

You can thaw frozen vegetables by placing them in a colander and running warm water over them until thawed. Or you can use the defrost setting on your microwave oven. You can also let the vegetables stand at room temperature for 1–2 hours, until thawed. Be sure to drain well after thawing so you don't add too much liquid to the recipe.

Lemon Chicken en Papillote

Lemon and chicken are perfect partners. The tart lemon tenderizes the chicken and adds great flavor. Serve these "packages" at the table and let your guests open them.

INGREDIENTS | SERVES 4

4 boneless, skinless chicken breasts

½ teaspoon salt

⅛ teaspoon lemon pepper

1 lemon, cut into thin slices, seeds removed

1 yellow summer squash, thinly sliced

1 zucchini, thinly sliced

¼ cup pine nuts

1. Preheat oven to 425°F. Cut four 12" × 18" pieces of cooking parchment paper. Fold in half, cut into a half-heart shape, and then unfold. Place chicken breasts on one side of the fold and sprinkle with salt and lemon pepper. Top with lemon slices.

2. Arrange summer squash and zucchini around chicken and sprinkle pine nuts over all. Fold hearts in half and seal the edges by tightly folding them together twice. Place on cookie sheets and bake for 10–15 minutes, until chicken registers 170°F on a meat thermometer. Serve immediately.

Grilled Turkey Tenderloin

The marinade for this simple recipe is a nice blend of sweet and spicy.
Serve the tenderloin with a mixed fruit salad and some toasted garlic bread.

INGREDIENTS | SERVES 4

1 pound turkey tenderloin
½ cup orange juice
2 tablespoons Dijon mustard
¼ cup honey
2 garlic cloves, minced
½ teaspoon salt
⅛ teaspoon pepper

The Tenderloin

Whether you are cooking beef tenderloin, pork tenderloin, or turkey tenderloin, remember that this popular cut is low in fat and should be cooked quickly. This cut comes from a part of the animal that isn't used much, so it is tender, with little connective tissue.

1. Prepare and preheat grill. Butterfly the tenderloin by cutting it in half lengthwise, being careful not to cut all the way through. Stop about 1 inch from the other side. Spread the tenderloin open, cover it with plastic wrap, and pound gently with a meat mallet or rolling pin to flatten.

2. For marinade, combine remaining ingredients in a large resealable plastic bag. Add the turkey, close the bag, and knead the bag, pressing the marinade into the turkey. Let stand at room temperature for 10 minutes.

3. Cook turkey about 6 inches above medium-hot coals for 5 minutes; brush with any leftover marinade. Turn turkey and cook for 4–6 minutes on second side, until thoroughly cooked. Discard any remaining marinade. Serve immediately.

Turkey Amandine

This recipe is a great way to use up leftover Thanksgiving turkey, and if you have gravy left
after the feast, use that! Serve over hot cooked couscous, mashed potatoes, or rice.

INGREDIENTS | SERVES 4

2 tablespoons olive oil
1 cup sliced carrots
2 cups chopped Grilled Turkey Tenderloin (see this chapter)
1 (14-ounce) jar turkey gravy
½ cup whipping cream
½ cup toasted sliced almonds

In heavy saucepan, heat olive oil over medium heat. Add carrots; cook and stir until crisp and tender, about 4–5 minutes. Add chopped turkey and stir. Add gravy and whipping cream and bring to a simmer. Cook for 3–5 minutes, until turkey and carrots are hot and tender. Sprinkle with almonds and serve.

Microwave Salsa Chicken

*Serve this delicious dish over couscous, topped with some sour cream,
chopped tomatoes, and diced avocado.*

INGREDIENTS | SERVES 4

1½ cups chicken broth

2 tablespoons chili powder

½ teaspoon salt

⅛ teaspoon cayenne pepper

4 boneless, skinless chicken breasts

1 cup chunky salsa

2 tablespoons tomato paste

2 tomatoes, chopped

Tomato Paste

Tomato paste is a concentrate of fresh tomatoes, sometimes made with seasonings like basil, garlic, and oregano. You can find it in cans or in tubes. Purchase it in tubes and you can add a small amount to particular dishes without having to store leftover paste.

1. Place chicken broth into a microwave-safe dish. Microwave on high for 3–5 minutes, until boiling. Meanwhile, sprinkle chili powder, salt, and cayenne pepper on the chicken and rub into both sides. Pierce chicken on the smooth side with a fork. Carefully place, smooth-side down, in hot liquid in dish.

2. Microwave the chicken on high power for 8 minutes; then remove dish from oven and carefully drain off chicken broth.

3. In small bowl combine salsa, tomato paste, and tomatoes and mix well. Turn chicken over, rearrange chicken in dish, and pour salsa mixture over. Return to microwave and cook for 2–6 minutes, checking every 2 minutes, until chicken is thoroughly cooked. Let stand for 5 minutes and serve.

Grilled Chicken Packets

This one-dish meal is so simple to make. You can make the packets ahead of time and keep them in the fridge until it's time to grill and eat.

INGREDIENTS | SERVES 4

4 boneless, skinless chicken breasts
½ teaspoon salt
⅛ teaspoon pepper
2 cups sliced mushrooms
3 garlic cloves, minced
1 cup pasta sauce
1½ cups shredded Gouda cheese

1. Prepare and heat grill. Tear off four 18" × 12" sheets of heavy-duty aluminum foil. Place chicken breasts in center of each sheet and sprinkle with salt and pepper. Divide mushrooms and minced garlic among foil sheets and top each with pasta sauce. Sprinkle with cheese.

2. Fold foil over ingredients and seal the edges of the foil packets, making double folds on all of the seams. Place over medium coals and cover grill. Cook for 20–25 minutes, rearranging once during cooking time, until chicken is thoroughly cooked. Serve immediately.

Sautéed Chicken Patties

Caramelized onions add great flavor to these tender chicken patties.
Serve them over mashed potatoes to soak up all the sauce.

INGREDIENTS | SERVES 4–6

4 tablespoons olive oil, divided

1 onion, finely chopped

1 teaspoon sugar

1 egg

2 cups panko, divided

½ teaspoon salt

⅛ teaspoon white pepper

1½ pounds ground chicken

1½ cups chicken broth

½ teaspoon dried marjoram leaves

Panko

Panko, or Japanese bread crumbs, are very light crumbs that make a coating exceptionally crisp and crunchy. You can substitute regular dry bread crumbs if you can't find them, but the coating won't be as crisp. Don't substitute soft, or fresh, bread crumbs, as the texture will be entirely different.

1. Heat 2 tablespoons olive oil in heavy sautée pan over medium heat. Add onion; cook and stir for 3 minutes, then sprinkle with sugar. Cook, stirring occasionally, until onion begins to turn light brown, 8–10 minutes.

2. Meanwhile, in large bowl, combine egg, ½ cup panko, salt, and pepper and mix well. Add caramelized onions; do not rinse pan. Add ground chicken to egg mixture and mix gently but thoroughly. Form into 6 patties and coat in remaining panko.

3. Add remaining olive oil to pan used to cook onions; heat over medium heat. Add chicken patties, 3 at a time, and sauté for 4 minutes. Carefully turn patties and sauté for 3–6 minutes longer, until thoroughly cooked. Repeat with remaining chicken patties. Remove all chicken patties to serving platter. Add chicken broth and marjoram to saucepan and bring to a boil over high heat. Boil for 2–3 minutes to reduce liquid; pour over chicken patties and serve.

Microwave Chicken Divan

This method of cooking chicken breasts in the microwave yields tender, moist chicken. Serve with a spinach salad and some fresh fruit.

INGREDIENTS | SERVES 4

1½ cups chicken broth

½ teaspoon salt

⅛ teaspoon pepper

½ teaspoon dried thyme leaves

4 boneless, skinless chicken breasts

1 (10-ounce) package frozen broccoli, thawed

1 (10-ounce) container refrigerated four-cheese Alfredo sauce

1 cup crushed round buttery crackers

1. Place chicken broth into a microwave-safe dish. Microwave on high for 3–5 minutes, until boiling. Meanwhile, sprinkle salt, pepper, and thyme on the chicken and rub into both sides. Pierce chicken on the smooth side with a fork. Carefully place, smooth-side down, in hot liquid in dish.

2. Microwave the chicken on high power for 8 minutes; then remove dish from oven and carefully drain off chicken broth.

3. Drain thawed broccoli and combine in medium bowl with Alfredo sauce. Rearrange chicken in dish, turn over, and pour broccoli mixture over; sprinkle with cracker crumbs. Return to microwave and cook for 3–6 minutes, checking every 2 minutes, until chicken is thoroughly cooked. Let stand for 5 minutes and serve.

Quick Chicken Cordon Bleu

Pancetta is Italian bacon that is cured with spices, but not smoked.
The deli department in your supermarket sells it thinly sliced.

INGREDIENTS | SERVES 4

1 cup grated Parmesan cheese, divided

4 boneless, skinless chicken breasts

8 slices pancetta

1 (14-ounce) jar Alfredo sauce

4 slices baby Swiss cheese

Deconstructing Recipes

One way to make recipes simpler to make is to deconstruct them. Chicken cordon bleu is typically made by stuffing ham and cheese into chicken breasts and then baking them. Wrapping the chicken in pancetta and topping with cheese results in the same taste but is much quicker to make.

1. Preheat oven to 400°F. Place ½ cup Parmesan cheese on a plate and dip chicken breasts into cheese to coat. Wrap pancetta around chicken breasts and place in a 2-quart casserole dish. Bake for 10 minutes.

2. In medium bowl, combine Alfredo sauce with remaining ½ cup Parmesan cheese.

3. Remove casserole from oven and pour Alfredo sauce mixture over chicken. Return to oven and bake for 10 minutes longer. Top each chicken breast with a slice of cheese and return to the oven. Bake for 5 minutes longer, or until chicken is thoroughly cooked and cheese is melted. Serve immediately.

Pesto Turkey Cutlets

The sauce for these cutlets is so delicious, you must serve this over hot cooked rice or couscous, with steamed broccoli or green beans on the side.

INGREDIENTS | SERVES 6

⅓ cup flour

1 teaspoon salt

1 teaspoon dried basil leaves

⅛ teaspoon white pepper

¾ cup grated Parmesan cheese, divided

2 eggs, beaten

12 turkey cutlets

3 tablespoons olive oil

1 (16-ounce) jar four-cheese Alfredo sauce

1 (10-ounce) container refrigerated pesto

1. In small bowl, combine flour, salt, basil, pepper, and ¼ cup Parmesan cheese and mix well. Break eggs into shallow bowl and beat well. Dip cutlets into egg, and then into flour mixture to coat. Place on wire rack.

2. Heat olive oil in heavy skillet over medium heat. Sauté cutlets, 4 at a time, for 3 minutes; then turn and cook for 2–3 minutes on other side. As cutlets are cooked, remove to a platter. When all cutlets are cooked, add Alfredo sauce to skillet; bring to a simmer.

3. Add pesto to skillet and stir to mix. Return cutlets to the pan with the sauce and heat for 1–2 minutes. Sprinkle with remaining ½ cup Parmesan cheese and serve immediately.

Cashew Chicken

A salty liquid made from fermented fish, fish sauce is a staple ingredient in Southeast Asian cooking. If fish sauce is unavailable, substitute 1 tablespoon of soy sauce.

INGREDIENTS | SERVES 3

¾ pound boneless, skinless chicken breast

2 tablespoons vegetable or peanut oil

1 tablespoon red curry paste

2 cloves garlic, chopped

1 yellow onion, cut into thin slices

¼ cup chicken broth

2 tablespoons oyster sauce

1 tablespoon fish sauce

2 scallions, chopped

1 teaspoon granulated sugar

½ cup roasted cashews

1 bunch cilantro sprigs, for optional garnish

1. Cut the chicken into bite-size pieces.

2. Heat the oil in a wok or heavy skillet. Add the red curry paste and the garlic. Stir-fry until the garlic is aromatic. Add the chicken and stir-fry on high heat for 4–5 minutes, until the chicken is white and nearly cooked.

3. Add the onions to the pan. Stir-fry for 2 minutes; then stir in the chicken broth, oyster sauce, and fish sauce. Stir in the scallions and the sugar. Stir in the cashews.

4. Continue cooking for another minute to combine all the ingredients and make sure the chicken is cooked through. To serve, garnish with cilantro sprigs.

Orange-Cilantro Chicken

On weekends or evenings when you have more time, add even more flavor to this dish by increasing the marinating time to 2 hours.

The Difference Between Grilling and Broiling

What separates grilling and broiling is more than whether or not the food is cooked indoors or outside on the grill. The main difference between these two cooking methods is the location of the heat source. In broiling, heat is applied to the food from the top, whereas in grilling the heat comes from the bottom. Both methods rely upon an intense direct heat that sears the food, giving it a rich flavor.

1. In a small bowl, whisk together the orange juice and olive oil. Whisk in lime juice, orange zest, cilantro, garlic, salt, pepper, and Tabasco sauce. Reserve ¼ cup of this mixture to use as a basting sauce.

2. Place a few diagonal cuts on the chicken so that the marinade can penetrate. Place the chicken in a large resealable plastic bag and add the marinade. Marinate the chicken for at least 5 minutes.

3. Preheat the broiler. Place the chicken on a rack that has been sprayed with nonstick cooking spray. Brush some of the reserved marinade on top. Broil the chicken, 9 inches from the heat source, for about 15 minutes, until the chicken is cooked through. Every 5 minutes, turn the chicken over and brush with the reserved marinade. Serve immediately.

Stir-Fry Chicken Cacciatore

Normally a slow simmered dish, this recipe transforms Italian chicken cacciatore into a quick stir-fry that is perfect for busy weeknights.

INGREDIENTS | SERVES 4

1 pound boneless, skinless chicken thighs

3½ tablespoons dry white wine, divided

1 teaspoon dried oregano

Black pepper, to taste

2 teaspoons cornstarch

1 shallot, peeled and chopped

¼ pound sliced fresh mushrooms

1 red bell pepper, seeded, cut into thin strips

3 tablespoons low-sodium chicken broth

3 tablespoons diced tomatoes with juice

½ teaspoon granulated sugar

3 tablespoons olive oil, divided

1 tablespoon chopped fresh oregano

Stir-Fry Tips

When stir-frying, always make sure the oil is hot before adding the food. Stir vegetables continually, to keep them from sticking to the bottom of the pan. When stir-frying meat, allow it to brown briefly before you begin stirring.

1. Cut the chicken into thin strips about 2–3 inches long. Place the chicken strips in a bowl and add 2½ tablespoons white wine, oregano, pepper, and cornstarch, adding the cornstarch last. Let the chicken stand while preparing the other ingredients.

2. While the chicken is marinating, cut the vegetables. In a small bowl, combine the chicken broth, diced tomatoes, and sugar. Set aside.

3. Heat 1 tablespoon oil in a wok or heavy skillet. When the oil is hot, add the chopped shallot. Stir-fry for a minute, until it begins to soften, and then add the sliced mushrooms. Stir-fry for a minute; then add the red bell pepper. Stir-fry for another minute, adding a bit of water if the vegetables begin to dry out. Remove the vegetables from the pan.

4. Heat 2 tablespoons oil in the wok or skillet. When the oil is hot, add the chicken. Let the chicken brown for a minute; then stir-fry for about 5 minutes, until it turns white and is nearly cooked through. Splash 1 tablespoon of the white wine on the chicken while stir-frying.

5. Add the chicken broth and tomato mixture to the middle of the pan. Bring to a boil. Return the vegetables to the pan. Stir in the fresh oregano. Cook, stirring, for another couple of minutes to mix everything together. Serve immediately.

Chicken with Havarti

Feel free to use either plain Havarti or Havarti with dill in this recipe.
Serve the chicken with steamed vegetables and cooked pasta.

INGREDIENTS | SERVES 4

4 tablespoons lemon juice
½ teaspoon garlic salt
¼ teaspoon black pepper
2 teaspoons fresh dill weed
4 boneless, skinless chicken breast halves
½ cup crumbled Havarti cheese

1. Preheat the broiler.

2. In a small bowl, combine the lemon juice, garlic salt, pepper, and dill weed. Use a pastry brush to brush the chicken breasts with the lemon juice mixture.

3. Spray a rack with nonstick cooking spray. Broil the chicken for 15 minutes or until cooked through, turning every 5 minutes. Brush any leftover lemon juice mixture on the chicken while broiling.

4. Sprinkle the crumbled cheese over the cooked chicken. Serve when the cheese is melted.

Easy Tandoori Chicken

Traditionally, tandoori chicken is marinated overnight in a spicy mixture of yogurt and seasonings. In this quick and easy variation, the chicken is pan-fried with the seasonings and served with a heated yogurt dressing.

INGREDIENTS | SERVES 4

1½ teaspoons ground coriander

1½ teaspoons ground cumin

1½ teaspoons ground cayenne pepper

½ teaspoon ground ginger

¼ teaspoon sugar

½ teaspoon garlic powder, or to taste

4 boneless, skinless chicken breast halves

¾ cup natural yogurt

2 tablespoons lemon juice

2 tablespoons vegetable oil

1 clove garlic, peeled, thinly sliced

1 shallot, peeled and chopped

Perfectly Cooked Chicken Breasts

One way to tell if a chicken breast is cooked is to press on it. Properly cooked chicken has a "springy" texture. If the chicken is too soft, it is not done, while chicken meat that is tough has been overcooked.

1. Combine the spices, sugar, and garlic powder in a small bowl. Rub over the chicken breasts to season.

2. In a small bowl, combine the yogurt and lemon juice. Set aside (do not refrigerate).

3. Heat the oil in a skillet on medium-high heat. Add the garlic and the chicken. Pan-fry for 3–4 minutes on one side until browned.

4. Add the shallot. Turn over the chicken and cook the other side until the chicken is cooked through (8–10 minutes total cooking time). While the chicken is cooking, briefly heat the yogurt in a saucepan over medium heat.

5. Remove the chicken to a serving plate and spoon yogurt mixture over chicken. Serve immediately.

Turkey Meatloaf

You can add extra flavor by using Italian seasoned bread crumbs in this recipe.

INGREDIENTS | SERVES 4

1 pound lean ground turkey

¼ cup ketchup

¼ cup water

½ medium onion, chopped

2 tablespoons instant basil and tomato soup mix

1 egg, beaten

½ teaspoon black pepper

¾ cup bread crumbs

1. In a large bowl, combine all the ingredients and stir, but do not overmix.

2. Spoon the mixture into a microwave-safe casserole dish and shape into a loaf.

3. Microwave on high heat for 10 minutes, and then for 5 minutes or as needed until the turkey is cooked and the juices run clear (total cooking time should be about 15 minutes).

4. Let stand for 5 minutes, and then pour any fat off the dish and serve.

Pan-Fried Garlic Chicken Thighs with Sun-Dried Tomatoes

There's almost no preparation required to make this flavorful chicken dish. Ready-to-use sun-dried tomatoes, such as Mariani's, are a great timesaver since they don't need to be softened before using.

INGREDIENTS | SERVES 2

1 pound (6–8 small) boneless, skinless chicken thighs
⅛ teaspoon garlic salt
¼ teaspoon black pepper
2 teaspoons olive oil
½ medium onion, thinly sliced
2 tablespoons sun-dried tomato strips
½ cup chicken broth
2 teaspoons lemon juice
1 tablespoon chopped fresh basil leaves

Cooking with Olive Oil

Loaded with heart-healthy monounsaturated fats, olive oil is a great choice for pan-frying, sautéing, and stir-frying. Just be sure to stick with the olive oils that don't break down at high heats (such as pure olive oil) and leave the extra-virgin olive oil for salads. Always wait until the olive oil is fully heated before adding the food.

1. Rinse the chicken thighs and pat dry. Rub the garlic salt and pepper over the chicken to season.

2. Heat the olive oil in a large skillet over medium heat. Add the chicken. Cook for 5–6 minutes, until browned on both sides, turning over halfway through cooking. Stir the chicken occasionally to make sure it doesn't stick to the pan.

3. Push the chicken to the sides of the pan. Add the onion and sun-dried tomato strips. Cook in the oil for about 3 minutes, until the onion is browned.

4. Add the chicken broth. Stir in the lemon juice.

5. Simmer for 8–10 minutes, until the liquid is nearly absorbed and the chicken is just cooked through. Stir in the basil leaves during the last 2 minutes of cooking. Serve immediately.

Chicken Breasts Stuffed with Ham and Cheese

This dish can be prepared in advance and refrigerated overnight.
It will take longer to cook if put into the oven directly from the refrigerator.

INGREDIENTS | SERVES 4

4 (6-ounce) skinless, boneless chicken breasts

¼ teaspoon seasoned salt

Freshly cracked black pepper, to taste

4 teaspoons Dijon mustard

4 ounces Black Forest deli ham (about 4 slices), cut into 1½-inch-wide strips

2 ounces deli Swiss or Gruyère cheese (about 2 slices), cut into 1½-inch-wide strips

1 tablespoon olive oil

1 egg, beaten

½ cup panko

Chopped fresh parsley, for garnish

1. Butterfly the chicken breasts and season with salt and pepper. Brush the inside of each breast with 1 teaspoon mustard. Lay equal portions of the ham and cheese over half of each breast, and fold back to the original shape. Secure the seam with a toothpick.

2. Preheat oven to 375°F.

3. Line a medium-sized baking dish with tinfoil and brush with the olive oil. Place the stuffed chicken breasts seam-side down in the baking dish. Brush the chicken with the beaten egg and evenly coat each breast with an equal amount of the panko crumbs. Bake uncovered until done, about 20–22 minutes. To check for doneness, cut through the bottom of a stuffed breast; the chicken should be cooked throughout without a trace of pinkness, and the cheese filling should be melted.

4. Let the chicken rest for a few minutes to allow the filling to set. To serve, place a breast on each serving plate and garnish with parsley. Serve hot.

CHAPTER 7

Beef and Pork

Greek Tenderloin Steak

Beef tenderloins are also called filet mignon. This method of preparing steak can be varied with different cheeses. Serve with a green salad and corn on the cob.

INGREDIENTS | SERVES 6

6 (4-ounce) beef tenderloin steaks

½ cup balsamic and oil vinaigrette

1 sweet red onion, chopped

2 cloves garlic, minced

1 tablespoon olive oil

¾ cup crumbled feta cheese with herbs

Easy Steak Doneness Tests

Put your hand palm up, and touch your thumb and index finger together. Feel the pad at the base of your thumb; that's what rare steaks feel like. Touch your thumb and middle finger together; the pad will feel like a medium-rare steak. Ring finger and thumb is medium, and thumb and pinky feels like a well-done steak.

1. Prepare and preheat grill. Place steaks in baking pan and pour vinaigrette over them. Let stand at room temperature for 10 minutes.

2. Meanwhile, in heavy skillet, cook onion and garlic in olive oil over medium heat until tender and just beginning to brown around the edges, about 6–8 minutes. Remove from heat and set aside.

3. Drain steaks and place on grill; cook, covered, 4–6 inches from medium heat for 7 minutes. Turn, cover, and cook for 4–8 minutes, until desired doneness. Uncover grill and top each steak with some of the feta cheese. Cover grill and cook for 1 minute, until cheese melts. Place steaks on serving plate and top with onion mixture. Serve immediately.

Spicy Cube Steaks

This comforting, old-fashioned recipe is delicious served with refrigerated mashed potatoes, heated with some sour cream and Parmesan cheese.

INGREDIENTS | SERVES 4

4 cube steaks
3 tablespoons flour
1 tablespoon chili powder
1 teaspoon salt
2 tablespoons olive oil
1 (14-ounce) can undrained diced tomatoes with green chilies
1 (10-ounce) can condensed nacho cheese soup
1 cup sliced mushrooms

Cube Steaks

Cube steaks are typically round steaks that have been run through a machine that pierces the steak all over to break up connective tissue, so the meat is more tender. You can pound your own round steaks using the pointed side of a meat mallet.

1. Place cube steaks on waxed paper. In small bowl, combine flour, chili powder, and salt and mix well. Sprinkle half of flour mixture over the steaks and pound into steaks using a rolling pin or the flat side of a meat mallet. Turn steaks, sprinkle with remaining flour mixture, and pound again.

2. Heat olive oil in large saucepan over medium-high heat. Add steaks; sauté for 4 minutes on first side; then turn and sauté for 2 minutes on other side. Remove steaks from saucepan.

3. Pour tomatoes and soup into pan; cook and stir until simmering, scraping up browned bits. Add steaks back to pan along with mushrooms; simmer for 15–20 minutes, until tender. Serve immediately.

Grilled Steak Kebabs

The combination of barbecue sauce and cola beverage adds nice spice and flavor to these easy grilled kebabs. Serve with hot cooked rice, a green salad, and some breadsticks.

INGREDIENTS | SERVES 4

1 pound sirloin steak
¾ cup barbecue sauce
2 tablespoons cola beverage
¼ teaspoon garlic pepper
8 ounces cremini mushrooms
2 red bell peppers, cut into strips

Grill Temperatures

Check the temperature of your grill by carefully holding your hand about 6 inches above the coals and counting how many seconds you can hold your hand steady before it gets too hot. If you can hold your hand for 5 seconds, the coals are low; 4 seconds, medium; 3 seconds, medium-high; and 2 seconds, high.

1. Cut steak into 1-inch cubes and combine with barbecue sauce, cola beverage, and garlic pepper in a medium bowl. Massage the marinade into the meat with your hands; let stand for 10 minutes.

2. Meanwhile, prepare vegetables and preheat grill. Thread steak cubes, mushrooms, and bell peppers onto metal skewers and place on grill over medium coals. Grill, covered, brushing frequently with remaining marinade, for 7–10 minutes, turning frequently, until steak reaches desired doneness. Discard any remaining marinade. Serve immediately.

Spicy Grilled Flank Steak

Grill seasoning contains lots of spices, usually including cumin, oregano, pepper, garlic, and sugar. Use it for hamburgers as well as grilled steaks.

INGREDIENTS | SERVES 4–6

3 garlic cloves
1 teaspoon salt
1 tablespoon grill seasoning
¼ teaspoon dry mustard
¼ teaspoon cayenne pepper
2 tablespoons balsamic vinegar
1½ pounds flank steak

It's All in the Slicing

Flank steak is a lean, flavorful cut that is tender only if sliced correctly. Look at the steak: you'll see parallel lines running through it. That's called the grain of the steak. When you cut the steak, cut against, or perpendicular to, those lines and the steak will be tender and juicy.

1. Prepare and heat grill. On cutting board, mince garlic cloves; then sprinkle with salt. Using the side of the knife, mash garlic and salt together to create a paste. Place in a small bowl and add remaining ingredients except flank steak; mix well.

2. Prick both sides of the steak with a fork and rub the marinade mixture into the steak. Let stand for 10 minutes.

3. Place steak on grill over medium coals and cover. Grill for 5 minutes; then turn steak, cover, and grill for 3–5 minutes longer, until medium-rare or medium. Let steak stand for 5 minutes, and then slice across the grain to serve.

Mini Meatloaf

Meatloaves made in muffin tins are cute, fun to make, and fun to eat.
Serve with some ketchup and frozen french fries to give your kids a treat.

INGREDIENTS | SERVES 6

2 eggs

½ teaspoon dried Italian seasoning

½ teaspoon onion salt

⅛ teaspoon garlic pepper

¾ cup soft bread crumbs

¾ cup ketchup, divided

1½ pounds meatloaf mix

1 cup shredded Colby-Jack cheese, divided

About Meatloaf Mix

Meatloaf mix is found in the meat aisle of the supermarket. It usually consists of one-third beef, one-third pork, and one-third veal, but read the label to find out what the blend is in your area. The veal lightens the mixture, and the pork adds a slightly different flavor and texture. Meatloaf made with all beef tends to be heavy.

1. Preheat oven to 350°F. In large bowl, combine eggs, Italian seasoning, onion salt, garlic pepper, bread crumbs, and ½ cup ketchup and mix well. Add meatloaf mix and ½ cup cheese and mix gently but thoroughly to combine.

2. Press meat mixture, ⅓ cup at a time, into 12 muffin cups. Top each with a bit of ketchup and remaining cheese. Bake at 350°F for 15–18 minutes, until meat is thoroughly cooked. Remove from muffin tins, drain if necessary, place on serving platter, cover with foil, and let stand for 5 minutes before serving.

Quick Beef Stroganoff

Beef Stroganoff is an elegant dish that usually takes a while to make,
but using precooked meat products means the dish is ready in about 20 minutes.

INGREDIENTS | SERVES 4

2 tablespoons olive oil

1 onion, chopped

1 (16-ounce) package fully cooked beef tips with gravy

1 (16-ounce) package frozen cut green beans, thawed and drained

4 cups egg noodles

1 cup sour cream

1. Bring a large pot of water to a boil. Meanwhile, heat olive oil in large skillet over medium heat. Add onion; cook and stir for 3–4 minutes, until crisp and tender. Add contents of beef package along with green beans. Bring to a simmer; cook for 6–7 minutes, until beef and green beans are heated.

2. When water is boiling, add egg noodles. Cook according to package directions, until al dente, about 4–5 minutes.

3. Meanwhile, stir sour cream into beef mixture, cover, and remove from heat. When noodles are done, drain well, place on serving platter, and spoon beef mixture on top. Serve immediately.

Cuban Pork Chops

Evoke a taste of the tropics with this simple, well-flavored recipe.
Serve it with a rice pilaf, spinach salad, and some cantaloupe slices drizzled with honey.

INGREDIENTS | SERVES 4

4 boneless pork loin chops

4 garlic cloves, finely chopped

2 teaspoons cumin seed

½ teaspoon dried oregano leaves

½ teaspoon salt

⅛ teaspoon cayenne pepper

2 tablespoons olive oil

¼ cup orange juice

2 tablespoons lime juice

1. Trim excess fat from pork chops. In small bowl, combine garlic, cumin, oregano, salt, and cayenne pepper and mix well. Sprinkle this mixture on both sides of chops and rub into meat. Let stand at room temperature for 10 minutes.

2. Heat olive oil in heavy saucepan over medium heat. Add pork chops and cook for 5 minutes. Carefully turn and cook for 5 minutes on second side. Add orange juice and lime juice and bring to a simmer.

3. Cover pan and simmer chops for 5–10 minutes, or until pork chops are tender and just slightly pink in the center and sauce is reduced. Serve immediately.

Ham Asparagus Wraps

The asparagus has to be cooked in this recipe because it doesn't bake long enough to soften. Use any flavor of cream cheese and bottled Alfredo sauce you like.

INGREDIENTS | SERVES 4

4 (¼-inch-thick) slices deli ham

½ cup soft cream cheese with garlic

12 spears Grilled Asparagus (see Chapter 10)

1 (10-ounce) jar garlic Alfredo sauce

½ cup grated Parmesan cheese

Preheat oven to 375°F. Place ham on work surface and spread each piece with some of the cream cheese. Top each with 3 spears of asparagus and roll up. Place in 12" × 8" glass baking dish and pour Alfredo sauce over all. Sprinkle with Parmesan cheese. Bake at 375°F for 15–20 minutes, until ham rolls are hot and sauce is bubbling. Serve immediately.

Ham Slices

For recipes that require you to enclose other ingredients in ham slices, do not use the thin slices of boiled ham meant for making sandwiches. You can use slices from spiral-sliced hams or go to the deli and ask for ham to be sliced from the whole ham.

Pork Chops with Onion Conserve

You'll have three pans cooking on the stove while making this recipe, but it still takes only 30 minutes!

INGREDIENTS | SERVES 4

½ cup golden raisins
1¼ cups orange juice, divided
¼ cup olive oil, divided
1 red onion, chopped
1 teaspoon sugar
4 center cut boneless pork chops
1 teaspoon salt
⅛ teaspoon pepper
1 teaspoon dried thyme

About Raisins

Raisins are dried grapes, but the way they are dried determines the color. Both golden and dark raisins are made from Thompson variety grapes, but the dark raisins are dried in the sun, while golden raisins are oven-dried. The sunlight causes the raisins to darken. Golden raisins may also be treated with sulfur dioxide; read labels carefully!

1. In small heavy saucepan, combine raisins and 1 cup orange juice; bring to a simmer over medium heat.

2. Meanwhile, in another heavy saucepan, heat 2 tablespoons olive oil over medium heat. Add red onion; cook over medium heat for 10 minutes, stirring frequently, until onion begins to turn brown. Add sugar to onion; cook for 2 minutes. Add raisin mixture; bring to a boil over high heat, and then reduce heat to low and simmer while cooking pork chops.

3. Meanwhile, sprinkle pork chops with salt, pepper, and thyme. Heat remaining 2 tablespoons olive oil in large skillet and add pork chops. Cook over medium heat, turning once, until pork is done, about 10 minutes. Remove pork from pan; cover to keep warm.

4. Add ¼ cup orange juice to drippings remaining in pan; turn heat to high and bring to a boil. Reduce heat and simmer for 2–3 minutes, until juice is reduced. Return pork chops to pan along with onion/raisin mixture. Cover and cook for 2 minutes; then serve immediately.

Stovetop Lasagna

Serve this super easy version of lasagna with a crisp green salad and some breadsticks.

INGREDIENTS | SERVES 4–6

1 pound bulk sweet Italian sausage

1 onion, chopped

1 (24-ounce) package frozen ravioli

1 (28-ounce) jar pasta sauce

1 teaspoon dried Italian seasoning

1½ cups Italian blend shredded cheese

1. Bring large pot of water to a boil. Meanwhile, in heavy skillet over medium heat, cook sausage and onion, stirring to break up sausage, until meat is browned. Drain sausage thoroughly and wipe out skillet.

2. Add ravioli to boiling water; cook until almost tender, about 1–2 minutes. Drain well.

3. In cleaned skillet, spread about 1 cup pasta sauce; then top with layers of sausage mixture, ravioli, and more pasta sauce. Sprinkle each layer with a bit of the dried Italian seasoning. Sprinkle top with cheese. Cover and cook over medium heat, shaking pan occasionally, until sauce bubbles, cheese melts, and mixture is hot, about 5–8 minutes. Serve immediately.

Pork and Apricot Skewers

This recipe is elegant enough for company. Serve with hot cooked rice and garlic bread, with a spinach salad on the side.

INGREDIENTS | SERVES 6

1½ pounds boneless pork tenderloin
1 cup apricot preserves
½ cup apricot nectar
12 dried whole apricots
2 onions
½ teaspoon dried thyme leaves

Kebabs

When you're making skewers or kebabs, there are different materials to choose from. Bamboo skewers must be soaked in water for at least 30 minutes before grilling so that they won't burn while the food is cooking. Metal skewers are more durable, but use caution because they get very hot when on the grill.

1. Prepare and heat grill. Cut pork into 1-inch cubes and place in medium bowl. Top with apricot preserves; let stand while preparing remaining ingredients.

2. In small saucepan, combine apricot nectar and dried apricots; bring to a boil over high heat. Reduce heat and simmer for 3 minutes. Remove apricots and set on wire rack to cool; pour hot nectar over pork cubes. Cut onions into 6 wedges each.

3. Drain pork, reserving marinade, and thread pork cubes, onion wedges, and apricots onto 6 metal skewers. Combine the reserved marinade with the thyme leaves in a small pan and bring to a boil over medium-high heat; reduce heat to low and simmer while skewers cook.

4. Grill skewers, covered, over medium coals for 5 minutes. Turn and brush with some of the simmering marinade. Cover and grill for 5–8 minutes longer, until pork is slightly pink in center and onions are crisp and tender; keep marinade simmering. Serve with the marinade on the side.

Ham and Cheese Penne

This simple one-dish dinner recipe can be made with any frozen vegetable combo. You can even eliminate the pasta if you use a vegetable combo that includes pasta!

Al Dente

When cooking pasta, al dente is a term used to indicate doneness. It means "to the tooth." Always test pasta by biting into it. When it's tender but still has a firmness to the center, it's done. Look at the pasta: you'll be able to see a small opaque line in the center after you bite it.

1. Bring a large pot of water to boil; cook penne according to package directions. Meanwhile, heat olive oil in large saucepan over medium heat. Add frozen vegetables; sprinkle with 2 tablespoons water. Cover and cook over medium heat for 4–5 minutes until vegetables are almost hot, stirring once during cooking time. Add ham and Alfredo sauce; bring to a simmer.

2. Drain pasta when cooked and add to saucepan with ham mixture. Stir gently; then simmer for 2–3 minutes longer, until vegetables and ham are hot. Sprinkle with Parmesan cheese and serve.

Grilled Orange Pork Tenderloin

This dish will definitely impress your guests. Serve along with corn and couscous, followed by Chocolate-Raspberry Pie (see Chapter 15) for dessert.

INGREDIENTS | SERVES 6–8

2 pounds pork tenderloin

1 teaspoon salt

⅛ teaspoon pepper

⅓ cup frozen orange juice concentrate, thawed

¼ cup honey

¼ cup Dijon mustard

1 tablespoon lemon juice

½ teaspoon dried oregano leaves

Butterflying Meats

Butterflying meat cuts the cooking time almost in half. You can butterfly just about any cut of meat. Use a sharp knife and cut slowly, being sure not to cut all the way through to the other side. Spread the cut meat out and, if desired, use a meat mallet to gently pound the meat and flatten it to an even thickness.

1. Prepare and heat grill. Cut pork tenderloins in half crosswise. Then butterfly the pork: cut the tenderloins horizontally in half, being careful not to cut through to the other side. Spread tenderloins open and place in large casserole dish. Sprinkle both sides with salt and pepper.

2. In medium bowl, combine remaining ingredients and mix well. Spread on all sides of tenderloins and let stand for 10 minutes.

3. Grill tenderloins 6 inches from medium coals, covered, turning once, for 14–17 minutes, until a meat thermometer registers 160°F. Brush with any remaining marinade after turning. Discard remaining marinade. Slice tenderloins across the grain to serve.

Sausage Stir-Fry

*Serve this fresh-tasting stir-fry over hot cooked rice with
chopped cashews on the side, along with a gelatin fruit salad.*

INGREDIENTS | SERVES 4

1 pound sweet Italian sausages

¼ cup water

2 tablespoons olive oil

1 onion, chopped

2 yellow summer squash, sliced

1 cup frozen broccoli florets, thawed

¾ cup sweet-and-sour sauce

Cooking Rice

Rice expands to three times its bulk when cooked. Each serving is about ½ cup, so if you want to serve six people, cook 1 cup of rice to make 3 cups. Combine 1 cup long-grain rice with 2 cups water and a pinch of salt in a saucepan. Cover, bring to a boil, reduce heat to low, and simmer for 15–20 minutes, until tender.

1. In large skillet, cook Italian sausages in water over medium heat for 6–8 minutes, turning frequently during cooking time, until water evaporates and sausages begin to brown. Move sausages to plate and cut into 1-inch pieces.

2. Drain fat from skillet but do not rinse. Return to medium-high heat, add olive oil, and then add onion. Stir-fry until onion is crisp and tender, 3–4 minutes. Add squash and broccoli; stir-fry for 4–5 minutes longer, until broccoli is hot and squash is tender. Return sausage pieces to skillet along with sweet-and-sour sauce. Stir-fry for 4–6 minutes, until sausage pieces are thoroughly cooked and sauce bubbles. Serve immediately.

Italian Crispy Pork Chops

This recipe is great for those who want to add some crunchiness to their pork.
Serve with rice and green beans for a balanced and delicious meal.

INGREDIENTS | SERVES 6–8

8 thin-cut boneless pork chops

2 eggs, beaten

2 tablespoons water

½ cup grated Parmesan cheese

1 cup panko

1 teaspoon dried Italian seasoning

½ teaspoon dried basil leaves

2 tablespoons butter

3 tablespoons olive oil

Make Your Own Panko

If you can't find panko bread crumbs, make your own bread crumbs from a fresh loaf of bread, spread crumbs on a baking sheet, and bake them in a 350°F oven for 5–8 minutes, until dry and crisp.

1. Place pork chops between two pieces of plastic wrap and pound with a rolling pin or meat mallet until about ⅓-inch thick.

2. In shallow bowl, combine eggs and water and beat until blended.

3. On shallow plate, combine cheese, panko, Italian seasoning, and basil and mix well. Dip pork chops into egg mixture and then into cheese mixture, pressing the cheese mixture firmly onto the chops. Place on wire rack when coated. Let stand for 10 minutes.

4. Heat butter and olive oil in a large skillet over medium-high heat. Fry the pork chops, 2–4 minutes on each side, until brown and crisp and just slightly pink inside. Serve immediately.

Southwest Pork Chops

These spicy pork chops are coated with layers of Tex-Mex flavor. Serve them with
hot mashed potatoes, a cooling fruit salad, and a lemon meringue pie for dessert.

INGREDIENTS | SERVES 6

3 tablespoons olive oil

6 (½-inch-thick) boneless pork chops

1 teaspoon salt

⅛ teaspoon cayenne pepper

1 tablespoon chili powder

1 chipotle chili, minced

2 tablespoons adobo sauce

½ cup salsa

1 (8-ounce) can tomato sauce

1. Place olive oil in heavy skillet and heat over medium heat.

2. Meanwhile, sprinkle pork chops with salt, cayenne pepper, and chili powder and rub into meat. Add pork chops to skillet and cook for 4 minutes.

3. Meanwhile, combine chipotle chili, adobo sauce, salsa, and tomato sauce in a small bowl.

4. Turn pork chops and cook for 2 minutes. Then add tomato sauce mixture to skillet, bring to a simmer, and simmer for 4–6 minutes, until chops are cooked and tender. Serve immediately.

Pressure Cooker Sausage Risotto

Your pressure cooker makes the most delicious risotto in less than half the time of traditional stovetop methods.

INGREDIENTS | SERVES 4

3 tablespoons olive oil, divided

1 pound bulk sweet Italian sausage

1 onion, finely chopped

2 cups Arborio rice

4 cups chicken stock, warmed

½ teaspoon dried Italian seasoning

½ cup grated Parmesan cheese

Pressure Cookers

There are two kinds of pressure cookers: those that cook on the stove and those that are self-contained. You can brown food in either type of cooker before adding all the ingredients, sealing the cooker, and bringing it up to pressure. Regulate the heat on the stovetop models by adjusting the stove burners.

1. Turn the pressure cooker to high and add 2 tablespoons of the oil. Cook the sausage until almost done, stirring to break up meat; then add the onion and cook until the sausage is done and the onion is crisp and tender, about 3 minutes. Add remaining olive oil and the rice; cook and stir for 2–4 minutes, until the rice is coated and opaque.

2. Add ½ cup of the stock and cook, stirring constantly, for 2–4 minutes, until the liquid is absorbed by the rice. Add the remaining stock and Italian seasoning and lock the lid into place. Pressure cook on medium for 8 minutes.

3. Let the pressure release, open the lid, and check the rice. If the rice isn't cooked al dente, lock the lid again and cook for 2–3 minutes longer. Release the pressure, open the lid, and stir in the Parmesan cheese until melted. Serve immediately.

Grilled Polish Sausages

Make extra Polish Sausages and save them for Easy Jambalaya (see Chapter 8).
This easy recipe is perfect for a summer cookout; serve potato salad and melon wedges on the side.

INGREDIENTS | SERVES 6

6 Polish sausages

1 cup beer

3 cups coleslaw mix

¾ cup coleslaw dressing

6 whole wheat hot dog buns, split

Sausages

Just about any sausage can be substituted for another. Just be sure to read the package to see if the sausages you choose are fully cooked or raw. The fully cooked sausages need only to be reheated, but the raw ones should be cooked until a meat thermometer registers 170°F.

1. Prepare and preheat grill. Prick sausages with fork and place in saucepan with beer. Bring to a boil over high heat; then reduce heat to low and simmer for 5 minutes, turning frequently. Drain sausages and place on grill over medium coals; grill until hot and crisp, turning occasionally, about 5–7 minutes.

2. While sausages are grilling, combine coleslaw mix and dressing in medium bowl and toss. Toast hot dog buns, cut-side down, on grill. Make sandwiches using sausages, coleslaw mix, and buns.

Beef and Broccoli Stir-Fry

Apple juice provides a convenient substitute for the rice wine or dry sherry that is normally used in Chinese marinades.

INGREDIENTS | SERVES 3

1 pound flank steak
1½ tablespoons soy sauce
1 tablespoon apple juice
2 teaspoons cornstarch
2 cups broccoli florets
¼ cup water
1 tablespoon oyster sauce
1 teaspoon granulated sugar
1 tablespoon vegetable oil

Speedy Stir-Frying

Stir-frying is one of the quickest cooking methods—it's easy to prepare a stir-fry meal in under 30 minutes. While it may seem time-consuming to marinate the meat, marinating helps tenderize the meat and adds extra flavor. Also, you can prepare the vegetables and sauce while the meat is marinating.

1. Cut the beef into thin strips about 2 inches long. (It's easiest to do this if the beef is partially frozen.) In a medium bowl, combine the beef with the soy sauce, apple juice, and cornstarch. Let the beef marinate for 15 minutes.

2. In a large saucepan with enough water to cover, blanch the broccoli for 2–3 minutes, until it is tender but still crisp. Remove the broccoli and rinse under cold running water. Drain.

3. In a small bowl, combine the water, oyster sauce, and sugar. Set aside.

4. Heat the oil in a heavy skillet over medium-high heat. Add the beef. Let brown for a minute, and then stir-fry until it loses its pinkness and is nearly cooked through.

5. Add the broccoli to the pan. Stir the sauce and pour it into the pan. Cook, stirring, to mix everything together and heat through (5 minutes). Serve immediately.

Quick Fried Beef with Onion-Cilantro Relish

Onion-cilantro relish is an easy side dish with a bit of spice that pairs nicely with plain fried beef. You can jazz it up a bit by adding a few slices of tomato or cucumber.

INGREDIENTS | SERVES 4

1¼ pounds flank steak

1½ tablespoons white wine vinegar

1½ tablespoons soy sauce

2 teaspoons cornstarch

1 medium sweet onion, minced

4 tablespoons minced green onion

1 cup chopped fresh cilantro

2 tablespoons lemon juice

½ teaspoon Asian chili sauce

½ teaspoon salt

2 tablespoons vegetable oil

1 garlic clove, thinly sliced

Or Broil It

This onion-cilantro relish would also pair very nicely with broiled steak. Instead of cutting the steak into thin strips, prepare it for broiling by rubbing with a garlic clove cut in half. Place on a rack and broil for 10–15 minutes, turning halfway through cooking, until the steak is cooked through and the juices run clear. Sprinkle the steak with salt and pepper during broiling.

1. Cut the beef across the grain into thin strips, about 2½–3 inches long. (It's easiest to do this if the beef is slightly frozen.) Place in a large bowl and stir in the white wine vinegar, soy sauce, and cornstarch, mixing in the cornstarch with your fingers. Let the beef stand while preparing the relish.

2. In a medium bowl, combine the onion, green onion, and cilantro. Stir in the lemon juice, chili sauce, and salt.

3. Heat the oil in a heavy skillet. Add the garlic and half the steak. Let sear for about 30 seconds; then stir-fry, moving the beef around the pan until it loses its pinkness and is cooked through. Remove the beef from the pan.

4. Repeat with the remaining half of the beef.

5. Serve the beef with the onion-cilantro relish.

Five-Ingredient Meatloaf

Parmesan cheese and tomato sauce are both good sources of umami, the meaty or savory flavor that is the secret ingredient in MSG (monosodium glutamate).

INGREDIENTS | SERVES 4

1½ pounds ground pork

¾ cup plus 2 tablespoons tomato sauce

¼ cup chopped onion

1 tablespoon balsamic vinegar

½ cup Parmesan cheese

Speedy Meatloaf Muffins

Placing individual portions in muffin tins reduces baking time and makes serving easy. Better still, leftover muffins can be frozen, making a quick and easy snack or midday meal. Bake the muffins at 350°F for 25–30 minutes until the muffins are cooked through.

1. In a large bowl, combine all the ingredients. For the tomato sauce, add ¾ cup and then add the remaining 2 tablespoons of sauce if more tomato flavor is desired.

2. Shape into a loaf and place in a microwave-safe casserole dish. Cover with microwave-safe wax paper.

3. Microwave on high heat for 15 minutes, 5 minutes at a time, rotating the dish a quarter turn between each cooking period. If the meatloaf is not cooked after 15 minutes, continue to cook for 1 minute at a time until done. (Total cooking time should be about 15 minutes.) The meatloaf is cooked when the internal temperature reaches 160°F.

4. Let stand for 5 minutes. Pour any fat off the dish and serve.

Skillet Shepherd's Pie

*If canned or packaged beef broth isn't available,
you can use 2 beef bouillon cubes dissolved in 1 cup of boiling water.*

INGREDIENTS | SERVES 4

1 pound ground beef

½ teaspoon salt

¼ teaspoon black pepper

½ medium onion, peeled and chopped

1 cup drained canned green beans

1 cup canned corn

1 portion Garlic Mashed Potatoes (see Chapter 10)

½ teaspoon paprika

1 cup beef broth

Leftover Mashed Potatoes

You don't have to wait until you're preparing a dish such as Skillet Shepherd's Pie to use leftover mashed potatoes—they can also be served alone as a side dish. Reheat the potatoes by frying them in 1–2 teaspoons of oil, or cook in the microwave with a bit of liquid, using the microwave's reheat setting or at 70 percent power.

1. Brown the ground beef in a large skillet on medium heat, using a spatula to break it up. Sprinkle the salt and pepper over the beef while it is cooking.

2. After the beef has been cooking for 5 minutes, add the onion. Cook for another 5 minutes, until the pinkness is gone from the beef and the onion is softened. Drain excess fat from the pan.

3. Add the green beans and corn to the pan.

4. Add the mashed potatoes. Stir in the paprika.

5. Add the beef broth. Simmer for 5 minutes, stirring, to heat everything through. Serve hot.

Rosemary Lamb Chops

This recipe can easily be doubled to serve eight people. Lamb cooked medium-rare will be pink on the inside and have a slightly firm texture.

INGREDIENTS | SERVES 4

4 lamb loin chops, about 1-inch thick, 3 ounces each

¼ teaspoon salt

⅛ teaspoon black pepper

2 teaspoons dried rosemary

2 tablespoons olive oil, divided

2 shallots, chopped

1 tablespoon red wine vinegar

1. Pat lamb chops dry with paper towels. Rub salt and pepper over the lamb chops to season. Rub the rosemary into the lamb chops.

2. Heat 1 tablespoon olive oil in a large skillet over medium-high heat. Add the lamb chops. Cook for 5 minutes; then turn over (turn the heat down if the lamb chops are cooking too quickly). Push to the sides of the skillet.

3. Heat 1 tablespoon oil in the middle of the skillet and add the shallots. Sauté the shallots while the lamb chops finish cooking (total cooking time for the lamb chops should be about 10 minutes). Drain any excess fat out of the pan while cooking.

4. Splash the lamb chops with the red wine vinegar during the last few minutes of cooking. Serve immediately.

Ground Pork Stroganoff

If you like, you can replace the chicken broth with dry white wine.
Serve the stroganoff over cooked rice or noodles.

INGREDIENTS | SERVES 4

2 cups ground pork

2 tablespoons margarine

1 medium onion, peeled and chopped

1 cup sliced fresh mushrooms

⅛ teaspoon nutmeg, or to taste

½ teaspoon dried basil

½ cup chicken broth

Salt and pepper, to taste

½ cup natural yogurt

**Using Chicken Bouillon
for Broth**

Chicken bouillon cubes are a handy substitute for store-bought or homemade chicken broth. To use, dissolve 1 bouillon cube in ½ cup of boiling water.

1. Brown the ground pork in a medium skillet over medium heat. Remove to a plate. Drain the excess fat from the pan.

2. While the ground pork is browning, melt the margarine in a separate large skillet. Add the onion and sauté for 2–3 minutes, until it begins to soften.

3. Add the mushrooms and cook for about 2 minutes, until the vegetables are softened. Stir in the nutmeg and dried basil.

4. Add the chicken broth and ground pork to the pan. Cook, stirring, for a minute to heat through. Taste and season with salt and pepper if desired.

5. Stir in the yogurt. Serve immediately over cooked rice.

Pork with Peaches

Be sure to use peaches that are not overripe and won't fall apart during stir-frying.

INGREDIENTS | SERVES 4

¾ pound pork tenderloin

1 tablespoon soy sauce

1 tablespoon apple juice

1½ teaspoons cornstarch

1 tablespoon water

2 tablespoons plus 1 teaspoon vegetable oil, divided

1 teaspoon minced ginger, divided

2 teaspoons curry powder

2 large peaches, thinly sliced

½ cup chicken broth

Black pepper, to taste

1. Cut the pork into 1-inch cubes. Place the pork in a medium bowl and toss with the soy sauce and apple juice. Let stand for 5 minutes.

2. In a small bowl, dissolve the cornstarch in the water.

3. Heat 2 tablespoons oil in a large skillet on medium-high heat. Add the pork and half the ginger. Cook, stirring constantly, until the pork is no longer pink and is nearly cooked through.

4. Push the pork to the sides of the pan. Add 1 teaspoon oil in the middle. Add the remainder of the ginger and the curry powder. Stir for a few seconds until aromatic. Add the sliced peaches. Cook for a minute, stirring continually, and then add the chicken broth. Add the cornstarch and water mixture, stirring to thicken.

5. Season with the pepper. Cook for another minute, stirring to mix everything together. Serve hot.

One-Dish Sausage and Rice

Using instant rice speeds up the cooking time of this simple, warming dish,
while using chicken broth instead of water to cook the rice adds extra flavor.

INGREDIENTS | SERVES 2

1 cup chicken broth

1 cup long-grain instant rice

2 tablespoons olive oil

1 shallot, peeled and chopped

1 teaspoon paprika

8 ounces cooked smoked sausage, thinly sliced

2 sprigs fresh parsley

Salt and pepper, to taste

Or Use Regular Rice

On evenings when you have a bit more time, try preparing One-Dish Sausage and Rice with regular long-grain rice. In a medium saucepan, bring the water and rice to a boil over medium heat. Let the rice cook until the water is nearly evaporated, add the sausage and parsley, reduce the heat, cover, and simmer until the liquid is absorbed and the rice is cooked. Let the rice sit for 5 minutes; then use a fork to fluff it up and mix in the sausage and parsley. The total cooking time will be about 25 minutes.

1. Bring the chicken broth to a boil in a medium saucepan. Stir in the rice, making sure all the grains are moistened. Remove from the heat, cover, and let stand for 5 minutes.

2. While the rice is cooking, prepare the other ingredients: Heat the olive oil in a large skillet over medium-high heat. Add the shallot. Sauté until softened, about 4 minutes (turn the heat down if the shallot is cooking too quickly). Stir in the paprika.

3. Stir in the sausage and parsley. Cook for a minute until the sausage is heated.

4. After the rice has been heating for 5 minutes, uncover and use a fork to fluff.

5. Stir the sausage and parsley into the cooked rice. Season with salt and pepper if desired. Serve immediately.

CHAPTER 8

Fish and Seafood

Shrimp Fettuccine

*Low-fat evaporated milk is a good substitute for heavy cream
because it is as thick as cream but contains much less fat.*

INGREDIENTS | SERVES 4–6

1 (16-ounce) package fettuccine

3 tablespoons olive oil

1 onion, finely chopped

1 pound raw medium shrimp

½ teaspoon salt

¼ teaspoon lemon pepper

1½ cups heavy cream or low-fat
evaporated milk

1 cup grated Parmesan cheese

Recipe Substitutions

You can substitute scallops, clams, oysters,
or cubed fresh fish fillets for shrimp in just
about any recipe. Scallops are cooked just
until opaque, clams and oysters until they
plump, and fish fillets until they turn
opaque and flake when tested with a fork.

1. Bring a large pot of water to a boil and cook fettuccine according to package directions.

2. Meanwhile, heat olive oil over medium-high heat in a large saucepan and add onion. Cook and stir for 4–5 minutes, until tender. Sprinkle shrimp with salt and pepper and add to saucepan; cook over medium heat for 4–5 minutes, until shrimp curl and turn pink. Add cream and heat for 2 minutes.

3. When pasta is cooked al dente, drain well and stir into shrimp mixture, tossing gently to combine. Cook over medium heat for 3–4 minutes, until sauce is slightly thickened. Add cheese and stir gently to coat. Serve immediately.

Shrimp Scampi Kebabs

Lemon and garlic are the main seasonings in Shrimp Scampi.
This is an easy way to make scampi on your grill. Serve with hot cooked rice.

INGREDIENTS | SERVES 6

3 lemons

¼ cup olive oil

4 cloves garlic, minced

1 teaspoon dried thyme leaves

½ teaspoon salt

⅛ teaspoon white pepper

1½ pounds large raw shrimp, cleaned

18 large mushrooms

2 yellow squash, cut into 1-inch pieces

Cleaning Shrimp

If the shrimp you buy still have the shell and tail on them, you must clean them before use. Cut a shallow slit along the back; remove the shell, tail, and legs; then rinse out the dark vein running along the shrimp, using your fingers to remove it if necessary.

1. Prepare and preheat grill. Using lemon zester, remove peel from 1 of the lemons. Place in medium bowl. Squeeze juice from the peeled lemon and add to peel in bowl. Cut remaining lemons into 6 wedges each and set aside.

2. Add oil, garlic, thyme, salt, and pepper to lemon mixture in bowl and mix well. Add shrimp and let stand for 10 minutes.

3. Drain shrimp, reserving marinade. Place shrimp, mushrooms, squash pieces, and lemon wedges alternately on twelve 8-inch-long metal skewers. Brush skewers with marinade; then grill 4–6 inches from medium-hot coals for 8–14 minutes, turning once, until shrimp are curled and pink and vegetables are tender. Brush skewers often with marinade. Discard any remaining marinade. Serve immediately.

Poached Salmon with Alfredo Sauce

You can find jarred Alfredo and other cheese sauces by the pasta sauces in the supermarket; they are a good substitute for the refrigerated sauces.

INGREDIENTS | SERVES 4

½ cup water

½ cup white wine or fish stock

4 (6-ounce) salmon fillets

1 tablespoon olive oil

1 onion, finely chopped

1 (10-ounce) container refrigerated Alfredo sauce

½ teaspoon dried basil leaves

½ cup grated Parmesan cheese

Poaching

Poaching is cooking meat or fruit in a liquid that is just below the boiling point. This method retains and concentrates the flavor of the food, and the results are juicy and tender. Fish is usually poached because the delicate flesh cooks gently with this method and does not dry out.

1. In a shallow saucepan large enough to hold fillets in a single layer, add water and wine. Bring to a boil over medium heat and add salmon. Reduce heat to low, cover pan, and cook for 8–10 minutes or until fish is opaque and flakes easily when tested with fork.

2. Meanwhile, in heavy saucepan, heat olive oil over medium heat. Add onion and cook until tender, about 4–5 minutes. Add Alfredo sauce and basil; cook and stir over low heat until sauce bubbles.

3. Place salmon on serving plates; cover with sauce and sprinkle with Parmesan cheese. Serve immediately.

Easy Jambalaya

Jambalaya is a festive Southern dish that usually takes hours to make.
Serve this easy version with some melon wedges, croissants, and ice cream sundaes for dessert.

INGREDIENTS | SERVES 4

1 (8-ounce) package yellow rice mix

2 tablespoons olive oil

1 onion, chopped

1 (14-ounce) can diced tomatoes with green chilies

1 (8-ounce) package frozen cooked shrimp, thawed

2 Grilled Polish Sausages (see Chapter 7), sliced

1. Prepare rice mix as directed on package.

2. Meanwhile, in large saucepan, heat olive oil over medium heat. Add onion; cook and stir for 4–5 minutes, until tender. Add tomatoes, shrimp, and sliced sausages; bring to a simmer and cook for 2–3 minutes.

3. When rice is cooked, add to saucepan; cook and stir for 3–4 minutes, until blended. Serve immediately.

Frozen Shrimp

You can buy frozen shrimp that has been shelled, deveined, and cooked. To thaw it, place in a colander under cold running water for 4–5 minutes, tossing shrimp occasionally with hands, until thawed. Use the shrimp immediately after thawing.

Shrimp de Jonghe

The bread crumb mixture for this elegant dish can be prepared ahead of time.
Purchase cooked, shelled, and deveined shrimp from your butcher.

INGREDIENTS | SERVES 6

3 cloves garlic, minced

½ teaspoon salt

½ cup butter, softened

1½ cups fine bread crumbs

¼ teaspoon dried marjoram leaves

¼ teaspoon dried tarragon leaves

⅛ teaspoon white pepper

2 pounds cooked, shelled shrimp, thawed if frozen

¼ cup lemon juice

1. Preheat oven to 425°F. In medium bowl, mash garlic with salt to form a paste. Add butter and beat until combined. Add bread crumbs, marjoram, tarragon, and white pepper and mix well.

2. Butter a 2-quart casserole dish. In large bowl, combine shrimp and lemon juice and toss to coat; then drain shrimp.

3. Layer shrimp and bread crumb mixture in prepared casserole dish. Bake for 15–20 minutes, until hot and bread crumbs begin to brown. Serve immediately.

Purchasing Shrimp

You can find cooked, shelled, and deveined shrimp in the meat aisle of the regular grocery store. This product is also stocked in the freezer section of the meat aisle; thaw according to package directions. Fresh cooked shrimp should be used within two days. It should smell sweet and slightly briny; if there is any off odor, do not buy it.

Shrimp Pesto Ravioli

You can use fish fillets, cut into cubes, in place of the shrimp, or substitute bay scallops.
Serve this easy dish with some breadsticks and a fruit salad.

INGREDIENTS | SERVES 4

1 tablespoon olive oil

1 red bell pepper, chopped

1 pound shelled, deveined large raw shrimp, thawed if frozen

1 (9-ounce) package refrigerated cheese ravioli

1½ cups water

¾ cup pesto sauce

½ cup grated Parmesan cheese

1. In large heavy skillet, heat oil over medium heat. Add red bell pepper and stir-fry for 3–4 minutes, until crisp and tender. Add shrimp; cook and stir for 4–6 minutes, until shrimp curl and turn pink. Remove shrimp and peppers from skillet.

2. Add ravioli and water to skillet and bring to a boil over high heat. Reduce heat to medium-high, cover, and simmer for 4–6 minutes, until ravioli are hot, stirring occasionally.

3. Drain off excess liquid and return shrimp and peppers to skillet. Cook over medium-high heat, stirring occasionally, until shrimp are cooked and mixture is hot. Stir in pesto, place in serving dish, sprinkle with cheese, and serve.

Honey Mustard Salmon

Honey and mustard make an irresistible flavor combination with rich and savory salmon fillets.
You can multiply this recipe for a larger crowd; marinating and cooking times remain the same.

INGREDIENTS | SERVES 4

⅓ cup honey mustard salad dressing

2 tablespoons honey

½ teaspoon dill seed

2 tablespoons butter, melted

4 (6-ounce) salmon fillets

Menu Ideas

Any fish dish is delicious served with a salad made from baby spinach. Toss together spinach, sliced water chestnuts, sliced mushrooms, and red bell pepper, and drizzle with some creamy garlic salad dressing. Top it with croutons or Parmesan shavings. Add some ready-to-bake bread-sticks and your meal is complete.

1. In shallow casserole dish, combine salad dressing, honey, dill seed, and butter and mix well. Add salmon fillets and turn to coat. Cover and let stand at room temperature for 10 minutes.

2. Prepare and preheat grill or broiler. Remove salmon from marinade and place, skin-side down, on grill or broiler pan. Cover and grill, or broil, 6 inches from heat for 8–12 minutes, until salmon is cooked and flakes when tested with a fork, brushing with remaining marinade halfway through cooking time. Discard remaining marinade. Serve immediately.

Fruity Tuna Steaks

Curry powder, orange juice, and apricot jam add great flavor to tender tuna steaks.
Because the steaks are simmered in the sauce, they pick up more flavor.

INGREDIENTS | SERVES 4

2 tablespoons olive oil

1 onion, chopped

2 teaspoons curry powder

⅓ cup frozen orange juice concentrate

2 tablespoons water

¼ cup apricot jam

Salt and pepper to taste

4 (6-ounce) tuna steaks

1. In heavy skillet, heat olive oil over medium heat. Add onion; cook and stir for 2 minutes. Sprinkle curry powder over onions; cook and stir for 2–3 minutes longer, until onions are crisp and tender.

2. Add orange juice concentrate and water to skillet, along with apricot jam and salt and pepper. Bring to a boil; then reduce heat to a simmer and add tuna. Cook for 8–10 minutes per inch of thickness, turning tuna once during cooking time, until fish flakes when tested with fork. You can serve tuna medium-rare if you like.

3. Place tuna on serving plate. If necessary, reduce sauce by turning heat to high and simmering until thickened, 3–4 minutes. Pour sauce over tuna and serve.

Steamed Spicy Scallops

A peppery wine sauce finished with butter coats these tender scallops that are steamed to perfection.

INGREDIENTS | SERVES 4–6

2 tablespoons olive oil

4 cloves garlic, minced

1 serrano pepper, minced

1 cup dry white wine

2 pounds sea scallops

1 teaspoon salt

⅛ teaspoon cayenne pepper

2 tablespoons butter

Scallops

There are three kinds of scallops available. Sea scallops are the largest, about 30 to the pound, and are white, sometimes with an orange tint. Bay scallops are smaller, about 50 to the pound, and are sweet and white with a hint of pink. Calico scallops, the smallest of all, are darker in color and not as tender.

1. In large saucepan, heat olive oil over medium heat. Add garlic and serrano pepper; cook and stir for 2–3 minutes, until fragrant. Add wine, reduce heat to low, and simmer while cooking scallops.

2. Meanwhile, place water in the bottom of a steamer and bring to a boil over high heat. Sprinkle scallops with salt and cayenne pepper and place in steamer top. Place over boiling water, cover, and steam scallops for 2 minutes. Gently stir scallops, cover again, and steam for 2–5 minutes, until scallops are opaque.

3. Remove serrano pepper sauce from heat and swirl in butter until melted. Place scallops on serving plate and top with sauce. Serve immediately.

Fish Creole

*You can use any mild white fish fillets in this flavorful recipe;
halibut, orange roughy, grouper, or cod would be good choices.*

INGREDIENTS | SERVES 6

½ cup chili sauce

1½ cups pasta sauce

2 cups medium cooked shrimp

2 tablespoons olive oil

6 (4- to 6-ounce) mild whitefish fillets

½ teaspoon salt

⅛ teaspoon red pepper flakes

2 tablespoons lemon juice

1. Preheat oven to 450°F. In medium saucepan, combine chili sauce and pasta sauce; bring to a boil over medium-high heat. Reduce heat to medium and simmer for 5 minutes, stirring frequently. Stir in shrimp, cover, and remove from heat.

2. Meanwhile, place oil in glass baking dish. Arrange fish in dish and sprinkle with salt, pepper flakes, and lemon juice. Bake for 8–10 minutes or until fish flakes easily when tested with a fork. Place on serving dish and top with shrimp sauce. Serve immediately.

Microwave Shrimp Scampi

This dish can be multiplied to serve more people. You must proportionally increase the microwave cooking time: if you double the shrimp, double the cooking time.

INGREDIENTS | SERVES 4

1 cup jasmine rice

2 cups chicken broth

2 lemons

½ cup butter

1½ pounds medium raw shrimp, cleaned

¼ teaspoon garlic powder

⅛ teaspoon garlic pepper

½ teaspoon garlic salt

Quick-Cooking Rice

You don't have to use instant rice when you want some in a hurry. Read labels at the grocery store. There are some kinds of rice, including Texmati and jasmine, that cook in only 15 minutes. As a bonus, these rice varieties are fragrant and full of flavor.

1. Combine rice and chicken broth in medium saucepan and bring to a boil over high heat. Cover pan, lower heat to medium-low, and simmer for 15 minutes.

2. Meanwhile, grate lemon zest from lemons and squeeze juice. Combine the zest, juice, and butter in microwave-safe dish. Microwave on high for 2 minutes. Sprinkle shrimp with garlic powder, garlic pepper, and garlic salt and add to butter mixture; toss to coat shrimp. Cover and microwave on high for 2 minutes. Uncover dish, stir shrimp, cover, and microwave on high for 1–3 minutes longer, until shrimp curl and turn pink.

3. Let shrimp stand, covered, for 2–3 minutes. Fluff rice with a fork. Serve shrimp and sauce over rice.

Coconut Shrimp Tempura

Baking the battered shrimp instead of deep-frying takes much of the work out of this classic appetizer. These taste delicious on their own, or you can serve them with a spicy dipping sauce, such as Asian chili sauce.

INGREDIENTS | SERVES 4

1 cup unsweetened coconut flakes

2 eggs, refrigerated

2 cups ice-cold water

2 cups rice flour

1 pound (about 24) large shrimp, peeled, deveined, tail on

Terrific Tempura Batter

Few fried foods are as irresistible as Japanese tempura, consisting of seafood or vegetables coated in a light, crispy batter. It's easy to make this restaurant favorite at home—just remember to use ice water and a cold egg, and to not overbeat the batter.

1. Preheat the oven to 450°F. Spray a baking sheet with nonstick cooking spray. Place the coconut flakes in a bowl.

2. In a medium bowl, beat the eggs and then stir in the ice water.

3. Stir in the flour until the batter has a runny consistency similar to pancake batter. Add more flour or ice water if needed.

4. Coat each shrimp in the batter, using your fingers to do so. Dip the shrimp into the coconut, holding it by the tail, and then lay it on the baking sheet. Continue with the remainder of the shrimp.

5. Bake the shrimp until it is golden brown on the bottom (4–5 minutes). Turn over and cook the other side until done. Serve immediately.

Baked Fish Fillets

Cooking the vegetables with the fish means they are flavored with the natural fish juices and lemony soy sauce mixture. Cooked rice is all that's needed to turn this into a complete meal.

INGREDIENTS | SERVES 4

1 tablespoon soy sauce

1 tablespoon lemon juice

2 teaspoons bottled minced ginger

Black pepper, to taste

½ teaspoon Asian chili sauce, or to taste

1 teaspoon salt

1 pound fish fillets, fresh

½ pound broccoli florets

10 baby carrots, cut in half

Selecting Fresh Fish

When choosing fish fillets, look for a clean smell and a firm texture, without any discoloration or brown spots. Avoid fish that have a strong fishy smell or yield to gentle pressure. When selecting whole fish, check for bright eyes and a shiny skin.

1. Preheat oven to 375°F.

2. In a small bowl, stir together the soy sauce, lemon juice, ginger, pepper, and chili sauce. Rub the salt over the fish fillets to season.

3. Cut four sheets of foil, each at least 12-inch square. Place each fish fillet in the middle of a sheet of foil and brush the fillet with a portion of the lemon juice mixture. Place ¼ of the broccoli and carrots around the fish.

4. Fold the foil over the fish and vegetables, crimping the edges to seal. Continue with the remainder of the fish fillets.

5. Bake at 375°F for 15–20 minutes, until the fish is cooked through and flakes easily (be careful not to overcook the fish). Serve immediately.

Easy Seafood Rice Pilaf

Microwaving the rice considerably shortens the cooking time in this simple shrimp and rice dish.

INGREDIENTS | SERVES 4

1½ cups long-grain white rice
3 cups chicken broth
1 tablespoon olive oil
1 onion, peeled, chopped
2 cloves garlic, finely chopped
½ teaspoon paprika, or to taste
1 teaspoon salt
¾ pound large shrimp, shelled, deveined
1 tablespoon lemon juice

1. Place the rice and broth in a microwave-safe casserole dish. Cover with microwave-safe plastic wrap. Cook the rice on high heat for 8 minutes.

2. Check and continue microwaving until the rice is cooked (about an additional 10 minutes). Do not stir the rice. Once the rice is finished cooking, let it stand for 5 minutes.

3. While the rice is cooking, heat the olive oil in a skillet on medium-high heat. Add the onion and garlic. Sprinkle the paprika over the onion. Sauté for 4–5 minutes, until the onion is softened (turn the heat down to medium if cooking too fast).

4. Sprinkle the salt over the shrimp and add to the pan. Splash the shrimp with the lemon juice and sauté until they turn pink (about 3–5 minutes), taking care not to overcook.

5. Fluff the rice with a fork. Stir in the shrimp mixture. Serve hot.

Shrimp Pad Thai Stir-Fry

Boiling the soaking water for the noodles shortens the amount of time it takes for them to soften. If you purchase shrimp that is already peeled and deveined, and soften the noodles ahead of time, this pad thai will be ready in under 15 minutes.

INGREDIENTS | SERVES 4

8 ounces rice stick noodles

2 tablespoons lemon juice

2 tablespoons white vinegar

1½ tablespoons tomato sauce

2 tablespoons brown sugar

2 tablespoons vegetable oil

2 teaspoons bottled minced garlic

1 tablespoon bottled chopped red jalapeño peppers

20 large shrimp, peeled, deveined

2 eggs, beaten

1 cup mung bean sprouts

1 cup chopped fresh cilantro leaves

⅓ cup chopped peanuts

A Southeast Asian Specialty

Thailand's signature noodle dish, pad thai—literally meaning Thai fried dish or mixture—has a universal appeal. The distinguishing characteristic of pad thai is the intriguing mixture of sweet-and-sour and spicy flavors. For an extra touch, serve the pad thai with an assortment of lime wedges, red chilies, and extra peanuts.

1. In a microwave-safe bowl, bring 4 cups of water to a boil (this will take 3–5 minutes). Remove the bowl from the microwave. Place the noodles in the boiling water to soften. In a small bowl, stir together the lemon juice, vinegar, tomato sauce, and brown sugar.

2. Heat the vegetable oil in a wok or large skillet. When the oil is hot, add the garlic and chopped jalapeños. Stir-fry for a few seconds; then add the shrimp. Cook until the shrimp turn pink (about 2 minutes).

3. Push the shrimp to the side of the skillet and add the beaten egg in the middle. Scramble the egg in the pan.

4. Add the softened noodles. Stir the lemon juice and tomato sauce mixture and pour over the noodles.

5. Stir in the mung bean sprouts. Stir in the cilantro leaves. Stir-fry for a couple of minutes to combine the ingredients. Garnish with the chopped peanuts before serving.

Sicilian-Style Swordfish

Lemon juice tenderizes the fish while olive oil disperses the flavor of the herbs in this easy recipe. If you don't have bottled minced garlic on hand, you can substitute ¼ teaspoon garlic powder or 2 minced garlic cloves.

INGREDIENTS | SERVES 4

⅓ cup olive oil
⅓ cup lemon juice
2 teaspoons bottled minced garlic
½ teaspoon dried oregano
2 teaspoons dried parsley
¼ teaspoon black pepper
4 swordfish steaks

1. Preheat the broiler. Spray the broiling rack with nonstick spray.

2. In a bowl, whisk together the olive oil, lemon juice, garlic, oregano, parsley, and pepper.

3. Pour the marinade into a large resealable plastic bag. Add the swordfish and close up the bag. Marinate for 10 minutes, turning once or twice to make sure the steaks are coated.

4. Place the swordfish on the broiling rack approximately 4 inches from the heat source. Broil for 4 minutes, turn, and cook for 4–6 minutes more, until the swordfish is just done. Serve immediately.

Seafood Au Gratin

If using frozen fish fillets, thaw before cooking. You can spice up the dish by adding a pinch of paprika to the white sauce.

INGREDIENTS | SERVES 4

4 tablespoons unsalted butter

3 tablespoons flour

½ teaspoon dried dill weed

¾ cup milk

¼ cup heavy cream or whipping cream

½ teaspoon ground nutmeg, or to taste

⅛ teaspoon black or white pepper, or to taste

1 teaspoon lemon juice

1 pound fish fillets

1 teaspoon salt

½ cup grated Cheddar cheese

1. Preheat the oven to 375°F. Spray an 8" × 8" baking dish with nonstick cooking spray.

2. In a small saucepan, melt the butter on low heat. Add the flour and blend it into the melted butter, stirring continually until it thickens and forms a roux (3–5 minutes). Stir in the dill weed.

3. Increase the heat to medium. Slowly add the milk and the cream, stirring with a whisk until the mixture has thickened. Stir in the nutmeg, pepper, and lemon juice.

4. Rub the salt over the fish to season. Lay the fish fillets out in the baking dish.

5. Pour the white sauce over the fish. Sprinkle the cheese on top.

6. Bake the fish for 25 minutes, or until it is cooked through. Serve immediately.

Teriyaki Shrimp

A combination of sweet and spicy flavors, Asian sweet chili sauce is available in the ethnic or international section of most supermarkets.

INGREDIENTS | SERVES 4

1 pound large shrimp, shelled, deveined, tail on

½ teaspoon salt

3 tablespoons vegetable oil, divided

1 teaspoon minced garlic

1 teaspoon minced ginger

1 teaspoon Asian sweet chili sauce

½ pound snow peas

⅓ cup teriyaki sauce

2 green onions, chopped into thirds

Quick-Cooking Seafood

Speedy cooking times make seafood the perfect choice for busy weeknights. In fact, the main concern when preparing fish and shellfish is to not overcook it. Overcooked seafood loses its natural juiciness and can be rather tough. Cook fish until the skin flakes easily with a fork. For shrimp and prawns, cook until the skin just turns pink.

1. Place the shrimp in a bowl and toss with the salt.

2. Heat 2 tablespoons oil in a large skillet over medium-high heat. Stir for a few seconds; then add the shrimp. Stir-fry the shrimp, stirring constantly, until they turn pink (about 2 minutes). Remove the shrimp from the pan.

3. Heat 1 tablespoon oil in the pan. Add the garlic, ginger, and chili sauce. Stir for a few seconds; then add the snow peas. Stir-fry for 2 minutes, stirring constantly. (Splash the snow peas with 1 tablespoon of water if they begin to dry out.)

4. Add the teriyaki sauce to the pan and bring to a boil.

5. Return the shrimp to the pan. Stir in the green onion. Stir-fry for a minute to combine all the ingredients. Serve hot.

Fish Stick Casserole

Here's a way to put leftover pasta and sauce to use.

INGREDIENTS | SERVES 2

1 cup frozen peas
2 cups leftover pasta with sauce
12 fish sticks
1 (10-ounce) can cream of mushroom soup

1. Preheat the oven to 425°F. Grease a 8" ×8" baking dish.

2. Place the frozen peas in a microwave-safe bowl. Cover with microwave-safe plastic wrap, leaving one corner open to vent steam. Microwave the peas on high heat for 2 minutes, and then for 30 seconds at a time, until cooked (total cooking time should be 2–3 minutes).

3. Spread 1 cup of the leftover pasta over the bottom of the baking dish. Carefully arrange the fish sticks on top. Stir together the soup and microwaved peas. Spoon over the fish sticks.

4. Spread the remaining cup of leftover pasta on top. Bake for 30 minutes, or until the fish sticks are fully cooked. Serve hot.

Pan-Fried Tilapia

*Breaded and pan-fried fish is a wonderful way to get your children to try fish.
Always attempt mild fish such as tilapia, mahi-mahi, or swordfish first.*

INGREDIENTS | SERVES 4

3 tablespoons olive or canola oil

1 cup flour or quick-mixing flour
(Wondra)

Garlic powder to taste

Salt and pepper to taste

2 eggs, beaten

4 tilapia fillets

1. Heat oil in skillet over low heat.

2. Mix flour with garlic powder, salt, and pepper.

3. Dip fish fillet in egg, and then flour mixture.

4. Pan-fry until golden brown, 5–6 minutes on each side, turning once. Serve hot.

The Benefits of Fish

Studies have proven that fish is one of the most important foods to incorporate into your diet. Include shellfish, such as shrimp, scallops, mussels, or clams, in pasta for a delicious fish dish. Even if fish is not one of your favorites, try to get your family to enjoy it in some fashion!

Pan-Seared Sea Scallops

Restaurant-quality sea scallops are now available to the general public.
Ask for fresh diver sea scallops; large, sweet, and succulent, these are a true treat!

INGREDIENTS | SERVES 4

4 tablespoons butter, divided

1¼ pounds large sea scallops, abductor muscle removed, rinsed and patted dry with paper towels

¼ teaspoon salt

Freshly cracked black pepper

¼ cup chopped shallots

½ cup chicken stock

2 tablespoons freshly squeezed lemon juice

1 teaspoon lemon zest

1 tablespoon chopped fresh parsley

Butter Facts

Butter rapidly absorbs flavors like a sponge. Regular butter can be stored in the refrigerator for up to 1 month, wrapped airtight. Unsalted butter should be stored for no longer than 2 weeks in the refrigerator.

1. Melt 3 tablespoons of the butter in a large nonstick skillet over medium-high heat. Season the scallops with salt and pepper and cook until seared, about 3–4 minutes per side. Transfer the scallops to a plate and tent with tinfoil to keep warm.

2. Add the remaining tablespoon of butter to the pan. Add the shallots and cook until soft, about 4 minutes, stirring frequently. Add the stock and lemon juice and bring to a simmer. Cook until slightly reduced, about 4 minutes.

3. Add the lemon zest and parsley and simmer for about 1 minute. Taste and adjust seasoning as desired. Transfer the scallops to serving plates and drizzle with the pan sauce. Serve hot.

Seared Ahi Tuna Steaks with Garlic

The success of this recipe depends on having fresh, high-quality fish.
The simple olive oil sauce lets the tuna shine through.

INGREDIENTS | SERVES 4

4 (8-ounce) ahi tuna steaks, 1-inch thick

½ teaspoon seasoned salt

Freshly cracked black pepper

3 tablespoons olive oil

4 tablespoons minced garlic

3 tablespoons Worcestershire sauce

Dash hot pepper sauce

1 tablespoon Dijon mustard

3 tablespoons freshly squeezed lemon juice

Roasting Garlic

Roasted garlic can usually be substituted for fresh garlic in most recipes. To roast garlic, cut off the very top of a garlic bulb to expose the tips of the cloves. Sprinkle the bulb with a little olive oil, salt, and pepper, and wrap in tinfoil. Bake in a 350°F oven for about 1 hour. Roasted garlic is a great spread on vegetables and a delicious flavor addition to sauces, soups, and stews. A full bulb will serve 4 adults and has 3g of carbohydrates per serving.

1. Heat a heavy nonstick skillet over high heat until wisps of smoke start to appear. Pat the tuna steaks dry with paper towels and season with salt and pepper. Add the tuna steaks to the skillet and quickly sear until the underside is a rich golden brown, about 2 minutes. Flip the steaks and brown the other side. (The steaks will be very rare in the center.) Reduce heat and cook for several more minutes if you prefer the tuna less rare. Transfer the steaks to a plate and tent with tinfoil to keep warm.

2. Allow the pan to cool slightly and then add the olive oil, garlic, Worcestershire, hot pepper sauce, and Dijon. Cook until the garlic is soft but not brown, about 2 minutes. Stir in the lemon juice and any accumulated juices from the tuna. Adjust seasoning to taste.

3. To serve, place the tuna steaks on serving plates and drizzle the sauce on top. Serve hot.

CHAPTER 9

Vegetarian

Spicy Vegetarian Chili

*You can use this chili in so many ways: from the topping for Taco Salad (see Chapter 3),
to filled stuffed baked potatoes, and as the base for enchiladas and burritos.*

INGREDIENTS | SERVES 4–6

2 (15-ounce) cans spicy chili beans, undrained

1 (14-ounce) can diced tomatoes with green chilies, undrained

1 (12-ounce) jar tomato salsa

1 tablespoon chili powder

1 green bell pepper, chopped

1 cup water

In a heavy saucepan, combine all ingredients. Bring to a boil; then reduce heat and simmer for 15–20 minutes, stirring occasionally, until peppers are crisp and tender and mixture is heated and blended. Serve immediately, topped with sour cream, grated cheese, and chopped green onions, if desired.

Canned Tomatoes

There are several different types of flavored tomatoes in the market. Fire-roasted tomatoes are broiled or roasted until the skins blacken; then they are chopped or diced. Tomatoes can be packed with garlic, or with green chilies; there are Mexican-seasoned tomatoes and Italian-seasoned tomatoes. Stock up on several kinds to add kick to your recipes.

Pesto Pasta

*This simple recipe is bursting with the flavors of summer.
You must only make it when tomatoes are ripe, sweet, and tender.*

INGREDIENTS | SERVES 4

1 pound linguine

2 tomatoes, seeded and chopped

1 (10-ounce) container basil pesto

½ cup toasted pine nuts

½ cup grated Parmesan cheese

1. Bring large pot of water to a boil and cook linguine according to package directions.

2. Meanwhile, in serving bowl, place tomatoes and pesto. When linguine is cooked al dente, drain well and add to serving bowl. Toss gently to coat pasta with sauce. Sprinkle with pine nuts and cheese and serve.

Tomatoes and Pierogies

You can use canned whole tomatoes in this recipe if the fresh ones are not in top condition.
Drain well and cut the tomatoes in half; add when directed in recipe.

INGREDIENTS | SERVES 4

1 cup vegetable broth

½ teaspoon dried thyme leaves

1 (16-ounce) package frozen pierogies

2 cups frozen baby peas

3 tomatoes, cut into wedges

Pierogies

Pierogies are large pasta half-rounds that are stuffed with mashed potatoes and seasonings, usually onion and cheese. They are a Polish or Hungarian specialty that is sold individually frozen. They cook in only a few minutes and can be dressed with any pasta sauce.

1. In heavy saucepan, combine vegetable broth and thyme. Bring to a boil over high heat. Add pierogies, bring to a simmer, lower heat to medium, and cover. Simmer for 5–7 minutes, until pierogies are almost hot.

2. Add baby peas and tomatoes, cover, bring to a simmer, and cook for 3–5 minutes longer, or until pierogies are heated through and vegetables are hot. Serve immediately.

Veggie Burritos

Burritos are made from flour tortillas rolled around a spicy seasoned filling.
Serve plain, or place in a baking pan, cover with enchilada sauce, and bake until bubbly.

INGREDIENTS | SERVES 4

2 tablespoons olive oil

1 onion, chopped

½ teaspoon crushed red pepper flakes

2 cups frozen broccoli and cauliflower combo, thawed

1 (15-ounce) can black beans, rinsed and drained

4 (10-inch) flour tortillas

1½ cups shredded pepper jack cheese

Frozen Vegetable Combos

Browse through your grocer's freezer aisle and you'll find almost endless combinations of frozen vegetables to add nutrition to your recipes in just one step. The combos range from broccoli, cauliflower, and carrots to baby corn, red peppers, and peas. They'll keep for a year in your freezer, so stock up!

1. Heat large skillet over medium heat. Add olive oil and onion; cook and stir for 3–4 minutes, until crisp and tender. Sprinkle with red pepper flakes; cook and stir for 1 minute.

2. Drain the vegetable combo well, and then add to the skillet; cook and stir for 3–5 minutes, until hot. Stir in black beans, cover, and let simmer for 3–4 minutes.

3. Meanwhile, warm tortillas by layering in microwave-safe paper towels and microwaving on high for 1–2 minutes. Spread tortillas on work surface, divide vegetable mixture among them, sprinkle with cheese, and roll up, folding in sides. Serve immediately.

Mushroom Risotto

Risotto is a creamy, rich dish of short-grain rice and vegetables.
Cooking constantly while stirring releases starch from the rice, which makes the mixture thick.

INGREDIENTS | SERVES 4–6

3 tablespoons olive oil

1½ cups assorted fresh mushrooms, sliced

½ teaspoon dried thyme leaves

1 cup arborio rice

4 cups vegetable stock

1 cup grated Parmesan cheese

2 tablespoons butter

Fresh Mushrooms

The variety of fresh mushrooms is staggering. In the regular grocery store, you can find portobello, cremini, button, chanterelle, shiitake, and porcini mushrooms. Use a combination for a rich, deep, earthy flavor in just about any recipe. Just brush them with a damp towel to clean; then slice and cook.

1. Place olive oil in large saucepan over medium heat. When hot, add the mushrooms and thyme. Cook and stir until mushrooms give up their liquid and the liquid evaporates, about 6–8 minutes. Then stir in rice; cook and stir for 3–4 minutes, until rice is opaque.

2. Meanwhile, heat vegetable stock in another saucepan; keep over low heat while making risotto. Add the stock to the rice mixture about 1 cup at a time, stirring until the liquid is absorbed.

3. When all the stock is added and rice is tender, remove from the heat, stir in cheese and butter, cover, and let stand for 5 minutes. Stir and then serve immediately.

Pasta with Spinach Pesto

Adding spinach to prepared pesto turns the color a bright green and adds flavor and nutrition, in addition to lowering the fat content.

INGREDIENTS | SERVES 8

½ cup frozen cut spinach

¾ cup grated Parmesan cheese, divided

1 (10-ounce) container prepared basil pesto

2 tablespoons lemon juice

1 (16-ounce) package campanelle or farfalle pasta

Pasta Shapes

There are hundreds of different pasta shapes on the market. Campanelle, which means "bellflowers," is a crimped and ruffled pasta that holds onto thick sauces. Farfalle, or butterfly-shaped pasta, is a good substitute, as is penne rigate or mostaccioli. Browse through the pasta aisle in your supermarket for more ideas.

1. Thaw spinach by running under hot water; drain well and squeeze with your hands to drain thoroughly. Combine in food processor or blender with ¼ cup Parmesan cheese, pesto, and lemon juice. Process or blend until mixture is smooth.

2. Meanwhile, cook pasta as directed on package until al dente. Drain well, reserving ½ cup pasta cooking water. Return pasta to pan and add pesto mixture and ¼ cup pasta cooking water. Toss gently to coat, adding more pasta cooking water if needed to make a smooth sauce. Serve with remaining ½ cup Parmesan cheese.

Linguine with Tomato Sauce

The combination of basil, tomatoes, and Brie cheese with hot pasta is simply sensational.
This recipe should only be made when tomatoes are in season.

INGREDIENTS | SERVES 4–6

5 large beefsteak tomatoes

⅓ cup olive oil

1 (12-ounce) box linguine pasta

½ teaspoon salt

¼ cup chopped fresh basil

1 (6-ounce) wedge Brie cheese

Soft Cheeses

Soft cheeses include Brie, Camembert, and Reblochon. These cheeses have a tangy flavor and very soft texture, making them difficult to work with. When you need to slice or grate these cheeses, place them in the freezer for about 15 minutes. The cheese will harden, making it easier to handle.

1. Cut tomatoes in half and squeeze out seeds. Coarsely chop tomatoes and combine in large bowl with olive oil.

2. Bring a large pot of water to a boil and cook linguine pasta as directed on package. Meanwhile, add salt and basil to tomatoes and toss gently. Cut Brie into small cubes and add to tomatoes.

3. When al dente, drain pasta and immediately add to tomato mixture. Toss, using tongs, until mixed. Serve immediately.

Tortellini in Wine Sauce

This elegant recipe is perfect for a spur of the moment dinner party.
You can keep all of these ingredients on hand and dinner will be on the table in under 15 minutes.

INGREDIENTS | SERVES 4

1 (14-ounce) package frozen cheese tortellini

2 tablespoons olive oil

3 cloves garlic, minced

½ cup white wine or vegetable broth

2 cups frozen baby peas

¼ teaspoon onion salt

¼ cup chopped flat-leaf parsley

1. Bring a large pot of water to a boil and cook tortellini as directed on package. Meanwhile, in a large saucepan, heat olive oil over medium heat. Add garlic; cook and stir for 2 minutes, until garlic just begins to turn golden. Add wine, peas, and salt and bring to a simmer.

2. Drain tortellini and add to saucepan with wine. Cook over low heat for 4–5 minutes, until mixture is hot and slightly thickened. Add parsley, stir, and serve.

Linguine with Peas

This recipe is so simple, yet packed full of flavor. You can make it with spaghetti or fettuccine as well; just make sure to serve it as soon as it's cooked.

INGREDIENTS | SERVES 4–6

1 pound linguine pasta
¼ cup olive oil
1 onion, chopped
3 cups frozen baby peas
½ cup toasted pine nuts
1 cup cubed Gouda cheese

Cooking Pasta

Pasta must be cooked in a large amount of salted, rapidly boiling water. The proportions are 1½ quarts of water for every 3 ounces of dried pasta. When finishing a dish by adding the pasta to a sauce, slightly undercook the pasta. Some of the residual heat from the sauce will continue to cook the pasta in the last few minutes.

1. Bring a large pot of salted water to a boil and cook pasta according to package directions.

2. Meanwhile, heat olive oil in a heavy saucepan over medium heat and add onion. Cook and stir for 5–7 minutes, until onions are tender. Add peas; cook and stir for 2–4 minutes longer, until peas are hot. Turn off heat and add pine nuts and Gouda cheese; cover and let stand while you drain pasta. Toss pasta with pea mixture and serve immediately.

Black Bean Unstructured Lasagna

Lasagna in under 15 minutes! Serve this wonderful dish with a fresh green salad drizzled with Italian dressing, some crisp breadsticks, and ice cream for dessert.

INGREDIENTS | SERVES 6–8

2 tablespoons olive oil

1 red bell pepper, chopped

1 (28-ounce) jar pasta sauce

½ cup water

1 (24-ounce) package frozen ravioli

1 (15-ounce) can black beans, rinsed and drained

1½ cups shredded pizza cheese

Modifying Equipment

If you don't have ovenproof pans or skillets, use heavy-duty foil to protect the handles. Wrap two layers of the foil around the handles and you can use the pans under the broiler. Foil can also be used to make a large pan smaller; just use it to build walls for the size pan you want. Fill the empty space with dried beans.

1. Preheat broiler. Heat olive oil in large ovenproof skillet over medium heat. Add bell pepper; cook and stir for 2–3 minutes, until crisp and tender.

2. Add pasta sauce and water; bring to a boil. Add ravioli, stir, bring to a simmer, and cook for 4–8 minutes, until ravioli are hot.

3. Add beans and stir. Sprinkle with cheese, place under the broiler, and broil until cheese is melted and begins to brown. Serve immediately.

Portobello Mushroom Burgers

Combining garlic and mayonnaise is a quick and easy way to make aioli, a garlicky sauce from France that complements everything from vegetables to meat, poultry, and seafood. This recipe can easily be doubled to serve 8.

INGREDIENTS | SERVES 4

4 portobello mushroom caps
2 tablespoons balsamic vinegar
1 tablespoon vegetarian chicken-flavored broth
2 garlic cloves, finely chopped
¼ cup mayonnaise
1 teaspoon lemon juice
¼ teaspoon cayenne pepper, or to taste
1 tablespoon olive oil
1 shallot, chopped
¼ teaspoon black pepper, or to taste
4 hamburger buns
4 romaine lettuce leaves

1. Wipe the mushrooms clean with a damp cloth and thinly slice.

2. In a small bowl, stir together the balsamic vinegar and vegetarian chicken-flavored broth. In a separate small bowl, stir together the garlic, mayonnaise, lemon juice, and cayenne pepper. Chill the mayonnaise mixture until needed.

3. Heat the oil in a large skillet over medium-high heat. Add the shallot and cook until tender, 4 minutes. Turn the heat down to medium and add the sliced mushrooms. Stir in the vinegar and broth mixture and the black pepper. Cook for 4–5 minutes, until the mushrooms are tender.

4. Lay out the hamburger buns in front of you. Put a lettuce leaf on the bottom of each bun. Spread 1 tablespoon of the garlic/mayonnaise mixture on the top of each bun and spoon ¼ of the sautéed mushrooms on top of the lettuce. Serve immediately.

French Cassoulet

Canned cannellini beans take the work out of soaking dried beans overnight. On nights when you're even more rushed than usual, replace the tomato and tomato sauce with 2 cups canned diced tomatoes.

INGREDIENTS | SERVES 4

2 teaspoons olive oil

2 cloves garlic, crushed

1 white onion, peeled and chopped

12 ounces Gimme Lean sausage-style meat substitute, cut into 1-inch pieces

1 medium tomato, chopped

1 cup tomato sauce

2½ cups drained white cannellini beans

1 bay leaf

1 tablespoon chopped fresh parsley

1½ teaspoons chopped fresh basil

¼ teaspoon salt, or to taste

Black pepper, to taste

1. Heat the oil in a large skillet on medium heat. Add the crushed garlic, onion, and Gimme Lean meat substitute. Sauté for 2–3 minutes.

2. Add the tomato, pressing down so that it releases its juices. Continue cooking for 2–3 more minutes, until the onion is softened.

3. Add the tomato sauce. Bring to a boil. Add the beans.

4. Add the bay leaf. Stir in the parsley, basil, salt, and pepper.

5. Turn the heat down and simmer, uncovered, for 5 minutes. Remove the bay leaf before serving.

Substituting Herbs

Dried herbs make a handy substitute when you don't have fresh chopped herbs on hand. When substituting dried herbs for fresh, always follow the ⅓ rule: use ⅓ the amount of dried herbs as fresh herbs that are called for in the recipe. In this recipe, for example, the fresh parsley and basil leaves could be replaced with 1 teaspoon dried parsley and ½ teaspoon dried basil.

Stuffed Red Peppers with Garlic Mashed Potatoes

It's hard to overestimate the health benefits of beans—while not completely replacing the protein found in meat, they are high in fiber, low in fat, and full of flavor.

INGREDIENTS | SERVES 4

½ cup leftover Garlic Mashed Potatoes (see Chapter 10)

1 tablespoon vegetarian chicken-flavored broth

½ teaspoon granulated sugar

⅛ teaspoon hot sauce, or to taste

½ cup drained canned black beans

2 medium red bell peppers, seeded, cut in half

1. Reheat the Garlic Mashed Potatoes in a small saucepan with the vegetarian chicken-flavored broth. Stir in the sugar and hot sauce. Remove from the heat.

2. In a small bowl, combine the mashed potatoes and beans. Carefully spoon ¼ of the mixture onto each bell pepper half.

3. Place the bell pepper halves in a microwave-safe baking dish. Cover with plastic wrap, leaving an opening in one corner for steam to vent. Microwave the peppers on high heat for 5 minutes.

4. Give the dish a quarter turn and microwave on high heat for 2 minutes, and then for 1 minute at a time until everything is heated through. Let stand for 5 minutes before serving.

Tofu Cacciatore

This quick and easy stir-fry allows you to enjoy the flavors of chicken cacciatore, traditionally a slowly simmered dish, on busy weeknights.

INGREDIENTS | SERVES 3

16 ounces soft tofu

1½ tablespoons olive oil

1 shallot, chopped

4 ounces vegetarian bacon substitute (such as Smart Bacon)

1 tomato, thinly sliced

½ cup canned mushrooms

⅓ cup vegetarian chicken-flavored broth

2 tablespoons tomato sauce

1 tablespoon chopped fresh basil

1 teaspoon chopped fresh thyme

½ teaspoon salt

Replacing Meat with Tofu

Protein-rich and low in calories, tofu makes a great substitute for meat in vegetarian cooking. Always be sure to drain the tofu ahead of time so that it can fully absorb the spices and other flavors in a dish. Also, to make up for the lack of the soluble fat in meat that disperses flavor, consider marinating the tofu in a flavorful marinade before cooking.

1. Remove the excess water from the tofu. Cut into 1-inch cubes.

2. Heat the olive oil in a large skillet over medium heat. Add the shallot and bacon substitute. Cook for 2 minutes; then add the tofu. Cook, stirring the tofu cubes gently, for 1–2 minutes, until the tofu cubes are browned and the shallot is softened.

3. Push the tofu to the sides of the pan and add the tomato in the middle, pressing down so that it releases its juices. Stir in the canned mushrooms.

4. Add the vegetarian chicken-flavored broth and tomato sauce. Bring to a boil.

5. Stir in the fresh basil and thyme. Stir in the salt. Cook for another minute, stirring to combine the ingredients. Serve hot.

Spicy Vegetable-Filled Tacos

The spicy combination of herbs and seasonings used to flavor the black beans are the same ones frequently used to marinade beef to make Tex-Mex fajitas.

INGREDIENTS | SERVES 6

6 taco shells

2 teaspoons vegetable oil

¼ cup chopped red onion

2 cups drained canned black beans

6 tablespoons vegetarian chicken-flavored broth

4 teaspoons lime juice

1 teaspoon Asian chili sauce

¼ teaspoon bottled minced garlic

¼ teaspoon ground cumin

¼ teaspoon salt

1 cup fresh shredded cabbage

¾ cup shredded Cheddar cheese

1. Preheat the oven to 350°F. Place the taco shells on an ungreased baking sheet. Bake for 5–10 minutes, until warm.

2. While the taco shells are heating, prepare the filling ingredients. Heat the vegetable oil in a saucepan over medium-high heat. Add the onion and sauté for 4–5 minutes, until softened.

3. Add the black beans. Stir in the broth, lime juice, chili sauce, minced garlic, cumin, and salt.

4. Remove the taco shells from the oven.

5. Fill each taco with a portion of the black bean mixture. Add the shredded cabbage. Sprinkle with cheese. Serve immediately.

Skillet Vegetarian Shepherd's Pie

The vegetarian version of Worcestershire sauce leaves out the anchovies. If not available, you can substitute ¾ teaspoon of soy sauce mixed with ¾ teaspoon of lemon juice.

INGREDIENTS | SERVES 2

1 tablespoon margarine

2 tablespoons chopped onions

1 cup baby carrots, cut in half

1 cup meat substitute, such as soy crumbles

½ cup vegetarian beef-flavored broth

1½ teaspoons vegetarian Worcestershire sauce

½ teaspoon dried oregano

¼ teaspoon salt, or to taste

¼ teaspoon black pepper, or to taste

1 cup leftover Garlic Mashed Potatoes (see Chapter 10)

1. Heat the margarine in a skillet. Add the onion and carrots and cook for 3–4 minutes, until softened.

2. Add the soy crumbles, vegetarian beef-flavored broth, and Worcestershire sauce.

3. Stir in the oregano, salt, and pepper. Cook for 5 minutes, or until the soy crumbles are heated through.

4. Stir in the mashed potatoes. Cook for another minute to heat through. Serve hot.

Microwave Garden Vegetable Lasagna

For a vegan version of this dish, replace the cottage cheese with crumbled firm tofu that has been combined with the seasonings, and the mozzarella cheese with mozzarella-flavored soy cheese.

INGREDIENTS | SERVES 4

2 cups crushed tomatoes

1¼ cups cottage cheese

¼ cup mozzarella cheese

¼ teaspoon dried basil

¼ teaspoon dried oregano

⅛ teaspoon black pepper

2 zucchini, thinly sliced

1 cup frozen spinach, thawed and drained

3 tablespoons Parmesan cheese

1. In a medium bowl, stir together the crushed tomatoes and the cottage cheese. Stir in the mozzarella cheese, basil, oregano, and pepper.

2. Lay out one of the zucchini in a deep-sided casserole dish that is microwave-safe. Add half of the spinach.

3. Spoon about half of the cheese and tomato mixture over the spinach. Repeat with the remainder of the zucchini, spinach, and cheese and tomato mixture.

4. Cover the dish with microwave-safe wax paper. Microwave on high heat for 3 minutes. Give the dish a quarter turn and microwave for 2 minutes at a time until the cheese is cooked (total cooking time should be 7–9 minutes).

5. Sprinkle the Parmesan cheese over the top. Let stand for at least 5 minutes before serving.

Tofu and Cashew Stir-Fry

Draining the tofu earlier in the day means that this simple stir-fry can go from kitchen to table in under 15 minutes.

INGREDIENTS | SERVES 4

1 pound firm tofu, drained
½ cup vegetarian chicken-flavored broth
¼ cup soy sauce
2 tablespoons lemon juice
1 teaspoon granulated sugar
1 teaspoon cornstarch
2 tablespoons vegetable oil
1 teaspoon minced ginger
2½ cups fresh stir-fry vegetables
2 tablespoons water, if needed
½ cup unsalted cashews

Freezing Tofu

Freezing tofu gives it a chewy, meatier texture. For best results, use firm or extra-firm tofu. Drain the tofu before freezing and wrap tightly in plastic. Use the tofu within 3 months.

1. Cut the tofu into ¾-inch cubes.

2. In a small bowl, stir together the vegetarian chicken-flavored broth, soy sauce, lemon juice, and sugar. Whisk in the cornstarch.

3. Heat the oil in a heavy skillet or wok over medium-high heat. Add the minced ginger. Stir for a few seconds; then add the stir-fry vegetables, pushing them around the pan constantly so that they don't burn. (Add 1–2 tablespoons water if needed to keep the vegetables from burning.) Stir-fry for 2–3 minutes, until they are tender but still crisp.

4. Add the tofu cubes. Cook for 1–2 minutes, gently stirring the cubes, until they are browned.

5. Stir the sauce and swirl into the pan. Bring to a boil and cook for about 2 more minutes to heat through. Stir in the cashews. Serve hot.

Sweet-and-Sour Tofu

Drained tofu acts like a sponge, absorbing the flavorful sweet-and-sour sauce.
For best results, be sure to use extra-firm tofu, which can hold its shape during stir-frying.

INGREDIENTS | SERVES 4

¼ cup pineapple juice

½ cup water

¼ cup vinegar

¼ cup brown sugar

2 tablespoons ketchup

2 teaspoons soy sauce

1 pound extra-firm tofu, drained earlier

2 tablespoons vegetable oil

2 thin slices ginger

2 ribs celery, sliced on the diagonal

1 medium red bell pepper, cut into chunks

1 cup straw mushrooms

1. In a small bowl, stir together the pineapple juice, water, vinegar, brown sugar, ketchup, and soy sauce.

2. Cut the tofu into 1-inch cubes. Heat the oil in a heavy skillet over medium-high heat. Add the ginger and let brown for 2 minutes. Remove the ginger.

3. Add the celery. Stir-fry for 2 minutes, stirring constantly. Add the red bell peppers. Add the straw mushrooms. Cook for another minute. (Splash the vegetables with 1–2 tablespoons of water if they begin to dry out during stir-frying.)

4. Add the tofu cubes. Cook, stirring, for about 1 minute to brown the tofu.

5. Stir the sauce and add it to the pan. Bring to a boil and cook for about 2 minutes, stirring, to thicken. Serve hot.

Zucchini Casserole

A wonderful soufflé-like dish. It is quite delicious—and low-fat.

INGREDIENTS | SERVES 4–6

3 cups zucchini, cut into bite-size pieces

¼ cup margarine

1 small onion, grated

2 cups carrots, grated

1 (10¾-ounce) can low-fat cream of mushroom soup

½ cup low-fat sour cream

1 (8-ounce) package seasoned bread crumb stuffing

¼ cup margarine, melted

½ cup grated Parmesan cheese

1. Preheat oven to 350°F.

2. In a large mixing bowl, combine zucchini, margarine, onions, carrots, cream of mushroom soup, and sour cream. Mix well.

3. Add ½ of the bread crumb stuffing and mix well.

4. Spray nonstick cooking spray into casserole dish. Pour zucchini mixture into casserole dish.

5. Mix remainder of bread crumb stuffing with melted margarine.

6. Sprinkle top of casserole with bread crumb mixture and Parmesan cheese.

7. Bake for 30 minutes or until golden brown. Serve hot.

CHAPTER 10

Sides

Duchess Potatoes

This recipe is a great way to use up leftover mashed or riced potatoes. You may need to add some more milk if you use leftover homemade potatoes, since they can dry out when refrigerated.

INGREDIENTS | SERVES 8

1 (12-ounce) package refrigerated mashed potatoes

1 egg, beaten

¼ cup grated Parmesan cheese

2 tablespoons sour cream

½ teaspoon dried basil leaves

2 tablespoons milk

2 tablespoons grated Parmesan cheese

Prepared Potatoes

You can find prepared refrigerated mashed potatoes in your supermarket's dairy aisle, or perhaps in one of the refrigerated end-caps at the end of an aisle. There are many different types of refrigerated prepared potatoes; look for hash brown potatoes and scalloped potatoes, too.

1. Preheat oven to 375°F. In large bowl, combine all ingredients except milk and 2 tablespoons Parmesan cheese and beat well until combined. Spoon or pipe mixture into 16 mounds onto parchment paper–lined cookie sheets. Brush with milk and sprinkle with 2 tablespoons Parmesan cheese.

2. Bake potatoes for 15–20 minutes, or until tops are beginning to brown and potatoes are hot. Serve immediately.

Green Beans with Red Peppers

You can buy frozen julienned green beans or frozen cut green beans. For this recipe, frozen cut green beans work best. The color combination of the deep green beans and the bright red peppers is very festive.

INGREDIENTS | SERVES 6

2 tablespoons olive oil

1 onion, finely chopped

3 cups frozen green beans

1 red bell pepper, cut into strips

1 tablespoon lemon juice

½ teaspoon salt

½ teaspoon dried thyme leaves

How to Julienne Bell Peppers

To julienne bell peppers, hold them upright on a cutting board. Cut off the four sides of the pepper from the stem and core. Remove any extra seeds or ribs. Place each piece skin-side down on the cutting board and cut the peppers into thin strips. Discard stem and core.

1. In heavy saucepan, heat olive oil over medium heat. Add onion; cook until onion is tender (about 4 minutes), stirring frequently.

2. Meanwhile, prepare green beans as directed on package and drain well. Add red bell pepper to saucepan with onions; cook and stir for 2–4 minutes, until tender. Add beans, lemon juice, salt, and thyme leaves; stir gently and cook until hot, about 2–3 minutes longer. Serve immediately.

Honey-Orange Carrots

These sweet and tart little carrots are perfect for a dinner party.
You can easily double or triple the recipe for a larger crowd.

INGREDIENTS | SERVES 4–6

1 (16-ounce) package baby carrots

2 cups water

2 tablespoons orange juice concentrate

2 tablespoons honey

2 tablespoons butter

¼ teaspoon dried thyme leaves

Baby Carrots

Baby carrots are actually large carrots that have been carefully trimmed and shaped. They are sweeter than the carrots you remember from your childhood because they are a different variety that is bred to grow faster, longer, and with a higher sugar content.

1. Rinse carrots and place in medium saucepan with water. Bring to a boil over high heat; then lower heat to medium and simmer carrots for 5–8 minutes, until just tender.

2. Drain carrots and return to pan. Stir in orange juice concentrate, honey, and butter; cook and stir over medium heat until sauce thickens and coats carrots, 2–4 minutes. Add thyme leaves and simmer for another minute; then serve.

Praline Sweet Potatoes

This recipe is excellent for an easy side dish for Thanksgiving.
Since it takes only about 20 minutes to make, you can prepare it just before serving.

INGREDIENTS | SERVES 6

2 (16-ounce) cans sweet potatoes in syrup

½ cup brown sugar, divided

½ cup butter, divided

¼ cup reserved sweet potato liquid

½ cup chopped cashews

3 tablespoons flour

⅛ teaspoon nutmeg

Sweet Potatoes

Sweet potatoes are usually canned in a sweet syrup, but some are canned in plain water; be sure to read the labels carefully. Sweet potatoes, whether canned or fresh, are a wonderful source of vitamins A and C; in fact, one serving can provide more than 400 percent of the recommended daily allowance of vitamin A.

1. Drain sweet potatoes, reserving ¼ cup liquid. Place drained sweet potatoes in saucepan over medium heat along with ¼ cup brown sugar, ¼ cup butter, and ¼ cup reserved liquid. Mash potatoes as they heat, stirring frequently. Place in 1½-quart microwave-safe casserole dish.

2. In small bowl, combine cashews, remaining ¼ cup brown sugar, flour, and nutmeg and mix well. Melt remaining ¼ cup butter and add to cashew mixture; mix until crumbly and set aside.

3. Microwave potatoes on high power for 2 minutes; then stir well. Sprinkle with cashew mixture and microwave on high 5–7 minutes longer, or until potatoes are hot. Serve immediately.

Smashed Potatoes

When you cube potatoes, they will cook in much less time.
This side dish is perfect to serve with a classic meatloaf.

INGREDIENTS | SERVES 6–8

6 russet potatoes

¼ cup butter

4 cloves garlic, minced

⅓ cup whole milk

½ teaspoon salt

1 tablespoon chopped fresh basil leaves

The Fluffiest Mashed Potatoes

Adding butter to the potatoes before adding liquid helps ensure that the potatoes will be fluffy. The fat in the butter helps coat the starch granules in the potatoes so they don't absorb too much liquid and become sticky or gluey. Use this rule every time you make mashed or smashed potatoes for best results.

1. Peel potatoes and cut into 1-inch cubes; as you work, place the potatoes in a large saucepan filled with cold water. When all the potatoes are prepared, bring to a boil over high heat. Cover pan, lower heat, and simmer potatoes for 15–20 minutes, until potatoes are tender when pierced with fork.

2. Meanwhile, combine butter and garlic in small saucepan and cook over medium heat, stirring frequently, until garlic is fragrant and tender, about 2 minutes. Remove from heat. In another small saucepan, combine milk, salt, and basil and heat until steam forms.

3. When potatoes are tender, drain thoroughly; then return potatoes to hot pan and shake for 1 minute over medium heat. Add butter mixture and mash with a potato masher. Then add milk mixture and stir gently. Serve immediately.

Crispy Broccoli Casserole

This casserole is so good, even your kids will like it! Any vegetable is improved by being smothered in cheese sauce and topped with crisp, buttered bread crumbs.

INGREDIENTS | SERVES 8

2 (16-ounce) packages frozen broccoli and cauliflower combo

1 (16-ounce) jar four-cheese Alfredo sauce

1 cup shredded Cheddar cheese

1½ cups soft bread crumbs

¼ cup butter, melted

1. Preheat oven to 375°F. Thaw vegetables according to package directions and drain thoroughly. Place in 13" × 9" glass baking dish. Top with the Alfredo sauce and sprinkle with the cheese.

2. In medium bowl, combine bread crumbs and butter and toss to mix. Sprinkle over cheese. Bake casserole at 375°F for 20–23 minutes, until the sauce is bubbling, vegetables are hot, and bread crumbs begin to brown. Serve immediately.

Grilled Asparagus

Grilling makes asparagus smoky, crisp, and tender.
The combination of butter and olive oil adds extra richness.

INGREDIENTS | SERVES 6

1 pound asparagus

2 tablespoons butter

1 tablespoon garlic-flavored olive oil

1 teaspoon seasoned salt

⅛ teaspoon pepper

1. Hold asparagus spears between your hands and bend until they snap; discard the tough ends.

2. Prepare and preheat grill. In small saucepan, melt butter with oil, salt, and pepper. Brush asparagus with this mixture; then place on grill 6 inches from medium coals. Cover and grill asparagus, brushing frequently with butter mixture, for 5–9 minutes, until tender. Serve immediately.

Flavored Olive Oils

You can find flavored olive oils at gourmet and specialty shops, and in the regular supermarket. Garlic oil, lemon oil, and herb oils are a great way to add complex flavor with just one ingredient. Please do not make your own flavored oils; the risk of food poisoning is just too great because of the oil's anaerobic (oxygen-free) environment.

Garlicky Green Beans

You can add more garlic to this simple and flavorful side dish if you like. Just be sure to stir constantly while the garlic and shallots are browning so they don't burn.

INGREDIENTS | SERVES 6

1 pound green beans
4 cups water
1 tablespoon olive oil
1 tablespoon butter
6 cloves garlic, peeled and chopped
1 shallot, peeled and chopped
½ teaspoon salt

Types of Garlic

There are several forms of garlic that you can buy. Garlic powder is powdered dried garlic; ⅛ teaspoon is equal to one clove. Garlic salt is garlic powder combined with salt; ¼ teaspoon is equal to one clove. And garlic paste in a tube is puréed, concentrated garlic; 1 teaspoon is equal to one clove of garlic.

1. Trim the ends off the green beans and cut each bean in half crosswise. Place in heavy saucepan and cover with water. Bring to a boil over high heat; then lower heat to medium and simmer for 5–8 minutes, until beans are crisp and tender.

2. Meanwhile, combine olive oil and butter in heavy saucepan and add garlic and shallot. Cook and stir over medium heat until the garlic is fragrant and turns light brown around the edges.

3. Drain beans and add to garlic mixture in pan, along with salt. Cook and stir over medium heat for 2–3 minutes, until beans are coated. Serve immediately.

Roasted Sugar Snap Peas

You can sometimes find stringless sugar snap peas in the market. If you can't, to remove the string, cut off the very end of the pea, pull the string off, and discard.

INGREDIENTS | SERVES 6

3 cups sugar snap peas
2 tablespoons olive oil
½ teaspoon dried marjoram leaves
½ teaspoon garlic salt
⅛ teaspoon pepper

About Sugar Snap Peas

Sugar snap peas are very sweet peas that are totally edible, including the pod. When purchasing, look for a bright green color with no dark or light spots and buy peas that are plump and crisp. Don't cook them too long; 2–3 minutes in boiling water is enough.

1. Preheat oven to 425°F. Remove strings from sugar snap peas, if desired. Place on baking sheet and sprinkle with remaining ingredients. Mix with your hands until the peas are coated.

2. Roast for 4–6 minutes, until peas just begin to brown in spots and are crisp and tender. Serve immediately.

Braised Carrots

Braising means cooking food covered in a small amount of liquid until tender.
The liquid is then reduced to a syrup and poured over the food to serve.

INGREDIENTS | SERVES 4

1 pound carrots

¾ cup water

¼ cup orange juice

1 tablespoon sugar

½ teaspoon salt

⅛ teaspoon white pepper

¼ teaspoon dried marjoram leaves

2 tablespoons butter

1. Peel carrots and cut diagonally into 1½-inch chunks; set aside. In a heavy saucepan, combine remaining ingredients. Bring to a boil over medium heat.

2. Add carrots to the pan and cover. Reduce heat to low and simmer carrots, covered, for 5–8 minutes, until carrots are soft when pierced with a knife. Remove the carrots from the pan and place on serving plate.

3. Increase heat to high and bring liquid to a boil. Boil for 3–5 minutes, until liquid is reduced and syrupy. Pour over carrots and serve.

Three-Bean Medley

This combination of beans is flavorful and delicious. And the sweet-and-sour salad dressing adds a nice punch of flavor. Serve it with a grilled steak and a mixed lettuce salad, with breadsticks on the side.

INGREDIENTS | SERVES 4–6

1 cup frozen green beans

1 cup frozen soybeans

1 cup frozen lima beans

½ cup sweet-and-sour salad dressing

¼ cup toasted pine nuts

1. Place the frozen green beans, soybeans, and lima beans in a heavy saucepan and cover with cold water. Bring to a boil; then reduce heat and simmer for 4–6 minutes, until all the beans are tender.

2. Drain beans thoroughly and return to saucepan. Add salad dressing and cook over medium heat until liquid comes to a boil and beans are glazed. Sprinkle with pine nuts and serve.

About Soybeans

Soybeans, also known as edamame, are grown in hairy pods; they are often served as a snack in the pod. The beans are high in complete protein and fiber and contain lots of isoflavones, which may help reduce the risk of cancer. And they taste great—nutty and sweet, with a buttery texture.

Broccoli Toss

When broccoli is properly prepared, the florets are bright green, tender, and mildly flavored.
Serve this simple side dish with a pasta casserole and a fresh fruit salad.

INGREDIENTS | SERVES 4–6

1 head broccoli, broken into florets

4 cups water

2 tablespoons olive oil

1 tablespoon butter

1 onion, chopped

3 cloves garlic, minced

2 tablespoons toasted sesame seeds

About Broccoli

The trick to cooking broccoli is to use a large amount of water and cook it, uncovered, very quickly. Use at least 4 cups of water for each head of broccoli. Follow these steps and your broccoli will be crisp, tender, and mildly flavored.

1. Place broccoli florets in large saucepan and cover with water. Bring to a boil; then reduce heat and simmer, uncovered, for 5–7 minutes, until crisp and tender.

2. Meanwhile, place olive oil and butter in a skillet over medium heat. Add onion and garlic; cook and stir for 4–6 minutes, until crisp and tender.

3. Drain broccoli thoroughly and add to skillet with onion and garlic. Toss to coat broccoli with onion mixture. Sprinkle with sesame seeds, toss gently, and serve.

Crunchy Puréed Squash

Frozen puréed squash is a fabulous convenience food that saves, literally,
hours of work in the kitchen. This hearty side dish is perfect for Thanksgiving.

INGREDIENTS | SERVES 6

1 (12-ounce) package frozen puréed winter squash

¼ cup orange juice

2 tablespoons maple syrup

½ teaspoon salt

⅛ teaspoon white pepper

1 cup granola

1. Preheat oven to 400°F. In large saucepan, combine the frozen squash with orange juice and bring to a simmer. Cook for 6–8 minutes, until the squash begins to thaw. Stir in maple syrup, salt, and pepper; continue cooking for 3–4 minutes longer, until squash is hot and smooth.

2. Place in 2-quart casserole dish and sprinkle with granola. Bake at 400°F for 12–15 minutes, until hot and granola browns slightly. Serve immediately.

Herbed Baby Potatoes

Baby potatoes cook quickly because they are so small.
Removing a strip of skin from the middle of the potatoes prevents splitting as they cook.

INGREDIENTS | SERVES 6

1 pound baby red-skinned potatoes
¼ cup butter
3 cloves garlic, minced
2 tablespoons fresh thyme leaves
2 tablespoons chopped fresh parsley
½ teaspoon salt
⅛ teaspoon white pepper

Preparing Fresh Herbs

To prepare herbs with tiny leaves, like oregano, rosemary, marjoram, and thyme, simply pull the leaves backward off the stem; chop if desired. Herbs with larger leaves, like sage, mint, and basil, should be rolled into a log and julienned.

1. Peel a strip of skin from the middle of each potato. Place potatoes in large pot and cover with cold water. Cover and bring to a boil over high heat. Uncover, lower heat, and cook potatoes until tender when pierced with a fork, about 12–14 minutes.

2. Meanwhile, combine butter and garlic in a small saucepan. Cook over medium heat for 2–3 minutes, until garlic is fragrant. Remove from heat.

3. When potatoes are done, drain thoroughly; then return potatoes to the hot pot. Let stand off the heat for 2–3 minutes, shaking occasionally. Place pot over medium heat and pour butter mixture over potatoes. Sprinkle with remaining ingredients, toss gently, and then serve.

Grilled Portobello Mushrooms

*Flavorful portobello mushrooms are a great choice for grilling—
cooking enhances their meaty flavor, and their high water content and thick texture
means they won't dry out during cooking or fall apart on the grill.*

INGREDIENTS | SERVES 4

1 pound portobello mushrooms
½ stick unsalted butter
¼ cup olive oil
2 tablespoons balsamic vinegar
1 shallot, chopped
½ teaspoon salt
½ teaspoon dried parsley
½ teaspoon dried basil leaves

1. Preheat the grill.

2. Wash the mushrooms and remove the stems.

3. In a small saucepan over low heat, melt the butter with the olive oil, balsamic vinegar, shallot, salt, parsley, and basil.

4. Place the mushroom caps on the grill with the gills facing upward. Brush the mushrooms with some of the melted butter mixture.

5. Grill the mushrooms for up to 10 minutes, or until they are tender, turning halfway and brushing frequently with the melted butter mixture. Serve hot.

Microwave French Fries

Preparing french fries in the microwave is quicker and healthier than deep-frying them in hot oil. Be sure not to overcook the potatoes or·they will deflate and become soft.

INGREDIENTS | SERVES 2

½ pound (2 medium) russet or red potatoes, peeled

¼ cup white vinegar

¼ teaspoon garlic salt

¼ teaspoon cayenne pepper

Quick-Cooking with Potatoes

One way to speed up the preparation time when you're cooking potatoes is to leave the peel on. Potato peels add a crunchy texture, and carry fiber and vitamin B2 (riboflavin). Just be sure to scrub the potato skin under cold running water to remove any pesticide residue or other toxins.

1. Scrub the potatoes under cold running water and use a paring knife to cut out any bruises or green spots. Cut into thin strips the size and shape of french fries.

2. Toss the cut potatoes in a bowl with the vinegar, stirring so that all the potato strips are coated.

3. Take approximately half the potato strips and arrange on a microwave-safe plate. Sprinkle the cut potatoes with the garlic salt.

4. Microwave the cut potatoes on high heat for 7 minutes, and then for 1 minute at a time until they are cooked through. (The potatoes will not brown like regular french fries, but will be fork-tender.)

5. Repeat with the remainder of the cut potatoes, sprinkling them with the cayenne pepper instead of garlic salt. Combine fries and serve.

Roasted Red Peppers

Roasting is a great way to bring out the sweet flavor of red bell peppers.
To add extra color, try using a combination of red and yellow bell peppers.
Green peppers can also be roasted; however, the flavor will not be as sweet.

INGREDIENTS | SERVES 4

4 red bell peppers
2 tablespoons olive oil

Versatile Peppers

Roasted red peppers add flavor to pasta dishes, heartier soups, and dips. You'll often find them used in combination with aromatic basil, pungent garlic, or cheese. Their sweet flavor pairs particularly well with goat cheese—for a quick snack, serve the roasted peppers and goat cheese on crusty bread.

1. Preheat the broiler and line it with aluminum foil. Cut the stems off the red peppers; cut the peppers in half and remove the seeds.

2. Place the peppers on the broiling pan with the skin-side facing up. Use a pastry brush to brush the peppers with the olive oil.

3. Broil the peppers for 15 minutes, or until most of the skin is blackened.

4. Use tongs to remove the peppers from the broiler and cover in aluminum foil or plastic wrap. Let the wrapped peppers stand for at least 10 minutes before removing the covering. Peel off the skins and cut into thin slices or squares as desired. Serve.

Stir-Fried Broccoli with Garlic

*Stir-frying has the advantage of being both quick and healthy—
the short cooking time means that vegetables retain more of their nutrients.*

INGREDIENTS | SERVES 3

2 tablespoons olive oil

2 garlic cloves, peeled and finely chopped

½ teaspoon red pepper flakes, or to taste

½ pound broccoli florets

⅛ teaspoon salt, or to taste

2 tablespoons water

1 red bell pepper, seeded, cut into chunks

2 teaspoons lemon juice

2 teaspoons soy sauce

1. Heat the olive oil in a large skillet on medium-high heat. Add the garlic cloves and red pepper flakes.

2. Add the broccoli. Stir briefly, sprinkling the salt over the broccoli while cooking, until the florets turn bright green.

3. Add the water and let the broccoli cook for 2–3 more minutes.

4. Add the red bell pepper. Stir in the lemon juice and soy sauce. Cook, stirring, for another minute. Serve immediately.

Preparing Vegetables ahead of Time

One way to speed up meal-preparation time is to chop several days' worth of vegetables ahead of time. Store the vegetables for each meal in a sealed bag in the refrigerator until ready to use.

Garlic Mashed Potatoes

Cooking the potatoes in the microwave speeds up the preparation time, since you don't have to wait for the water to boil.

INGREDIENTS | SERVES 6

4 medium red potatoes
4 tablespoons butter or margarine
¼ cup milk
2 teaspoons garlic powder, or to taste
½ teaspoon salt, or to taste

1. Wash and peel the potatoes. Cut them roughly into bite-size chunks.

2. Place the potatoes in a deep microwave-safe dish and cover with water.

3. Microwave the potatoes on high heat for 10 minutes. Give the dish a quarter turn and continue microwaving for 1–2 minutes at a time until the potatoes are cooked through and can easily be pierced with a fork. (Total cooking time should be about 15 minutes.) Drain.

4. Place the potatoes in a large bowl. Add the butter or margarine and use a fork or a potato masher to whip the potatoes. Gradually add the milk until the potatoes have reached the desired consistency (do not add more milk than is needed). Stir in the garlic powder and salt. Serve hot.

Spaghetti Squash

Shhh—the children will be sure they are eating spaghetti. It looks like spaghetti, but tastes even better!

INGREDIENTS | SERVES 3–4

1 large spaghetti squash, cleaned
1 tablespoon trans fat–free margarine
3–4 tablespoons Parmesan cheese

1. Pierce the skin of the squash with a fork in about 5–6 places and microwave for 2–3 minutes.

2. Cut the squash in half (lengthwise) and scoop out the seeds.

3. Use fork to scrape into strands and place in a small serving bowl.

4. Blend squash with margarine and sprinkle with Parmesan cheese.

5. Serve immediately while still warm.

Oven-Roasted Asparagus and Parmesan

Medium-sized stalks of asparagus work best for this recipe.
The pencil-thin stalks tend to burn at the tips, and the thick stalks require peeling.

INGREDIENTS | SERVES 4

1½ pounds asparagus, bottoms trimmed
1 tablespoon olive oil
½ teaspoon salt
Freshly cracked black pepper, to taste
¼ cup freshly grated Parmesan

1. Preheat oven to 450°F.

2. In a large mixing bowl, combine the asparagus, olive oil, salt, and pepper. Toss to evenly coat the asparagus. Line a baking sheet with parchment paper and lay out the asparagus in a single layer.

3. Bake until crisp and tender, about 8 minutes, depending on the thickness. Sprinkle the cheese on top, and bake until the cheese melts, about 2 minutes. Taste and adjust seasoning as needed. Transfer to a serving platter and serve hot.

Roasted Zucchini

This recipe features little prep time and easy cleanup—just one pan for mixing and cooking. You can substitute yellow squash for half the zucchini for a variation in color.

INGREDIENTS | SERVES 4

1 tablespoon olive oil

2 cups zucchini rounds (about ½-inch thick)

½ teaspoon salt

Freshly cracked black pepper, to taste

2 tablespoons minced red onion

1 garlic clove, minced

1 teaspoon lemon zest

1. Preheat oven to 425°F.

2. Combine the olive oil, zucchini, salt, and pepper in an 8" × 8" baking dish with sides. Use a rubber spatula to stir and coat the zucchini evenly with the oil and seasonings. Bake, uncovered, for about 12 minutes, stirring once midway through cooking.

3. Add the red onion, garlic, and lemon zest, stirring to combine. Bake until the zucchini is tender, about 5 minutes. Transfer to a serving platter and serve hot.

CHAPTER 11

Pasta, Rice, and Other Grains

Basic Cooked Instant Rice

Using instant rice (also called quick-cooking rice) speeds up the cooking time considerably. While these general instructions should work for most types of instant long-grain cooked rice, be sure to follow the package directions if they are different.

INGREDIENTS | SERVES 2

¾ cup water

¾ cup cooked instant long-grain rice

⅛ teaspoon salt, or to taste

Black pepper, to taste

1. Bring the water to a boil in a medium saucepan.

2. Stir in the rice, making sure it is thoroughly wet. Stir in the salt and pepper.

3. Remove the rice from the heat. Cover the saucepan and let stand for 5 minutes, or until the water is absorbed.

4. Fluff up the rice with a fork and serve.

Easy Flavored Rice

Cooking rice in broth, juice, or another liquid is a great way to add extra flavor. Feel free to load up the rice by stirring in ½ cup of golden sultana raisins.

INGREDIENTS | SERVES 4

¾ cups chicken broth

¾ cup coconut milk

½ teaspoon curry powder

1½ cups cooked instant long-grain rice

2 teaspoons margarine

¼ teaspoon salt, or to taste

Black pepper, to taste

1. Bring the chicken broth, coconut milk, and curry powder to a boil in a medium saucepan.

2. Stir in the rice, making sure it is thoroughly wet. Stir in the margarine, salt, and pepper.

3. Remove the saucepan from the heat.

4. Cover the saucepan and let stand for 5 minutes. Fluff up with a fork and serve.

Mexican Fried Rice

This spicy side dish would go nicely with a less highly seasoned main dish.

INGREDIENTS | SERVES 4

3 tablespoons vegetable oil, divided

½ medium yellow onion, finely chopped

1 tablespoon jarred chopped jalapeño peppers

1 tomato, diced

1 cup canned corn niblets

3 cups cold cooked rice

½ teaspoon ground cumin

2 green onions, finely sliced

¼ teaspoon salt, or to taste

⅛ teaspoon black pepper, or to taste

How to Cook Long-Grain Rice

Cooking rice the traditional way gives you an alternative to always having to use instant rice on nights when time is limited. To cook the rice, bring the rice and water to boil in a medium saucepan, using 2 cups water for every cup of rice. When the water is boiling, turn the heat down to medium-low and partially cover. Continue cooking until "holes" start to appear in the rice. Cover fully, turn the heat down to low. Let the rice steam for at least 15 minutes more, until the water is fully absorbed.

1. Heat 1½ tablespoons oil in a nonstick skillet over medium heat. Add the onion. Cook for 4–5 minutes, until the onion is softened.

2. Stir in the chopped jalapeño peppers. Stir in the tomato. Cook for a minute and stir in the canned corn. Remove the vegetables from the pan.

3. Heat 1½ tablespoons oil in the pan. Add the rice. Cook, stirring, for 1–2 minutes, until heated through. Stir in the ground cumin.

4. Return the vegetables to the pan. Stir in the green onions. Stir to mix everything together. Season with the salt and pepper. Serve hot.

Easy Apple Risotto

Traditionalists insist that the only way to make risotto is to stand over the pot, painstakingly stirring the liquid into the rice. However, simply letting the rice simmer in broth and apple juice does a reasonably good job, leaving you free to prepare the rest of the meal.

INGREDIENTS | SERVES 4

2 tablespoons olive oil

1 medium red apple, cored and sliced

1 teaspoon cinnamon, or to taste

1 cup Arborio short-grain rice

2 tablespoons golden raisins

1½ cups chicken broth

1 cup apple juice

3 tablespoons shredded Cheddar cheese

Rustic Risotto

A classic dish from northern Italy, risotto is famous for its rich, creamy texture. The distinctive flavor and texture of risotto come from using a super-absorbent rice with grains that stick together when cooked. Arborio is the most popular rice for making risotto in North America, but other varieties of Italian rice, such as carnaroli, can also be used.

1. Heat the olive oil in a large skillet on medium-high heat. Add the apple and cinnamon. Cook, stirring, for about 2 minutes, until the apples start to become crisp.

2. Add the rice and cook for about 2 minutes, until the grains start to become shiny and translucent. Stir in the raisins.

3. Add the chicken broth and apple juice.

4. Turn the heat down to low, cover, and simmer for 20 minutes.

5. Stir in the cheese and serve.

Creamy Risotto Side Dish

*This won't have quite the same texture and flavor as authentic risotto,
but it's a good stand-in for nights when you're in a hurry.*

INGREDIENTS | SERVES 4

1 cup frozen baby peas
1 cup Arborio or other short-grain rice
2 cups chicken broth, divided
½ teaspoon dried basil leaves
½ teaspoon dried oregano
½ teaspoon garlic powder
⅛ teaspoon black pepper, or to taste
1 teaspoon salt, divided
⅓ cup shredded Parmesan cheese

1. Place the frozen peas in a microwave-safe casserole dish. Cover with microwave-safe plastic wrap, leaving one corner open to vent steam. Microwave the peas on high heat for 2 minutes, and then for 30 seconds at a time until cooked (total cooking time should be 2–3 minutes).

2. Add the rice and 1½ cups broth. Stir in the basil, oregano, garlic powder, pepper, and ½ teaspoon salt. Cover the dish with microwave-safe plastic wrap and microwave for 5 minutes.

3. Stir in ½ cup broth and ½ teaspoon salt. Microwave on high for 5 more minutes.

4. Stir, cover, and microwave for 5 minutes, or until the liquid is mainly absorbed and the rice grains are tender.

5. Stir in the Parmesan cheese. Serve hot.

Healthy Brown Rice

*While instant brown rice is a quick and easy alternative to making regular brown rice,
it can be hard to find. Another option is to make brown rice ahead of time and reheat it later.*

INGREDIENTS | SERVES 4

1 cup brown rice
2¼ cups water

Bring the rice and water to boil in a medium saucepan. Reduce the heat to low-medium. Cook the rice, uncovered, until the water is absorbed (40 minutes). Let stand for 10 minutes. Fluff and serve.

Rice Reheating Tips

For safety's sake, it's important to cool down and refrigerate the cooked rice within 2 hours after cooking. To reheat, combine the rice with 1–2 tablespoons water in a saucepan and cook over low heat, or heat in the microwave (follow your microwave's instructions for reheating food).

Steamed Coconut Rice

*Microwave basmati rice takes less time to make and still has
the rich nutty flavor of regular boiled scented rice.*

INGREDIENTS | SERVES 6

1½ cups scented rice

1 tablespoon margarine

2 shallots

1¼ cups coconut milk

1¾ cups water

½ teaspoon salt

Or Cook It the Regular Way

Another way to cut down on the time it
takes to prepare rice for dinner is to boil
the rice in advance so that it just needs to
be reheated. To cook basmati rice on the
stovetop, sauté the margarine and shallots
in a skillet until the shallots are softened.
Add the rice, coconut milk, water, and salt
and bring to a boil, uncovered. Turn down
the heat to medium and boil, uncovered,
until the liquid is nearly absorbed (10–12
minutes). Continue cooking for a few more
minutes until the water is absorbed.

1. Rinse the rice in cold water and drain.

2. Place the margarine and chopped shallots in a
   microwave-safe 3-quart casserole dish. Microwave on
   high heat for 1½ minutes, stir, and then microwave for
   30 seconds at a time until the shallots are tender.

3. Add the coconut milk, water, rice, and salt. Microwave
   on high for 10 minutes.

4. Stir the rice. Cover the dish with microwave-safe wax
   paper. Microwave for 3 minutes and then for 1 minute
   at a time until the liquid is absorbed.

5. Remove the dish from the microwave. Let stand for 5
   minutes. Fluff and serve.

Spanish Rice Side Dish

*This simple side dish is incredibly easy to make. To turn it into a main meal,
simply add 2 cups of cooked shrimp or leftover cooked chicken.*

INGREDIENTS | SERVES 4

⅔ cup tomato juice

1⅓ cups water

2 cups instant rice

½ teaspoon salt, or to taste

⅛ teaspoon black pepper

1 tablespoon olive oil

2 cloves garlic, chopped

1 onion, chopped

1 teaspoon paprika, or to taste

1 green bell pepper, chopped into chunks

1. In a saucepan, bring the tomato juice and water to a boil. Stir in the rice, salt, and pepper. Remove from the heat, cover, and let stand for 5 minutes.

2. While the rice is cooking, prepare the vegetables: Heat the olive oil in a heavy skillet or wok on medium-high heat. Add the garlic and onion. Sprinkle the paprika over the onion and sauté for about 2 minutes, until the onion begins to soften.

3. Add the green pepper and continue cooking until the vegetables are softened.

4. Stir the cooked vegetables into the rice. Fluff with a fork before serving.

Easy Italian Rice Pilaf

This comforting dish is full of flavor without being too heavy.
Reduced-sodium chicken broth is available in resealable cartons in many supermarkets.

INGREDIENTS | SERVES 4

1 tablespoon olive oil

2 shallots, peeled and chopped

1 teaspoon bottled minced garlic

1 tablespoon chopped sun-dried tomato strips

1 cup chopped red bell pepper

1 cup drained canned mushrooms

¼ teaspoon cayenne pepper

1 tablespoon balsamic vinegar

2¼ cups reduced-sodium chicken broth

2 cups instant white rice

1. Heat the olive oil in a large skillet on medium heat. Add the shallots, garlic, and sun-dried tomato strips. Sauté for 3–4 minutes, until the shallots are softened.

2. Add the chopped bell pepper and the mushrooms. Sprinkle the cayenne pepper on top. Splash the vegetables with the balsamic vinegar. Cook until the vegetables are softened (total cooking time is about 5 minutes).

3. Add the chicken broth. Bring to a boil.

4. Stir in the instant rice. Cover and let stand off heat for 5 minutes. Serve hot.

Angel Hair Pasta with Shrimp

You can sprinkle ½ cup Parmesan cheese over the cooked shrimp and pasta.
To reduce the preparation time, feel free to use leftover cooked pasta.

INGREDIENTS | SERVES 4

3 quarts water

1½ teaspoons salt

¾ pound angel hair pasta

1 tablespoon olive oil

2 cloves garlic, minced

2 shallots, chopped

1 teaspoon dried basil

1 teaspoon dried oregano

1 tomato, chopped

1 pound peeled, deveined shrimp

2 tablespoons lemon juice

¼ cup light cream

¼ teaspoon black pepper

Pasta Cooking Tips

The key to making perfect pasta is to use plenty of water, giving the pasta room to move around, and stirring it to separate the strands. Ideally, pasta should be cooked until it reaches the al dente stage.

1. Bring a large pot with the water and salt to a boil. Add the pasta to the boiling water. Cook until the pasta is cooked al dente. (Prepare the vegetables and shrimp while the pasta is cooking.)

2. Heat the olive oil in a skillet. Add the garlic and shallots. Sprinkle the dried basil and oregano over the shallots. Sauté for 3–4 minutes, until softened.

3. Add the tomato and the shrimp. Sauté the shrimp until they turn pink.

4. Add the lemon juice and cream. Cook until thickened. Stir in the pepper. Keep warm.

5. Drain the cooked pasta in a colander. Place in a large bowl. Toss the pasta with the sauce. Serve immediately.

Basic Stir-Fried Noodles

Linguine and spaghetti both make handy substitutes for Chinese egg noodles.
If you like, stir-fry ½ pound of fresh spinach leaves with the noodles.

INGREDIENTS | SERVES 4

2 quarts water

1 teaspoon salt

½ pound linguine

2 teaspoons soy sauce

½ teaspoon granulated sugar

1 tablespoon red wine vinegar

2 tablespoons vegetable oil

1 teaspoon bottled minced garlic

Marvelous Mian

They may not have the same intriguing shapes as Italian pasta, but there are many varieties of Chinese noodles, called mian. Delicate rice noodles, made from rice flour and water, are frequently added to soups and sometimes salads. Made with wheat flour and egg, thick fresh Shanghai noodles are more than able to hold their own in stir-fries, absorbing the flavors of the sauce they are cooked with.

1. Bring a large pot with 2 quarts of water to a boil with the salt. Add the linguine to the boiling water. Cook for 3–4 minutes, until the linguine is cooked al dente. Drain in a colander.

2. In a small bowl, stir together the soy sauce, sugar, and red wine vinegar.

3. Heat the oil in a skillet over medium-high heat. Add the minced garlic. Stir for a few seconds; then add the noodles.

4. Stir for 1 minute; then pour in the sauce.

5. Stir-fry for 1–2 more minutes, until the noodles are heated through. Serve hot.

Pasta Primavera

Traditionally, pasta primavera is loaded with fresh spring vegetables (the word primavera means "spring"), but using canned vegetables helps you enjoy this Italian specialty on busy weeknights. Feel free to use homemade Roasted Red Peppers (see Chapter 10) or store-bought bottled roasted peppers.

INGREDIENTS | SERVES 4

2 tablespoons olive oil

1 white onion, peeled, chopped

1 zucchini, chopped

1 teaspoon dried basil

1 teaspoon dried oregano

1 cup drained canned asparagus tips

1 cup roasted red peppers

½ cup tomato sauce

½ cup light cream

½ teaspoon salt, or to taste

¼ teaspoon black pepper, or to taste

½ pound leftover cooked whole wheat spaghetti

½ cup shredded Parmesan cheese

1. Heat the olive oil in a skillet over medium-high heat. Add the onion. Sauté for 2–3 minutes; then add the zucchini. Sprinkle the basil and oregano over the onion while it is cooking. Sauté until the vegetables are softened, 4–5 minutes, turning the heat down to medium if needed.

2. Add the canned asparagus and the red peppers. Cook for 1 minute on medium heat.

3. Add the tomato sauce and cream. Cook, stirring, until it begins to bubble and thicken slightly. Stir in the salt and pepper. Turn down the heat and keep warm.

4. Reheat the cooked pasta. Place the pasta in a bowl and toss with the primavera sauce. Sprinkle with the Parmesan cheese. Serve hot.

Five-Ingredient Spaghetti and Meatballs

*There are a number of good premade tomato sauces on the market—choose your favorite.
Use your preferred frozen vegetables in this recipe—spinach, cauliflower,
and a frozen stir-fry vegetable mix are all good choices.*

INGREDIENTS | SERVES 4

24 frozen meatballs

3 cups frozen vegetables

¾ pound leftover cooked spaghetti

3 cups premade tomato sauce

¾ cup grated Parmesan cheese

Cooking Pasta in the Microwave

Don't have leftover pasta on hand, and there's no time to cook a new batch? You can quickly cook pasta in the microwave. First, heat the water in a microwave-safe dish. Add the noodles—stirring to make sure they are completely covered with the water—and cook on high heat until tender. The exact cooking time will depend on the amount of pasta to be cooked—count on at least 4 minutes for 8 ounces of dried egg noodles.

1. Place the frozen meatballs in a microwave-safe dish. Microwave on high heat for 2 minutes, and then for 30 seconds at a time if needed until the meatballs are cooked.

2. Place the frozen vegetables in a microwave-safe dish. Cover and microwave on high heat for 3 minutes, and then for 1 minute at a time until cooked.

3. Reheat the pasta.

4. Heat the premade tomato sauce in a saucepan over medium heat.

5. Toss the pasta with the tomato sauce. Stir in the meatballs and vegetables. Sprinkle the Parmesan cheese on top. Serve hot.

Garlic Noodles with Bacon

Here is a quick and easy way to jazz up leftover pasta.
You can use other types of long pasta in this recipe, such as linguine or angel hair pasta.

INGREDIENTS | SERVES 4

8 ounces leftover cooked spaghetti

3 slices bacon

3 tablespoons margarine

2 tablespoons cream cheese

2 teaspoons bottled minced garlic, or to taste

1 cup half-and-half

⅓ cup grated Parmesan cheese

½ teaspoon dried basil, or to taste

½ teaspoon dried oregano, or to taste

Black pepper, to taste

Serving Leftover Pasta

The easiest way to reheat leftover cooked pasta is to place it in a colander and quickly rinse it under hot running water, moving your fingers through to separate the strands. To reheat pasta in the microwave, place in a microwave-safe bowl covered with wax paper or plastic wrap. Microwave on high heat for 1 minute, and then for 30 seconds at a time until the pasta is heated through.

1. Reheat the spaghetti.

2. Place the bacon on a plate covered with a paper towel. Lay two more paper towels over the bacon. Microwave on high heat for 2 minutes, and then for 1 minute at a time until the bacon is cooked. Remove and chop.

3. Melt the margarine in a saucepan over low heat. Whisk in the cream cheese. Stir in the garlic.

4. Turn the heat up and add the half-and-half. Add the Parmesan cheese and continue stirring with a whisk until the mixture has thickened. Stir in the basil, oregano, and pepper.

5. Place the cooked pasta in a large bowl. Toss with the sauce and bacon. Serve hot.

Greek Macaroni and Cheese

Here is a more adult version of the kid's favorite mac 'n' cheese, made by adding cheese and herbs traditionally used in Greek cooking to a basic white sauce and serving over pasta. You can use any small tubular pasta as the macaroni, including traditional macaroni noodles.

INGREDIENTS | SERVES 3

½ pound leftover tubular pasta, cooked

4 tablespoons unsalted butter

3 tablespoons flour

1 teaspoon bottled minced garlic

1 cup whole milk

⅓ cup crumbled feta cheese

¼ teaspoon ground nutmeg, or to taste

1 teaspoon dried mint

¼ teaspoon black pepper, or to taste

1 teaspoon lemon juice

1. Reheat the pasta.

2. Melt the butter in medium saucepan on very low heat. Add the flour and blend it into the melted butter, stirring continually until it thickens and forms a roux. Stir in the garlic.

3. Turn the heat up to medium-low and slowly add the milk and cheese. Stir in the ground nutmeg and the dried mint. Continue stirring with a whisk until the mixture has thickened.

4. Stir in the pepper and lemon juice.

5. Toss the pasta with the sauce and serve immediately.

Microwave Lasagna

With flavorful marinara sauce, this dish doesn't really need any extra seasoning.
But if you like, you can add a pinch of dried oregano, basil, or parsley.

INGREDIENTS | SERVES 2

½ pound ground beef

1 cup crushed tomatoes

1½ cups marinara sauce

1½ cups grated mozzarella cheese

1½ cups ricotta cheese

12 oven-ready lasagna noodles

1. Crumble the ground beef into a microwave-safe bowl. Microwave the beef on high heat for 5 minutes. Give the dish a quarter turn and microwave on high heat for 4 more minutes. Make another quarter turn and microwave for 1 minute at a time until the beef is cooked through. Remove from the microwave and drain the fat.

2. Combine the ground beef with the crushed tomatoes and marinara sauce. Stir in the cheeses.

3. Lay out four of the lasagna noodles in a large bowl or a 1-quart microwave-safe casserole dish. (Break the noodles if needed to fit into the container.) Spoon ⅓ of the sauce mixture over the noodles, spreading evenly. Add two more layers of the noodles and sauce.

4. Cover the dish with wax paper. Microwave on high heat for 7–8 minutes, until the cheeses are cooked. Let the lasagna stand for 10 minutes before serving.

Rotini with Perfect Peanut Sauce

Of course, any shape noodle can be used for this recipe. An important tip is to use healthier peanut butter, without trans fat (or partially hydrogenated vegetable oil), and a whole wheat noodle.

INGREDIENTS | SERVES 4–6

½–¾ pound whole wheat rotini pasta noodles

Peanut Sauce:

4–5 tablespoons trans fat–free peanut butter

2 teaspoons brown sugar

2 garlic cloves, peeled and minced

2 tablespoons canola oil

2 tablespoons reduced-sodium soy sauce

1 tablespoon cider vinegar

1 tablespoon sesame oil

4–5 tablespoons hot water

1. Bring a large pot of water to a boil. Cook the pasta until just soft. Drain and set aside.

2. In a medium bowl, combine the peanut butter, brown sugar, garlic, canola oil, soy sauce, cider vinegar, and sesame oil. Blend well.

3. Add the hot water and mix until you reach a creamy consistency.

4. Add the sauce to the pasta. Serve immediately for best flavor.

A Really Neat Twist on Pasta

Peanut butter with pasta? Now that Japanese/Asian food is so popular, why not prepare this pasta dish with a peanut sauce? To increase the protein level for this dish, add sliced chicken or cooked shrimp—more protein will always keep the children satiated. It's yet another way to have them eat whole wheat pasta, too, without complaints!

CHAPTER 12

Pizza, Burgers, and Wraps

English Muffin Pizzas

*These little pizzas can be topped with just about anything. Use cooked ground beef,
drained chopped green chilies, and pepper jack cheese for Mexican pizzas;
or chopped ham, drained pineapple tidbits, and Colby-Jack cheese for Hawaiian pizzas.*

INGREDIENTS | SERVES 6–8

8 English muffins, split and toasted

1½ cups pizza sauce

1 (6-ounce) jar sliced mushrooms, drained

1 cup pepperoni, sliced

2 cups shredded mozzarella cheese

1. Preheat oven to broil. Place English muffin halves on baking sheet and top each one with pizza sauce. Layer mushrooms and pepperoni over pizza sauce. Sprinkle cheese over pizzas.

2. Broil pizzas, 4–6 inches from heat source, for 2–4 minutes or until pizzas are hot and cheese is melted, bubbly, and beginning to brown. Serve immediately.

Mexican Chicken Pizzas

*These individual pizzas are full of Tex-Mex flavor.
Serve them with a simple fruit salad and an ice cream pie for dessert.*

INGREDIENTS | SERVES 8

8 flour tortillas

1 (16-ounce) can refried beans

½ cup taco sauce

½ teaspoon dried oregano

1 tablespoon chili powder

2 (9-ounce) packages refrigerated grilled cooked chicken strips

2 cups shredded pepper jack cheese

1. Preheat oven to 400°F. Place tortillas on two cookie sheets and bake for 5–8 minutes until tortillas are crisp, reversing the cookie sheets halfway through cooking time and turning tortillas over once.

2. In small bowl combine beans, taco sauce, oregano, and chili powder and mix well. Spread evenly over baked tortillas. Top with chicken strips and cheese. Bake for 12–18 minutes, or until pizzas are hot and cheese is melted and beginning to brown, reversing cookie sheets halfway through cooking time. Cut into wedges and serve.

Spinach Cheese Pizzas

Nutmeg really helps to bring out spinach's rich flavor.
This may seem like a strange addition to pizza, but try it—you'll like it!

INGREDIENTS | SERVES 6–8

6 bagels, split and toasted
2 tablespoons olive oil
1 onion, chopped
1 (8-ounce) can pizza sauce
¼ teaspoon ground nutmeg
1 cup frozen chopped spinach, thawed
1½ cups shredded mozzarella cheese

1. Preheat broiler. Place bagels on a cookie sheet.

2. In heavy saucepan, heat olive oil over medium heat and add onion; cook and stir for 4–6 minutes, until onion is tender. Add pizza sauce and nutmeg; bring to a simmer.

3. Meanwhile, drain the thawed spinach in a colander or strainer; then drain again by pressing between paper towels. Spread bagel halves with pizza sauce mixture and top evenly with the spinach. Sprinkle with cheese. Broil 6 inches from heat for 4–7 minutes, until cheese melts and sandwiches are hot. Serve immediately.

Meatball Pizza

This simple pizza can be made with cooked and drained ground beef or sausage instead of the meatballs. Serve with a green salad and carrot sticks.

INGREDIENTS | SERVES 4

1 (14-inch) prepared pizza crust

1½ cups pizza sauce

½ teaspoon dried oregano leaves

½ teaspoon dry mustard

½ (16-ounce) bag frozen meatballs, thawed

1 cup frozen onion and bell pepper stir-fry combo

2 cups shredded pizza cheese

Pizza Cheese

Pizza cheese is usually a blend of Cheddar, mozzarella, and provolone or Monterey Jack cheeses, and sometimes Parmesan or Romano. It's available preshredded in the dairy section of your supermarket. You can substitute Co-Jack cheese for the pizza cheese blend—it is a blend of Colby and Monterey Jack cheeses.

1. Preheat oven to 400°F. Place pizza crust on a cookie sheet. In small bowl, combine pizza sauce with oregano and dry mustard and mix well. Spread over pizza crust.

2. Cut meatballs in half and arrange, cut-side down, on pizza sauce. Sprinkle with onion and bell pepper stir-fry combo, and then with pizza cheese. Bake at 400°F for 18–23 minutes, or until crust is golden brown and cheese has melted and begins to brown. Serve immediately.

Funny Face Pizza

*This is just a cute way to get the children involved in making their pizza—
including those great vegetables, too!*

INGREDIENTS | SERVES 4–6

1 (1-pound) prepared pizza crust
(preferably whole wheat)

1 (24-ounce) jar spaghetti or pizza sauce

2 cups shredded low-fat mozzarella
cheese

Oregano, chopped parsley, pepper, and
garlic powder, to taste

1 cup steamed broccoli florets

1 olive

4 large carrots, grated

2 round zucchini slices

1 thin slice red pepper

1. Preheat oven to 350°F.

2. Lay out pizza crust on a large piece of aluminum foil,
   sprayed with nonstick cooking spray.

3. Cover pizza crust with tomato sauce, mozzarella
   cheese, and spices.

4. Decorate with vegetables, using grated carrots for hair
   and eyebrows. Use an olive for the nose and broccoli
   florets for the eyes. Use red pepper slice for the mouth
   and zucchini for the cheeks; or use different vegetable
   favorites and your imagination.

5. Cook pizza according to package directions. Serve hot.

Sloppy Joes

Invented to cope with a meat shortage during World War II,
sloppy joes are a favorite with kids, who like their soupy texture.

INGREDIENTS | SERVES 4

1½ pounds ground beef
½ yellow onion, chopped
½ green bell pepper, diced
1 cup water
1 cup tomato paste
2 tablespoons brown sugar
¼ teaspoon paprika, or to taste
¼ teaspoon garlic powder
¼ teaspoon black pepper, or to taste
4 hamburger buns
⅓ cup shredded Cheddar cheese

Sloppy Joes with Sizzle

Feel free to jazz up this basic recipe for
Sloppy Joes by replacing the tomato paste
with your favorite prepared salsa, or the
water with tomato soup.

1. Place the ground beef in a large skillet and brown over medium heat. After the beef is halfway cooked, add the onion and bell pepper. Continue cooking until the beef is browned and the onion is softened, about 10–12 minutes.

2. Add the water. Stir in the tomato paste. Stir in the brown sugar, paprika, garlic powder, and pepper.

3. Bring to a boil. Turn down the heat, cover, and simmer for about 10 minutes, until the mixture is heated through and reaches desired thickness.

4. Spoon the beef mixture over the hamburger buns. Sprinkle with shredded cheese and serve.

Turkey Sloppy Joes

Not a fan of hamburger buns? You can also make sloppy joes with sandwich buns, on a loaf of French or Italian bread, or even with tortilla or nacho chips.

INGREDIENTS | SERVES 4

1½ pounds ground turkey

1 medium onion, chopped

1 green bell pepper, chopped into chunks

½ cup water

1 cup ketchup

3 tablespoons brown sugar

3 tablespoons red wine vinegar

¾ teaspoon ground cumin, or to taste

¼ teaspoon black pepper

4 hamburger buns

⅓ cup crumbled Havarti cheese

1. Brown the ground turkey in a large skillet over medium-high heat.

2. Add the onion and bell peppers. Cook for 4–5 more minutes, until the onion is softened. Drain the fat out of the pan.

3. Add the water, ketchup, brown sugar, and red wine vinegar. Stir in the cumin and pepper. Turn the heat down to low and simmer, uncovered, for 15 minutes.

4. Spoon the turkey mixture over the hamburger buns. Sprinkle the crumbled cheese on top. Serve immediately.

Chicken Salad Pitas

Purchase the best whole grain bread—the first label on the ingredient list should be "whole wheat flour," not "enriched wheat flour." Look for anywhere from 3–5 grams of fiber per slice of bread.

INGREDIENTS | SERVES 1

3 ounces solid white chicken

1–2 tablespoons low-fat mayonnaise

1 teaspoon celery salt (optional)

1 teaspoon garlic powder (optional)

1 medium whole wheat pita

Mash chicken with low-fat mayonnaise. Add spices, if desired. Put in pita bread and serve.

They Won't Be Sharing with Their Classmates

The rest of the lunchbox should include: ½–1 cup of berries or a small banana; you can add a little chopped lettuce and tomato to the sandwich, for the older kids; and a smart snack, such as pretzels or low-fat popcorn (for children older than 5–6 years old). Your kids won't trade this lunch.

Basic Chicken Wraps

Cream cheese is the "glue" that holds this wrap together.
It's very simple to flavor the cream cheese for a nice twist.

INGREDIENTS | SERVES 4

3 ounces cream cheese, at room temperature

1 tablespoon mayonnaise

1 tablespoon fresh lemon juice

¼ teaspoon seasoned salt

Freshly cracked pepper, to taste

2 (8-inch) low-carb tortillas, at room temperature

2 cups sliced or cubed cooked chicken

½ cup thinly sliced red onion

1 cup baby spinach leaves

Wrap Favorites

Wrap sandwiches have long been a favorite for folks on the fly. Easy to prepare in advance and wrap in plastic film, these quick sandwiches are delicious and easy to eat.

1. Mix together the cream cheese, mayonnaise, lemon juice, salt, and pepper in a small bowl (or use a food processor to blend until smooth).

2. Place the tortillas on a clean work surface. Spread half of the cream cheese mixture on the upper third of each tortilla, about ½ inch from the edge. Place half of the chicken on the lower third of each tortilla. Top each with onions and spinach.

3. Roll up each wrap: Starting from the bottom, fold the tortilla over the filling and roll upward, compressing slightly to form a firm roll. Press at the top to "seal" the wrap closed with the cream cheese mixture. Cut the sandwich in half and wrap in plastic film. Refrigerate until ready to serve.

Chicken and Spinach Wrap

This recipe takes advantage of store-bought rotisserie chicken and the beautiful selection of prepped veggies and greens at the salad bar.

INGREDIENTS | SERVES 1

1 (8-inch) low-carb wrap, flavor of your choice

2 tablespoons flavored cream cheese spread

⅓ cup sliced or shredded rotisserie chicken or cooked chicken breast

½ cup spinach leaves

¼ cup peeled and shredded carrots

1 tablespoon sliced black olives

1 tablespoon sliced red onions

Salt, to taste

Freshly cracked black pepper, to taste

Carrot Facts

Carrots are a great source of beta-carotene and vitamin A. Know that ¼ cup of regular carrots contains 3g of carbohydrates and ¼ cup of baby carrots contains 5g of carbohydrates. However, studies have shown that beta-carotene is most effective when derived from natural foods and not from supplements. Carrots are a carb expenditure well worth it.

1. Place the wrap on a clean, dry work surface. Spread the cream cheese on the upper quarter of the wrap, about 1 inch from the edge.

2. Spread the chicken in an even layer on the lower quarter of the wrap, about 1 inch from the edge. Top with the spinach, carrots, olives, and onions, equally distributed across the wrap. Sprinkle with salt and pepper.

3. Fold the bottom edge of the wrap over the filling and compress carefully, without tearing the wrap. Roll upward, away from you, using the cream cheese to seal the wrap closed. Cut in half on the bias for serving, or wrap halves airtight in plastic wrap for later.

Taco Salad Wrap

This is a really fun "mishmash" salad with many new flavors for the children.
Depending on their spice tolerance, you can heat it up or mild it down.
Try different types of beans and vegetables, and see what they like the most.

INGREDIENTS | SERVES 4

1 pound lean ground beef

1 (16-ounce) can kidney beans, rinsed and drained

1 teaspoon chili powder (optional)

1 teaspoon garlic powder

8 whole wheat flour or corn tortillas

½ head romaine lettuce, chopped finely

2 medium ripe tomatoes, chopped finely

1 cup black olives, chopped

1 (10-ounce) jar mild taco sauce (optional)

1. In a medium skillet over medium heat, cook ground beef until cooked through, about 8–10 minutes. Drain fat from meat.

2. In a medium mixing bowl, combine beef, beans, chili powder, and garlic powder.

3. Wipe the skillet with a paper towel and then warm each tortilla in the skillet over low heat for 1–2 minutes.

4. On a plate, divide the meat and bean mixture equally over the tortillas.

5. Divide the lettuce, tomatoes, and olives over each tortilla.

6. Top each with 2 tablespoons of taco sauce, if desired.

7. Fold tortilla over and wrap. Serve immediately or cover in plastic wrap for later.

California-Style BLT Wraps

Eliminate the avocado if you're going to make this in advance—it will oxidize and look unappealing.

INGREDIENTS | SERVES 4

3 ounces cream cheese, at room temperature

2 tablespoons mayonnaise

¼ teaspoon seasoned salt

Freshly cracked pepper, to taste

2 (8-inch) low-carb tortillas, at room temperature

6 slices smoked bacon, cooked

¼ cup diced avocado

¼ cup seeded and diced ripe tomato

1 cup chopped romaine hearts

Wrap Facts

These wrap recipes are based on 4 servings, which is derived from using 2 wraps to make 2 sandwiches, each cut in half, for a total of 4 halves, or 4 servings. These are considered lunch-sized portions. It's best to have the wraps at room temperature for ease of handling. If needed, microwave them for 5–10 seconds until they're pliable. Cold wraps tend to crack and make a mess.

1. Mix together the cream cheese, mayonnaise, salt, and pepper in a small bowl (or use a food processor to blend until smooth).

2. Place the tortillas on work surface. Spread half of the cream cheese mixture on the upper third of each tortilla, about ½ inch from the edge. Place half of the bacon on the lower third of each tortilla. Top each with the avocado, tomato, and lettuce.

3. Roll up each wrap: Starting from the bottom, fold the tortilla over the filling and roll upward, compressing slightly to form a firm roll. Press at the top to "seal" the wrap closed with the cream cheese mixture. Cut the sandwich in half and wrap in plastic film. Refrigerate until ready to serve.

Spicy Italian Sausage Pizza Wraps

Tortillas are the crust for these satisfying pizza-like treats.
It's too messy to eat flat or open-faced, so fold 'em over.

INGREDIENTS | SERVES 2

1 teaspoon olive oil
6 ounces spicy bulk Italian sausage
⅓ cup chopped yellow onion
1 teaspoon dried Italian seasoning
4 ounces pizza sauce
2 (8-inch) low-carb tortillas
½ cup shredded mozzarella
⅓ cup shredded Parmesan cheese
Red pepper flakes, to taste

Is the Oil Hot Enough?

The oil should be shimmering with ripples. You can drop in a few bread crumbs and they should start to bubble and fry. If the oil is smoking, the oil is too hot and you should remove the pan from the heat immediately. Never put a hot pan under cold water to cool. It can result in a dangerous situation.

1. Heat the oil in a heavy nonstick skillet over medium-high heat. Cook the sausage, stirring and breaking up larger pieces, until cooked through, about 6 minutes. Use a slotted spoon to transfer the sausage to a bowl.

2. Remove and discard all but 1 tablespoon of the fat from the skillet. Cook the onion until soft, about 4 minutes, stirring frequently. Add the Italian seasoning, pizza sauce, and the reserved sausage. Stir to combine and cook until heated through and starting to simmer, about 2 minutes. Taste and adjust seasoning as desired.

3. To serve, place each tortilla in the center of a serving plate. Place half of the sausage mixture on each tortilla, spreading it about ½ inch from the edges. Sprinkle the cheeses on top and add red pepper flakes to taste. Fold over and serve hot.

Bull's-Eye Soy Burger

This is a vegetarian dish that is fun to prepare and loaded with calcium.
Reports show high intakes of calcium may keep blood pressure lower.

INGREDIENTS | SERVES 6

6 frozen prepared soy burgers

6 slices low-fat white American cheese

6 slices low-fat Cheddar cheese

6 tablespoons ketchup

24 sticks of celery, washed and tops cut off

Sneak in a Little Vegetarianism—You Can't Go Wrong!

Most children tend to shy away from vegetarian food items (many adults, too). Begin to introduce some soy products to the kids, as studies show us that soybeans—as a source of protein, iron, and fiber, and as a nonanimal source of fat—are quite healthy for them.

1. In medium skillet, spray nonstick cooking spray. Pan-fry soy burgers on low heat until cooked through.

2. With white American cheese slices, cut off edges, making round slices. With Cheddar cheese slices, cut off edges, creating smaller round slices.

3. To assemble bull's-eye burger, place burger on a serving plate. Top with white American cheese, and then with Cheddar cheese. Place 1 tablespoon ketchup on top of the Cheddar cheese.

4. To create the bull's-eye stand, place 2 celery stalks at base of the burger, about 2 inches apart. Cut celery stick in half and place halves on top of the burger, with their tips touching.

5. Cut another celery stick in half, and then cut halves lengthwise. Place one trimmed half between the bottom celery sticks, horizontally, close to the burger. Place the final trimmed half smack in the middle of the ketchup dollop. Serve immediately.

The Basic Burger

Experiment with your basic burger by trying out the three different cooking methods.

INGREDIENTS | SERVES 4

1¼ pounds ground round beef
½ teaspoon seasoned salt
Freshly cracked black pepper, to taste

Getting the Basics Down

There are many versions of the basic burger; some contain egg yolk, bread crumbs, and any other number of additions. This is the simplest basic burger; therefore, the quality of the ground meat is key. Be sure not to overhandle the meat when forming hamburger patties. Use a very light touch and make sure you don't compact the meat too much. Don't use a spatula to press down on the patty while cooking, either, because you'll press out the natural juices and lose both juiciness and flavor.

1. Lightly mix the ground round with salt and pepper and form into 4 evenly sized patties. Cook by your choice of the following methods:

2. **To grill:** Clean grill rack and lightly oil to prevent sticking. Preheat grill to medium-high. Cook for about 5 minutes per side for medium, turning once. Transfer burgers to a plate and tent with foil to keep warm. Let rest for 1–2 minutes to allow the juices to reabsorb. Serve hot. If using an indoor grill, follow manufacturer's directions.

3. **To broil:** Clean broiler rack and lightly oil to prevent sticking. Set broiler rack 4 inches from heat source. Preheat broiler to medium-high. Cook for about 5 minutes per side for medium, turning once. Transfer burgers to a plate and tent with foil to keep warm. Let rest for 1–2 minutes to allow the juices to reabsorb. Serve hot.

4. **On stovetop:** Heat 2 tablespoons oil in a large, nonstick skillet over medium-high heat. Cook for about 5 minutes per side for medium, turning once. Transfer burgers to a plate and tent with foil to keep warm. Let rest for 1–2 minutes to allow the juices to reabsorb. Serve hot.

Bacon Burgers

With a winning combination of flavors including bacon and sharp Cheddar with a hearty basic burger, this is definitely a grill-time recipe.

INGREDIENTS | SERVES 4

1¼ pounds ground round beef

¾ teaspoon seasoned salt

⅛ teaspoon freshly cracked pepper

¼ cup crispy bacon crumbles

8 (1-ounce) slices sharp Cheddar cheese

Nothing Beats a Good Burger on the Grill!

Lean burgers are a staple in the diet plan of many people who are controlling carbs. A bunless burger is really no different from the classic Salisbury steak preparation that was popular in the 1970s. It was named after a nineteenth-century physician who recommended that his patients reduce their starch intake and eat plenty of beef.

1. Lightly mix the ground round with the seasoned salt, pepper, and bacon crumbles and form into 4 evenly sized patties.

2. Clean and oil grill rack and preheat grill to medium-high. Cook the burgers for about 5 minutes on each side for medium. Add 2 slices of cheese per burger during the last 2 minutes of cooking.

3. Transfer the burgers to a plate and tent with foil to keep warm. Let rest for 1–2 minutes to allow the juices to reabsorb. Serve hot.

Pizza Burgers

*Get the kids—this is a family favorite. An easy recipe that
you can cook on the grill, in the broiler, or on the stovetop.*

INGREDIENTS | SERVES 4

1¼ pounds ground round beef
½ teaspoon garlic salt
¼ teaspoon red pepper flakes
½ teaspoon dried Italian seasoning
6 ounces pizza sauce
8 (1-ounce) slices mozzarella cheese

1. Lightly mix the ground round with the garlic salt, pepper flakes, and Italian seasoning and form into 4 evenly sized patties.

2. Clean and oil grill rack and preheat grill to medium-high. Cook the burgers about 5 minutes on each side for medium. During the last 2 minutes of cooking, top each burger with a generous tablespoon of the pizza sauce and 2 slices of cheese per burger.

3. Transfer the burgers to a plate and tent with foil to keep warm. Let rest for 1–2 minutes to allow the juices to reabsorb. Serve hot.

South of the Border Burgers

*Spicy salsa equals spicy burgers; mild salsa equals mild burgers!
This recipe works well on the grill, in the broiler, or on the stovetop.*

INGREDIENTS | SERVES 4

1¼ pounds ground round beef
½ teaspoon garlic salt
¼ teaspoon red pepper flakes
4 (1-ounce) slices pepper jack cheese
1 cup quality salsa, such as Frontera brand
¼ cup canned jalapeño slices
¼ cup chopped fresh cilantro

Indoor or Outdoor?

The little indoor grills that are popular these days, such as the George Foreman Grill, are a convenient and easy alternative to using the larger outdoor charcoal or gas grills.

1. Lightly mix the ground round with the garlic salt and pepper flakes and form into 4 evenly sized patties.

2. Clean and oil grill rack and preheat grill to medium-high. Cook the burgers for about 5 minutes on each side for medium. During the last 2 minutes of cooking, top each burger with a slice of cheese.

3. Transfer the burgers to a plate and tent with foil to keep warm. Let rest for 1–2 minutes to allow the juices to reabsorb. Serve hot, topped with the salsa, jalapeños, and cilantro leaves.

Spicy Turkey Cheeseburgers

Lots of spices make these burgers very flavorful. You could make a Tex-Mex sandwich spread to put on the hamburger buns by combining mayonnaise with some chopped chipotle peppers and adobo sauce.

INGREDIENTS | SERVES 4

½ cup bread crumbs

1 egg, beaten

½ teaspoon salt

¼ teaspoon cayenne pepper

¼ teaspoon cumin

1 teaspoon chili powder

1¼ pounds ground turkey

4 slices pepper jack cheese

4 whole wheat hamburger buns

Make Recipes Your Own

Once you get the hang of making a recipe quickly, think about varying the ingredients to make it your own. For instance, Spicy Turkey Cheeseburgers could be made with chutney, curry powder, and Havarti or provolone cheese. Or make them Greek burgers with feta cheese, chopped olives, and some dried oregano leaves.

1. Prepare and preheat grill or broiler. In large bowl, combine bread crumbs, egg, salt, cayenne pepper, cumin, and chili powder and mix well. Add turkey and mix gently but thoroughly until combined. Form into 4 patties.

2. Cook patties, covered, 4–6 inches from medium heat for about 10 minutes, turning once, until thoroughly cooked. Top each with a slice of cheese, cover, and cook for 1 minute longer, until cheese melts. Meanwhile, toast the cut sides of hamburger buns; make sandwiches with turkey patties and buns. Serve hot.

Spicy Chicken Burgers

You can substitute ground turkey or pork for the chicken.
Adjust the quantity of pepper sauce to control the spiciness.

INGREDIENTS | SERVES 4

1 pound ground chicken

¼ cup finely chopped yellow onion

¼ cup finely chopped red bell pepper

1 teaspoon minced garlic

¼ cup thinly sliced scallions

½ teaspoon hot pepper sauce

1 teaspoon Worcestershire sauce

Salt, to taste

Freshly cracked black pepper, to taste

1. Clean and oil broiler rack. Preheat broiler to medium.

2. Combine all the ingredients in a medium-sized bowl, mixing lightly. Form into 4 patties. Broil the burgers for 4–5 minutes per side until firm through the center and the juices run clear. Transfer to a plate and tent with tinfoil to keep warm. Allow to rest 1–2 minutes before serving.

Hot Stuff about Hot Sauce

Tabasco is a trademarked name and product held by the McIlhenny family since the mid-1800s. It is produced in Louisiana and is manufactured from tabasco peppers, vinegar, and salt. The peppers are fermented in barrels for three years before being processed for the sauce.

CHAPTER 13

Smoothies and Juices

Strawberry-Banana Smoothie

*Use frozen fruit to make smoothies rich and creamy. Peel and slice
ripe bananas and keep them in the freezer for this delicious breakfast or snack.*

INGREDIENTS | 4 (1-CUP) SERVINGS

2 frozen bananas

1 cup fresh or frozen sliced strawberries

1 cup low-fat vanilla or strawberry yogurt

1½ cups orange juice

½ cup Cheerios cereal

1. Place bananas, strawberries, yogurt, and orange juice in a blender and blend until smooth.

2. Pour into glasses and top with a spoonful of Cheerios.

Pineapple-Peach Juice

*Nothing starts kids' engines better in the morning than a glass full of manganese.
This trace mineral, contained in high doses in pineapple, is an essential coenzyme for energy production.*

INGREDIENTS | 4 (½-CUP) SERVINGS

1½ cups fresh pineapple

1 peach, pitted

3 tablespoons water

1. Run both the pineapple and the peach through the juicer.

2. Mix thoroughly together. If juice is too thick, dilute with the water a tablespoon at a time until it's the consistency your kids like.

Stress-Free Mornings

Feeding kids and getting them out the door in the morning can be challenging. For less mess and stress, prepare juices the night before and store in the fridge. This means no spills to wipe or appliances to clean when you are trying to get out the door. This is the perfect recipe for storing overnight. The citrus in the pineapple keeps the drink from browning better than an apple-based juice. Fresh, homemade juices can be stored safely in the fridge for 24–48 hours.

Cucumber-Melon Juice

After an overnight fast, this fresh juice is the perfect way to get kids going in the morning. The refreshing zing of cucumber mixed with the sweet taste from the melons will wake them up and jump-start their engines. No more groggy zombies!

INGREDIENTS | 1 (1-CUP) SERVING

1 cucumber, peeled
½ honeydew melon or cantaloupe

Water-Soluble Vitamin C

Essential vitamins are the vitamins we can only obtain through our diet. Fat-soluble vitamins, such as vitamins A, D, E, and K, can be stored in our bodies for a long period of time, but water-soluble vitamins, like vitamin C, cannot be stored and need to be eaten daily! One cup of cantaloupe has over 100 percent of the daily requirement for vitamin C. Drinking fresh juices with ingredients such as cantaloupe and cucumbers can help kids meet their daily need for vitamin C. Serving these vitamin C–rich juices first thing in the morning can put your mind at ease.

1. Peel cucumber and juice it.

2. Scoop flesh out of melon and juice the flesh only.

3. Stir the two fruit juices together thoroughly until dissolved in each other.

Melon-Orange Juice

Combining oranges, honeydew melon, and watermelon in this drink gives kids plenty of vitamin C for the day. School and playground viruses won't stand a chance in your home with a daily dose of this drink.

INGREDIENTS | 3 (½-CUP) SERVINGS

½ honeydew melon, peeled
½ orange, peeled
½ cup watermelon, rind removed

1. Combine all three fruits in the juicer, one after the other.

2. Juice all three fruits and collect in a single container. Stir before serving.

Swiss Muesli

Enjoy this juice disguised as oatmeal. Swiss muesli is uncooked oatmeal soaked overnight in a liquid in the refrigerator. Start with 1 cup of rolled oats. Add 1–1½ cups juice to the oats, cover, and put in the fridge overnight. In the morning, add nuts, dried fruit, fresh fruit, or seeds. Mix the cold-soaked oats in the morning and enjoy.

Strawberry-Cantaloupe Juice

You can smell a cantaloupe even before cutting into it. The delicious fruity aroma will tempt kids on a weekend morning as they try to decide what they are hungry for. Once they smell the melon, they'll be craving this melon juice.

INGREDIENTS | 3 (½-CUP) SERVINGS

½ cantaloupe, rind removed

1 cup strawberries

1. Feed cantaloupe and strawberries through the funnel of a juicer, one after the other.

2. Collect the juice into a container and stir before serving.

Using Juice for Syrup

Pancakes, waffles, and French toast all taste better with a little syrup on top. You can make your own syrup with no sugar added just by using some homemade juice. Take 2 cups of homemade juice, like the one in this recipe. Mix together 1 tablespoon cornstarch with 1 tablespoon cold water. Put juice and cornstarch in a saucepan on the stove. Bring juice to a boil over medium heat and cook for about 7–8 minutes, stirring continuously. Remove from heat and use it to top your pancakes or waffles. Although you can store it for several days in the fridge, you will want to warm it right before use to prevent it from thickening up.

Peach-Grape Juice

The kids will want you to save some fresh grapes and peaches for this juice. Store a portion of the grapes and peaches in the refrigerator to ensure there are some left after snacking. In the fridge your fruit will last from 7–10 days, rather than 2–4 days on the counter.

INGREDIENTS | 3 (½-CUP) SERVINGS

2 peaches, pitted

1 cup red grapes

¼ lemon, peeled

1. Juice the peaches and grapes, and then the lemon.

2. Collect into a pitcher and stir well before serving.

Quick After-School Snacks

Making your own after-school snacks is easy, smart, and cost-effective. Anytime you have fruits and vegetables out to prep for juicing, consider setting one or two of each fruit or veggie aside to prepare for snacks. Cleaning and cutting up fruit and veggies so they're ready to grab in the fridge means your kids are more likely to do so.

Grape-Apple Juice

Drink this grape-apple-lemon juice with an egg, cheese, and lettuce sandwich for breakfast.
A breakfast with whole grains, protein, dairy, veggies, and fruit is a great way to start the day.

INGREDIENTS | 3 (½-CUP) SERVINGS

1 cup red grapes
1 apple, cored
½ lemon, peeled

1. Juice the grapes, apple, and lemon into one container.

2. Stir juices together so they are thoroughly mixed. Serve.

Invisible Writing

Teach your kids a chemistry lesson, use up the lemon juice, and have fun while you're doing it. Juice the other half of your lemon and put the juice in a small bowl. Use paintbrushes to paint lemon juice onto a piece of paper in shapes, letters, or pictures. Let the paper dry. Hold the paper up to a light bulb until the paper heats up. The picture painted by the lemon juice will darken and the image will become visible. The acid in the lemon weakens the paper and turns brown when heated. Try other fruit juices and see what different colors you can make!

Banana-Berry Smoothie

Recruit the kids to help in making this drink. Bananas and clementines can be peeled by most children.
The rest of the ingredients don't need to be cut at all.

INGREDIENTS | 4 (1-CUP) SERVINGS

1 cup spinach
1 banana, peeled
1 cup strawberries
1 cup blueberries
1 cup blackberries
2 clementines or tangerines
1 cup water

1. Combine spinach, banana, strawberries, blueberries, blackberries, clementines, and ½ cup water in a high-powered blender and blend.

2. Continue to blend and add the remaining ½ cup water until drink is smooth. Serve.

Engage the Kids in the Kitchen

Teaching kids to learn their way around the kitchen can never be started too soon. From the moment they can pick up a spoon, drop food into a blender, or flip a switch, they can be part of meal prep. Smoothies are the perfect beginning for young chefs. They can learn to follow a recipe, prepare the drinks, and serve them to the family. Kids are so proud of accomplishments such as these and are generally anxious to try their own creations.

Lemon-Apple Smoothie

Summertime and lemonade go hand in hand, but lemonade is loaded with sugar. Start a new tradition of summertime and lemon smoothies, and your kids will be well hydrated with less sugar.

INGREDIENTS | 4 (1-CUP) SERVINGS

2 apples, peeled and cored

4 lemons, peeled

1 tablespoon honey

2 cups water

1 cup ice

1. Combine apple, lemons, honey, and 1 cup water in a blender and blend for 30 seconds.

2. Add the remaining 1 cup water and ice and blend until smooth and thoroughly mixed. Serve.

Honey

Even though honey is sweeter, it is actually better for your kids than table sugar. Honey contains vitamins and minerals such as vitamin B, magnesium, potassium, and calcium. Table sugar has been stripped of its nutrients. The enzymes in table sugar are mostly destroyed, while honey keeps its enzymes. Lastly, honey is less likely to spike blood sugar because it is absorbed more slowly into the bloodstream. Honey has also been shown to have a soothing effect on sore throats. So next time you have a choice, choose honey.

Cucumber Smoothie

Your kids don't need to be particularly fond of cucumbers to love this smoothie. The sweet orange flavor is what they'll notice when they are asking for more.

INGREDIENTS | 4 (1-CUP) SERVINGS

2 cucumbers, peeled

2 oranges, peeled

¼ inch ginger, peeled

1 cup orange juice

1 cup ice

1. Place cucumbers, oranges, ginger, and ½ cup orange juice in a blender and blend for 30 seconds on low.

2. Take off lid and push food onto blades. Add remaining ½ cup juice and ice and put lid back on. Blend on high until smooth. Serve.

Let Your Kids Choose

Smoothies are a great way to let kids make good choices. As you get into a routine of smoothie making, kids will begin to learn what things they enjoy in their smoothies. Letting them choose between spinach and romaine lettuce, cucumbers and carrots, or water and orange juice gives them ownership of the drink and lets them be in charge. Once they feel like they were integral in getting this smoothie to the table, they will be less picky and more likely to drink it.

Melon-Citrus Juice

This refreshing juice is a thirst quencher! This juice is a healthy and more hydrating alternative to carbonated drinks normally taken to a picnic or to the pool in the summer.

INGREDIENTS | 2 (½-CUP) SERVINGS

2 cups watermelon, rind removed
2 oranges, peeled

1. Place watermelon and oranges in a juicer.

2. Run the fruit through the juicer until you have 1 full cup of juice. Stir to combine and serve.

Vitamin C Powerhouse

With both oranges and watermelon in this juice, one serving provides 85 mg of vitamin C. The recommended daily allowance (RDA) for kids ages one to eight years old for vitamin C is 15–25 mg. This drink helps children meet—and exceed—those recommended levels. Vitamin C is essential for those kids who get exposed to germs on a regular basis, as it helps boost their immune systems.

Blackberry Juice

When kids are away from home for the day, send along this blackberry juice. When it's tough to control what kinds of foods they'll be eating when you aren't around, you can be grateful they are getting some superfoods during the day from this juice.

INGREDIENTS | 2 (½-CUP) SERVINGS

2 pints blackberries
½ lemon, peeled
1 banana

1. Push blackberries, lemon, and banana through a juicer and juice completely.

2. Collect into a pitcher and stir to combine the juices well. Serve.

DIY: Fruit Leather

The ingredients in this juice recipe are perfect for delicious homemade fruit leather. First, use the fruit to make your juice. Second, use the exact same amounts of fruit, and add into a saucepan over medium heat. Stir the fruit until it begins to break down. Add a small amount of your juice to dilute the fruit in your saucepan. Take the fruit and juice mix from your saucepan and purée it in a blender or food processor. Line a baking sheet with plastic wrap and pour your fruit onto the wrap. Let the pan dry in the sun, or place in an oven at 140°F (or the lowest oven setting) for several hours until the fruit is no longer sticky to the touch. Peel the fruit leather from the plastic wrap and eat it!

Cucumber Lemonade

As a sugar-free sports drink, this sour juice may be just what some child athletes need to get hydrated. One ounce of lemon juice contains six times more potassium than 1 ounce of a lemon-flavored sports drink, without the artificial colors and sweeteners.

INGREDIENTS | 2 (½-CUP) SERVINGS

2 cucumbers, peeled
1 lemon, peeled

1. Push the cucumbers and lemon through a juicer and juice until all food has gone through.

2. Collect juice in one glass and stir to combine. Serve.

Juicing Lemons

Juicing lemons and limes without a juicer is not only possible but quite simple. There are a few tricks to extracting the most juice out of these citrus fruits. Trick number one: warm up a lemon or lime in the microwave for about 20–30 seconds. The juice of a warm fruit will flow much more freely than the juice of a cold one. Second, roll the fruit around on the counter with the palm of your hand. This will break up some of the membranes of the fruit. Then the fruit is ready to cut and squeeze.

Garden Juice

Forget about spending the next day trying to use up your zucchini for bread. Spend 5 minutes and juice it instead. Adding some apples to this zucchini juice brings out the sweetness of the fall flavors.

INGREDIENTS | 2 (½-CUP) SERVINGS

1 green zucchini
3 carrots, peeled
2 red apples, cored

1. Juice the zucchini, carrots, and apples into one large glass.

2. Stir the juices together until they are thoroughly combined. Serve.

Repurpose Pulp

Depending on the condition of your pulp after running fruits and vegetables through the juicer, there may be something you can do with it. If your pulp is very dry, the best thing to do with it may be to turn it into a compost pile, or bury it in your garden to promote soil turnover. However, if your pulp still has a little water to it, you can use it in baked goods, such as muffins. Be sure to use organic fruits and vegetables, or wash your fruits and vegetables thoroughly, if you are using the pulp. Using pulp from this recipe, with the carrots, zucchini, and apples, would make a delicious addition to zucchini bread or carrot cake.

Icy Island Dream

*No need to head to the tropics to have a taste of the islands at home.
A ripe papaya, a juicy pineapple, and some bright red strawberries can take you
and your kids on a mini vacation, even in the middle of winter.*

INGREDIENTS | 3 (½-CUP) SERVINGS

1 cup pineapple, peeled

7 large strawberries, hull intact

½ papaya, seeds removed

1. Take pineapple, strawberries, and papaya, place in a juicer, one after the other, and juice.

2. Collect juice from all three fruits into one container and stir before serving to combine.

Strawberry Delights!

When you purchase a pound of strawberries, save seven strawberries for this juice and use the rest to have some fun. Instead of frosting sugar-filled cookies, let kids decorate nutrient-filled strawberries. Using toothpicks and clean, dry strawberries, dip them in melted chocolate. Before the chocolate sets, dip a second time in sprinkles, nuts, shredded coconut, or sugar crystals. Let dry completely on wax paper and enjoy.

Pineapple Smoothie

*Escape to the tropics with this pineapple-and-orange medley of flavors.
Pineapple's high amount of manganese is perfect for giving athletes energy
while at the same time reducing inflammation due to injury.*

INGREDIENTS | 4 (1-CUP) SERVINGS

1 cup spinach

2 cups pineapple, peeled and cored

1 orange, peeled

2 apples, peeled and cored

1 tablespoon flax meal

2 cups orange juice

1. Take spinach, pineapple, orange, apples, flax meal, and 1 cup orange juice and place in a high-powered blender. Blend until smooth.

2. Add the remaining orange juice and continue to blend until it reaches desired consistency. Serve.

Finding Recipes

Have a system for flagging recipes your kids particularly like so you can quickly go back to them without scouring all your cookbooks to find them again. If your kids love this pineapple smoothie, and you noticed they drank it without complaint, use Post-it Page Markers or Half-inch Flags to mark the page. Color coordinate according to which child liked it. Susie's favorite recipes could all be flagged with red Post-it tabs, while Johnny's could be all green.

Cherry Smoothie

The anti-inflammatory properties of cherries make this smoothie perfect for active kids. Prepare this drink for afternoon refreshment, after a long day of playing outside. Freeze extra cherries to float on top of the drink.

INGREDIENTS | 4 (1-CUP) SERVINGS

1 cup spinach

2 cups cherries, pitted

1 apple, cored and peeled

Pulp of 1 vanilla bean, or 1 teaspoon vanilla extract

2 cups water

1. Combine spinach, cherries, apple, vanilla bean, and 1 cup water in a blender. Blend until smooth.

2. Add remaining 1 cup water and blend again until all ingredients are well incorporated. Serve.

Cherries

A 2010 study published in the *Journal of the International Society of Sport Nutrition* found tart cherry juice reduced pain during long-distance running. The antioxidants in the cherries seemed to protect against damage caused by trauma to the muscles. The benefit of the cherry juice was seen in both participants in the study who drank the juice prior to an endurance event as well as during the event. Cherry juice's anti-inflammatory properties can benefit regular athletes as well as endurance athletes.

Lemon-Melon Smoothie

This smoothie delivers ultimate hydration for kids on those hot summer days. It's hard sometimes to come in from the heat and fun just to drink a glass of water, but delivering this cool, refreshing smoothie to them during play is a hydrating treat they'll take a break for.

INGREDIENTS | 4 (1-CUP) SERVINGS

1 cup romaine lettuce

2 cups seedless watermelon

2 cups cantaloupe

½ lemon, peeled

½ lime, peeled

2 cups water

1. Combine romaine, watermelon, cantaloupe, lemon, lime, and 1 cup water in a blender and blend about 30 seconds.

2. Add remaining 1 cup water and blend until smoothie is desired consistency. Serve.

The Watermelon Bowl

Don't toss the watermelon rind after making this smoothie. Cut the watermelon in half across the middle to scoop out the flesh for the smoothie. Keep the watermelon rind intact. Use a melon baller to scoop balls of cantaloupe, watermelon, and honeydew melon. Add to your watermelon bowl; then add strawberries, blueberries, and chopped pineapple. Grate ginger over the top and stir. Your watermelon bowl fruit salad makes a beautiful and fun centerpiece!

The Purple Cow

The bone benefits in this drink don't end with the calcium in the milk! Both blackberries and blueberries contain small amounts of magnesium and phosphorus that work synergistically to build and maintain bones.

INGREDIENTS | 3 (½-CUP) SERVINGS

1 cup blueberries
1 pint blackberries
½ cup skim milk

1. First juice the blueberries and then the blackberries in a juicer, and collect in a single container.

2. Stir the milk into the juice. Serve.

Vitamin D and Bone Health

Both osteoporosis and osteopenia, diseases characterized by bone weakening, are becoming more and more common despite an increase in the amount of calcium in our diets. Researchers have begun taking a look at the impact of vitamin D on bone health and its role in bone development. Also referred to as the "sunshine vitamin," vitamin D regulates the absorption and excretion of calcium and phosphorus. When our calcium levels are low, vitamin D allows us to absorb more calcium from our food. When our calcium levels are high, we absorb less calcium during digestion. Without vitamin D, this process couldn't be regulated, and we would possibly be deficient in important bone-building calcium even when our diets are rich with it.

Peary Punch

Even with the spinach, kids will still drink it up because of the sweetness of the smoothie. Extra bonus: no kids running wild on a sugar high.

INGREDIENTS | 2 (1-CUP) SERVINGS

½ cup spinach
2 pears, peeled and cored
1 banana, frozen and peeled
½ cup soy milk or low-fat milk
3–4 ice cubes

Combine all ingredients in a blender. Mix until well incorporated. Serve.

Not Just for Popeye

Although Popeye was the one to bring attention to the muscle-building benefits of spinach, there are many more reasons to eat spinach that he didn't share. Calorie for calorie, spinach is actually higher in protein than most other vegetables. This is important to provide the necessary nutrients for growing kids.

Banana Split Smoothie

This chocolate smoothie hits the spot. Adding honey to smoothies changes kids' perception from it being a drink for health to it being a dessert drink. What they may not realize, however, is that although this dessert smoothie tastes like ice cream, the honey used to sweeten it comes packed with B vitamins.

INGREDIENTS | 2 (1-CUP) SERVINGS

8 ounces soy milk or low-fat milk
1 tablespoon honey
2 bananas, frozen
1 tablespoon cocoa powder

Place milk, honey, frozen bananas, and cocoa powder in a blender and blend until well incorporated. Serve.

The Power of Cocoa

Cocoa powder is an ingredient with amazing benefits for children. The antioxidants in cocoa powder can help kids have healthier skin, combat diarrhea, improve insulin sensitivity, or soothe a cough; plus it improves visual as well as verbal memory!

Triple Berry Blastoff

Triple the berries for triple the antioxidants, triple the vitamins, and triple the delicious flavor. Including romaine lettuce adds almost 100 percent of your vitamin K intake for the day.

INGREDIENTS | 4 (1-CUP) SERVINGS

1 cup romaine lettuce
1 pint blueberries
1 pint raspberries
2 pints strawberries
2 bananas, peeled
1 cup vanilla almond milk
1 cup Greek-style yogurt

1. Combine lettuce, blueberries, raspberries, strawberries, bananas, and vanilla almond milk in a blender and blend until smooth.

2. Add Greek-style yogurt and blend until thoroughly mixed. Serve.

Freezing Strawberries

There is no question, freezing your own strawberries is a money saver. You can grow your own, or head over to a local picking farm. First, cut the stems out of your unwashed strawberries. Make sure strawberries are completely dry. Lay them on a wax paper–lined cookie sheet and freeze them for 2–4 hours, until they begin to be firm. This way the strawberries will freeze separately and not in one big clump. Then, scoop all the strawberries into a freezer-safe bag for storing in the freezer. They will last 10–12 months.

Kiwi Crush

Use half of a lemon for this delicious smoothie, and use the other half of the lemon for party decorations. Float half a lemon in a shallow vase with some yellow and blue hydrangeas floating with it. Serve the smoothie on the table alongside the centerpiece.

INGREDIENTS | 4 (1-CUP) SERVINGS

2 cups mangoes, peeled and pitted

2 tangerines, peeled

4 kiwis, peeled

½ lemon, peeled

2 cups water

1. Combine mangoes, tangerines, kiwis, lemon, and 1 cup water in a blender and blend thoroughly, about 30 seconds.

2. Add remaining 1 cup water and blend again for at least 60 seconds, or until fruit is completely smooth. Serve.

Types of Water

With many types of water to choose from—tap, distilled, filtered, bottled—it can be overwhelming to decide which is best. Tap water is free and regulated to control harmful substances, but your city may allow things in your water that you aren't comfortable with, like fluoride. Distilled water tastes great, but vital minerals have been filtered out of it. Filtered water tastes great, retains some important minerals, but may be pricey. Bottled water is convenient, but it is less regulated and what's in it is generally a mystery without testing it in a lab. All the smoothies in this book taste great with any water you choose.

Agua Melon Fresca

Although seedless watermelon is available for purchase, black seeds in watermelon are safe to eat. Return black seeds to the top of your smoothie and your drink will look like a ladybug.

INGREDIENTS | 4 (1-CUP) SERVINGS

2 cups watermelon, seeds and rind removed

2 bananas, peeled

1 cup plain yogurt

1 cup ice (optional)

1. Combine watermelon, bananas, and yogurt in a blender and blend until smooth.

2. Add ice if desired and blend until smoothie is the consistency desired. Serve.

Make Vegetables the Star

The amount of energy to produce 1 pound of fruits or vegetables versus 1 pound of meat is significantly less. To minimize the carbon footprint from your family, consider more fruits and vegetables for your meals as a way to cut back on energy expended to produce your food. Anytime you can have a salad be the star of your dinner, or a smoothie be the focus of your breakfast, you'll be saving energy. Fruit and vegetable smoothies are a great way to replace a high-energy-consuming meal with a low one.

Watermelon-Berry Smoothie

Watermelon juice, first sticking to little hands and eventually sticking to your floor and shoes, can be such a mess. Blend up watermelon this summer for your next picnic party, serve outside in cups with straws, and sticky shoes will be a thing of the past.

INGREDIENTS | 4 (1-CUP) SERVINGS

2 cups watermelon

1 cup raspberries

1 cup pineapple, peeled and cored

1 cup vanilla yogurt

Take watermelon, raspberries, pineapple, and yogurt and place in a blender. Blend for 30 seconds, or until smooth. Serve.

Watermelon Shapes

Watermelon is an easy fruit to be creative with. Slice watermelon about 1-inch thick and remove the rind. Using cookie cutters, cut into watermelon to create shapes. Place shapes on skewers if they are small, or stack on a plate for a snack. Watermelon shapes can be decorated even further with some fresh basil, mint, or even sliced almonds.

Luscious Lemon Slushy

This citrus lemon slushy might remind you of a drink that you get at the local fair. The fair drink, however, doesn't include any real lemon at all! It includes sugar, ice, and some artificial flavoring. Party guests will enjoy the real thing and be asking for more.

INGREDIENTS | 4 (1-CUP) SERVINGS

2 lemons, peeled

2 tablespoons honey

2 cups pineapple juice

2 cups ice

1. Take lemons, honey, and pineapple juice and place in a blender. Blend until smooth.

2. Add ice and blend until slushy. Serve.

Citrus-Themed Party

There are so many fun things you can do with a citrus-themed party, beyond serving a citrus smoothie. Slice oranges, lemons, and limes and fill a vase with the sliced fruit for a centerpiece. Have party décor like balloons and crepe paper in yellow and orange colors. Use a bowl of whole cloves and an orange; then have the kids puncture the orange with their cloves for their own party favor to take home. Have a blind taste-test game: Use pineapple, lemon, oranges, or grapefruit and have the kids guess which flavor they taste. Of course, follow the party with a tangy citrus lemon drink, and the kids will enjoy every minute.

Lemon-Lime Fizz

Eight ounces of your typical lemon-lime soda served at birthday parties contains a whopping 25 grams of sugar! When you add the cake and ice cream, kids will have consumed more sugar than they need in a whole week. This lemon-lime soda has all the party pizzazz of the real thing without all that sugar!

INGREDIENTS | 4 (1-CUP) SERVINGS

3 lemons, including the rind

3 limes, including the rind

4 cups sparkling water

Healthy Parties

Replacing traditional party food with healthier fare may be easier than you think. Most kids come for the party, games, and friends. The food can be healthy, and also be part of the fun. Fruit pizzas, fruit salad served in ice cream cones, fruit juice Popsicles, frozen smoothies made into ice cream, air-popped popcorn, and baked potato chips can all be part of the party.

1. Cut lemons and limes to fit in juicer.

2. Juice the lemons and limes and pour equally into 4 glasses.

3. Top off with 1 cup of sparkling water in each glass. Serve.

Kiwi Fizz

A fruit soda actually made with fruit seems like a blast from the past. Today's fruit-flavored soda, like orange soda or fruit punch, has zero fruit. This fruit soda is mostly fruit and still fizzy.

INGREDIENTS | 4 (½-CUP) SERVINGS

2 red apples
3 kiwis, peeled
1 cup sparkling water

Party Drink Ideas

Change any fruit juice into a party drink with the simple addition of sparkling water. Add fun touches to the kids' cups such as mini drink umbrellas, swirled paper straws, strawberries suspended in ice cubes, frozen cherries, sliced lemons, star fruit on the end of a skewer, or even a scoop of ice cream in the glass. Use markers and stickers to decorate white paper, wrap the decorative paper around each cup, and add each child's name.

1. Juice apples and kiwis.

2. Mix together juice from apples and kiwis and divide into 4 glasses.

3. Pour ¼ cup sparkling water over juice in each cup and stir before serving.

CHAPTER 14

Cookies and Other Sweet Treats

Layered Brownies

Cream cheese and brownies are natural partners. This is a dual-use recipe; you end up with layered brownies for tonight's dessert, and plain brownies for this weekend!

INGREDIENTS | SERVES 9

1 (14-ounce) package rich and fudgy brownie mix

⅓ cup sugar

1 egg

1 (3-ounce) package cream cheese, softened

1 cup semisweet chocolate chips

Low-Fat Products in Baking

You can use low-fat cream cheese, low-fat milk, and low-fat sour cream in baking, but do not use low-fat or whipped margarines or butter. Those ingredients can contain a lot of water, which will ruin the structure of your baked products.

1. Preheat oven to 375°F. Spray 2 (9" × 9") square pans with baking spray and set aside.

2. Prepare brownie mix as directed on package. Pour half of batter into one prepared pan and set aside. In small bowl, combine sugar, egg, and cream cheese and beat until smooth and blended.

3. Pour half of remaining brownie batter into second prepared pan. Top with cream cheese mixture, and then pour last part of brownie batter over cream cheese mixture; marble with a knife.

4. Bake both pans of brownies for 19–22 minutes, or until tops look dry and shiny. Remove from oven and immediately sprinkle cream cheese brownies with the chocolate chips; cover that pan with foil and let stand for a few minutes. Remove foil and spread chips evenly over brownies. Let cool completely and cut into bars.

Marshmallow Treats

This is a twist on the traditional combination of Rice Krispies bars. Peanut butter and chocolate are added to toasted rice flakes cereal, which is then formed around large marshmallows. The finished cookies look like popcorn balls.

INGREDIENTS | YIELDS 12 COOKIES

4 cups miniature marshmallows

¼ cup peanut butter

2 tablespoons butter

4 cups toasted rice flakes cereal

1 cup miniature chocolate chips

12 large marshmallows

Substitutions

For a nice treat, you can substitute many things for the large marshmallows in these easy cookies. You can use chocolate Kisses, either milk chocolate or dark; miniature candy bars; dates; or dried apricots. Or you don't need a filling at all! The cereal mixture can also be pressed into a 13" × 9" pan and cut into bars.

1. Combine miniature marshmallows, peanut butter, and butter in large microwave-safe bowl. Microwave on high for 1–3 minutes or until marshmallows are melted, stirring once during cooking time. Stir well to combine. Add rice cereal and miniature chocolate chips and mix well.

2. Form a scant ½ cup cereal mixture around each large marshmallow and form a ball, using greased hands. Refrigerate about 10–15 minutes, until firm. Wrap in cellophane and store at room temperature.

Streusel Grape Bars

Grapes are a surprising and fresh filling for this rich oatmeal bar. Serve them with a fork at the end of a company dinner, or cut into small squares and tuck into lunchboxes.

INGREDIENTS | YIELDS 16 BARS

1 cup flour
½ cup quick-cooking oats
½ cup brown sugar
⅛ teaspoon allspice
⅓ cup butter, melted
1 cup chopped red grapes
2 tablespoons grape jelly

Grapes

Almost all the grapes sold in produce departments today are seedless. They are called "table grapes" to distinguish them from grapes used to make wine. You can buy red, green, or blue-black grapes. Varieties include Flame, Thompson Seedless, Red Globe, Autumn Royal, and Christmas Rose.

1. Preheat oven to 350°F. In large bowl, combine flour, oats, brown sugar, and allspice and mix well. Add melted butter; stir until mixture forms crumbs. Press half of crumbs into 9" × 9" pan and set aside.

2. In small bowl, combine grapes with jelly and mix well. Spoon over crust in pan and spread evenly. Sprinkle grapes with remaining crumb mixture. Bake for 15–20 minutes, or until bars are light golden brown. Cool and cut into bars.

Graham Fudge Squares

These no-bake bars have the most wonderful rich flavor and texture from the cinnamon graham cracker crumbs.

INGREDIENTS | YIELDS 36 SQUARES

1 cup sugar

¾ cup flour

½ cup butter

1 (15-ounce) can sweetened condensed milk

2 cups semisweet chocolate chips, divided

1½ cups cinnamon graham cracker crumbs

1. Grease 9" × 9" pan with butter and set aside. In heavy saucepan, mix sugar, flour, butter, and sweetened condensed milk. Bring to a boil over medium-high heat, stirring constantly. Let boil for 1 minute, stirring constantly. Remove from heat and add 1¼ cups of the chocolate chips. Stir until chocolate melts and mixture is smooth.

2. Add graham cracker crumbs and mix well. Spread in prepared pan and press down. In microwave-safe bowl, place remaining ¾ cup chocolate chips. Microwave on medium power (50 percent) for 1 minute. Remove and stir until smooth. Pour over bars and spread to cover. Chill in freezer for 10–15 minutes; then cut into bars to serve.

Easy Fudge

Use just about anything as the additions in this easy candy—candy-coated chocolate pieces, gumdrops, peanuts, chopped candy bars, macadamia nuts, or toffee bits would all be wonderful.

INGREDIENTS | SERVES 8–10

1 (12-ounce) package semisweet chocolate chips

½ cup milk chocolate chips

1 (15-ounce) can sweetened condensed milk

1 cup chopped cashews

1 cup miniature marshmallows

Sweetened Condensed Milk

Sweetened condensed milk was invented in the 1800s to prevent food poisoning in infants and children that was caused by lack of pasteurization and refrigeration. It's a combination of milk and sugar with 50 percent of the water removed. Keep a can or two on hand because it's a great ingredient for making fudge and candies.

1. Grease an 8" × 8" pan with butter and set aside. In medium microwave-safe bowl, combine semisweet chocolate chips, milk chocolate chips, and sweetened condensed milk. Microwave on 50 percent power for 2–4 minutes, stirring once during cooking time, until chocolate is almost melted. Remove from microwave and stir until chocolate melts.

2. Stir in cashews until mixed; then stir in marshmallows. Spread into prepared pan and let stand until cool. Cut into bars to serve.

Grasshopper Cookies

These easy cookies are based on the plain chocolate wafer cookies that are used to make the old-fashioned chocolate dessert of cookies layered with cream.

INGREDIENTS | YIELDS 30 COOKIES

1 (7-ounce) jar marshmallow crème
½ teaspoon peppermint extract
3–5 drops green food coloring
1½ cups powdered sugar
1 (12-ounce) package semisweet chocolate chips, divided
1 (10-ounce) package chocolate wafer cookies

Marshmallow Crème

Marshmallow crème, also known as marshmallow fluff, is a fat-free product usually made of corn syrup, sugar, egg whites, and vanilla. It will keep, unopened, in a cool place for about a year. To measure it, first oil the measuring cup so that the crème will slip right out.

1. Place marshmallow crème in medium bowl and mix in peppermint extract and green food coloring. Stir in powdered sugar until blended; then stir in ¾ cup chocolate chips.

2. Place cookies on a wire rack and top each with a spoonful of the marshmallow crème mixture; spread to edges. Place in freezer for 10 minutes.

3. Meanwhile, place remaining 1¼ cups chocolate chips in glass measuring cup. Heat at 50 percent power in microwave oven until chips are almost melted, about 1½ minutes. Stir until chips are melted and mixture is smooth.

4. Remove cookies from freezer. Spoon some of the chocolate mixture over each cookie to coat. Return to freezer for a few minutes to harden chocolate. Store in airtight container at room temperature.

Macadamia Coconut Bars

The saltiness of the buttery round cracker crumbs helps temper the sweetness of the remaining ingredients in these easy bar cookies.

INGREDIENTS | YIELDS 36 BARS

2 cups buttery round cracker crumbs

¾ cup butter, melted

1½ cups chopped macadamia nuts

1 (14-ounce) can sweetened condensed milk

1½ cups coconut

Don't Use Evaporated Milk!

Many cooks, especially beginning cooks, tend to confuse sweetened condensed milk with evaporated milk. Doing so will ruin your recipes! Sweetened condensed milk is very thick and sweetened, while evaporated milk is simply milk with some water removed. Read labels!

1. Preheat oven to 350°F. In medium bowl, combine cracker crumbs with melted butter. Press into 13" × 9" pan. Sprinkle nuts over the crust; then evenly drizzle with sweetened condensed milk. Sprinkle coconut over milk.

2. Bake for 22–26 minutes, or until edges are golden brown and bars are almost set. Let cool; then cut into bars.

Chocolate Chow Mein Clusters

Kids love this sweet treat, but for a more adult version, you can add 2–3 teaspoons of liqueur. Grand Marnier, amaretto, or kirsch brandy are all good choices. If chocolate macaroon candy is unavailable, feel free to use chocolate rosebuds.

INGREDIENTS | SERVES 4

2 cups dry crispy chow mein noodles

2 cups coconut chocolate macaroon candy

⅓ cup light cream

Chocolate Melting Tips

Unfortunately for cooks with a sweet tooth, chocolate scorches easily when heated. When melting chocolate in the microwave, always be sure to stir the chocolate between cooking periods. For stovetop melting, make sure the bottom of the bowl containing the chocolate does not come in contact with the heated water.

1. Place the chow mein noodles in a large bowl.

2. To melt the coconut chocolate macaroon candy on the stovetop, place the macaroons and cream in a bowl over a saucepan half-filled with water, making sure the water doesn't touch the bottom of the bowl. Bring the water to a near boil over medium-low heat, stirring the chocolate macaroon candy constantly so that the chocolate doesn't burn.

3. To melt the chocolate in a microwave, place the chocolate macaroon candy and cream in a microwave-safe bowl. Melt on high heat for 1 minute, stir, and continue microwaving for 30 seconds at a time until the chocolate is melted.

4. Stir the chocolate into the noodles. Chill for 10–15 minutes before serving.

Skillet Bars

The secret to this recipe is to use quick-cooking oats, which are thinner than regular cooking oatmeal and have been steamed.

INGREDIENTS | SERVES 6

3 cups quick-cooking oats
3 tablespoons butter
¾ cup brown sugar
¾ cup granulated sugar
1½ cups dried fruit and nut mix
¾ cup unsweetened evaporated milk

1. Place the quick-cooking oats in a large mixing bowl. Set aside.

2. In a large skillet, melt the butter on medium-low heat. Add the sugars and cook until they are dissolved and bubbling.

3. Stir in the dried fruit, stirring to mix it in with the dissolved sugar. Push to one side of the skillet.

4. Turn the heat up to medium and add the evaporated milk in the other half of the skillet. When the milk is just starting to boil, stir to mix it in with the dried fruit and sugar mixture.

5. Pour the mixture into the bowl with the quick-cooking oats and mix thoroughly. Press into a greased 8" × 8" or 9" × 9" baking pan. Chill before serving.

Microwave S'mores

*The classic campfire treat, invented in the early twentieth century,
s'mores are easy to make at home in a microwave oven.*

INGREDIENTS | SERVES 6

12 whole graham crackers (2-part square)

1 cup semisweet chocolate chips

½ cup mini marshmallows

Stovetop S'mores

Don't have a microwave? Don't worry; you don't need to start up a campfire in the backyard—s'mores can also be made on the stovetop. Just melt the marshmallows and chocolate over low heat, following the instructions for melting chocolate in Chocolate Chow Mein Clusters (see this chapter). Spread the chocolate mixture over half the graham crackers and lay the remaining crackers on top, pressing down to make a sandwich.

1. Lay 6 graham crackers in a microwave-safe shallow baking dish.

2. In a small bowl, stir together the chocolate chips and marshmallows.

3. Arrange the chocolate and marshmallows over the graham crackers.

4. Microwave on high heat for 1½ minutes, and then for 15–30 seconds at a time until the chocolate and marshmallows are melted.

5. Remove and top each s'more with a graham cracker to make a sandwich.

Basic Peanut Butter Cookies

While rolling the cookies, keep the remainder of the cookie dough covered in plastic wrap so that it doesn't dry out. Feel free to replace the chocolate chips with raisins if desired.

INGREDIENTS | SERVES 10

1 cup chunky peanut butter

1 cup margarine, room temperature

½ cup granulated sugar

½ cup brown sugar

1 teaspoon vanilla extract

1 large egg

¾ cup chocolate chips

1 teaspoon baking soda

½ teaspoon salt

1½ cups all-purpose flour

Freezing Cookies

Freshly baked cookies can be frozen and enjoyed later. To freeze, place the cookies in individual resealable plastic bags, or between layers of wax paper in a sealed container. For best results, do not freeze the cookies for longer than 3 months.

1. Preheat the oven to 375°F. Grease two 9" × 13" baking sheets.

2. In a large mixing bowl, stir together the peanut butter, margarine, sugars, vanilla extract, and the egg, mixing well. Stir in the chocolate chips.

3. In a separate medium mixing bowl, stir the baking soda and salt with the flour. Gradually stir the flour mixture into the creamed peanut butter mixture with a wooden spoon.

4. Roll the dough into balls about 1–1½ inches in diameter. Place on the baking sheets, approximately 2 inches apart. (You will have more cookies than can fit on the 2 sheets and will need to use one of them again.) Press down in the middle of each cookie with a wet fork.

5. Bake for 12 minutes, or until the cookies are browned around the edges and a toothpick placed in the middle comes out clean. Cool and store in a sealed container.

Cranberry Chews

Dried cranberries and lemon juice add a tart flavor to these chewy cookies.
This recipe yields about 40 cookies.

INGREDIENTS | SERVES 8

1½ cups all-purpose flour
½ teaspoon baking soda
¾ teaspoon ground cinnamon
½ teaspoon salt
1½ sticks unsalted butter, softened
¾ cup granulated sugar
1 large egg
1 tablespoon lemon juice
¾ cup dried cranberries

1. Preheat the oven to 350°F. Grease two 9" × 13" baking sheets.

2. In a bowl, stir together the flour, baking soda, ground cinnamon, and salt.

3. In a separate large mixing bowl, use an electric mixer to mix together the butter and sugar. Gradually beat in the egg and lemon juice. Blend in the flour mixture. Stir in the dried cranberries.

4. Drop a heaping teaspoon of dough onto the baking sheet. Space the cookies on the cookie sheets about 2 inches apart. (You will have more cookies than can fit on the 2 sheets and will need to use one of them again.) Press down gently with a wet fork.

5. Bake the cookies for 10 minutes, or until the edges are golden brown and crisp. Remove and let cool. Store in a sealed container.

Chocolate Chip Macaroons

This is a very simple recipe—and so much fun to eat!

INGREDIENTS | SERVES 8

1 egg
¼ cup sugar
7 ounces shredded coconut
3 tablespoons margarine
1 teaspoon vanilla extract
4 ounces mini chocolate morsels

The Trans Fat Story—the Unhealthiest Fat Ever Created

Trans fats, or partially hydrogenated vegetable oil, as it is usually listed on the label, is the most dangerous type of fat you can eat. Why are trans fats so harmful? Hydrogenation, or the addition of hydrogen to a somewhat healthy fat, is very dangerous to arteries. Learn to read not only the Nutrition Facts label on all food products but, even more importantly, the actual ingredient list. If the words "partially hydrogenated vegetable oil" or "partially hydrogenated vegetable shortening" appear anywhere within the ingredient list, choose another product.

1. Preheat oven to 325°F.

2. Mix egg, sugar, and coconut in a medium bowl.

3. Melt margarine in microwave (melt on high, uncovered, for 30–45 seconds), and then add margarine and vanilla to the bowl. Mix well.

4. Fold in chocolate morsels.

5. Spray nonstick cooking spray onto baking sheet. Drop dough by heaping tablespoons onto baking sheet. Bake for 15–20 minutes. Cool and store in a sealed container.

Crispy Oatmeal Crisps

Use "quick-cooking" oatmeal, not an instant oatmeal. In fact, instant oatmeal does not contain as many of the cholesterol-lowering properties as the regular.

INGREDIENTS | SERVES 16–18

3 eggs

1 teaspoon cinnamon

1 teaspoon vanilla

½ teaspoon salt

1½ cups granulated sugar

2 tablespoons margarine, melted and cooled

4 teaspoons baking powder

3½ cups quick-cooking oatmeal

A Healthful Twist on a Cookie?

This is a light oatmeal cookie, thin and crispy. Though a fairly basic cookie recipe, it has enough oatmeal to be able to give cholesterol-lowering benefits—it's certainly better than a brownie! Indulge the kids once in a while. Teach that it is acceptable to have a sweet treat; however, offer two cookies and a glass of cold low-fat milk, not six cookies!

1. Preheat oven to 350°F. Place aluminum foil on several cookie sheets. Spray with cooking spray.

2. Using an electric mixer, beat eggs until foamy.

3. Add cinnamon, vanilla, salt, and sugar. Beat 2–3 minutes until thick and well blended.

4. Add melted margarine and mix. Stir in baking powder and oats.

5. Using a rounded teaspoon, drop batter onto cookie sheet, about 2 inches apart. Continue to stir remaining batter occasionally, as the liquid will start to settle.

6. Bake for 10 minutes, until cookies appear thin and lightly colored, darker on the rim and lighter in the center. When cookies are done, immediately slide the cookies off the cookie sheet and cool before serving.

Mint Cookies

*For really magnificent cookies, feel free to add chopped walnuts or dark chocolate chips—
just a little healthy antioxidant thrown in.*

INGREDIENTS | SERVES 12–15

⅔ cup margarine, softened

¾ cup sugar

⅓ cup firmly packed dark brown sugar

1 egg

1 teaspoon vanilla extract

1 (1-ounce) square unsweetened chocolate, melted

1½ cups all-purpose flour

1 (10-ounce) package mint chocolate morsels

1. Preheat oven to 325°F. In a mixing bowl, beat margarine at medium speed with an electric mixer.

2. Gradually add white and brown sugars. Mix well. Add egg, vanilla extract, and melted chocolate and continue to beat. Gradually add flour until batter is smooth.

3. By hand, stir in mint morsels.

4. Spray nonstick cooking spray on a baking sheet. Using a teaspoon, drop large teaspoons-full of dough onto the baking sheet.

5. Bake 10–15 minutes. Cool on a wire rack before serving.

Cookie Monster Cookies

*There's a little health thrown into this chocolate chip, peanut butter, oatmeal cookie—
again, feel free to leave in some of these goodies, or take them out.*

INGREDIENTS | SERVES 10–20

2 eggs
¼ cup honey
1 cup peanut butter
1 cup oatmeal flakes, lightly toasted
1½ teaspoons vanilla extract
¼ cup canola oil
3 tablespoons sugar-free pancake syrup
¼ cup low-fat milk
1½ cups flour
½ cup mini chocolate chips

1. Preheat oven to 350°F. In a medium mixing bowl, beat eggs until creamy. Add honey and peanut butter. Mix well.

2. Add oatmeal flakes, vanilla, oil, pancake syrup, and milk. Add flour gradually, and then stir in chocolate chips. Blend until batter is smooth.

3. Spray nonstick cooking spray onto a baking sheet. Drop batter by teaspoons onto baking sheet.

4. Bake 8–10 minutes, just until golden brown. Cool before serving.

Almond Cookies

These are great alone or with a fruit dessert. Store in an airtight container.
To crisp, put in a low-temperature oven for 1–2 minutes.

INGREDIENTS | YIELDS 72 COOKIES

Sugar substitute for baking equal to 7 tablespoons granulated sugar

3 egg whites, at room temperature

½ cup finely ground blanched almonds

⅓ cup cake flour

1 teaspoon Cointreau

¼ teaspoon vanilla extract

Sweet Tooth

Adding sweet spices such as cinnamon, nutmeg, or cardamom will enhance the perception of sweetness in your desserts.

1. Preheat oven to 425°F. Oil two 17" × 14" baking sheets or line them with parchment paper.

2. In a large bowl, stir together the sugar substitute and egg whites until the whites are frothy and the sugar substitute is dissolved. Add the remaining ingredients and whisk until the batter is somewhat smooth.

3. Place rounded teaspoon-sized dollops of dough onto the prepared baking sheets, leaving a 1-inch space between each cookie.

4. Bake in the oven for 5–6 minutes, or until the edges turn golden. Remove from oven and transfer the cookies to a wire rack. Let cool completely before serving.

CHAPTER 15

Desserts

Caramel-Apple Parfaits

Choose crisp and tart apples for this simple fall dessert. Granny Smith apples would be a good choice because they hold their shape well even when cooked.

INGREDIENTS | SERVES 8

½ cup sugar

1 teaspoon cinnamon

3 apples, peeled and chopped

½ cup butter

4 cups vanilla ice cream

8 shortbread cookies, crumbled

½ cup chopped toasted pecans

Cooking Apples

There are apples that are best for eating out of hand, and those best for cooking. Cooking apples include McIntosh, Cortland, Rome Beauty, Jonathan, Haralson, and Granny Smith. The best apples for eating out of hand include Honeycrisp, Gala, Red Delicious, and new varieties including Sweet Sixteen and Honeygold.

1. In medium bowl, combine sugar, cinnamon, and apples and toss to coat.

2. Melt butter in a heavy saucepan and add apple mixture. Cook over low heat for 10–12 minutes, or until apples are tender and sauce is lightly caramelized. Remove from heat, pour mixture into a heatproof bowl, and let stand for 10 minutes, stirring occasionally.

3. Make parfaits with apple mixture, ice cream, crumbled shortbread cookies, and pecans. Serve immediately.

Chocolate-Raspberry Pie

*You can find prepared chocolate cookie pie crusts in the baking aisle
of your supermarket. Or make your own by combining 2 cups chocolate cookie
crumbs with ⅓ cup melted butter and pressing the mixture into a 9-inch pie pan.*

INGREDIENTS | SERVES 8

1 cup semisweet chocolate chips

1 (8-ounce) package cream cheese, softened

1 (9-inch) chocolate cookie pie crust

¼ cup raspberry jelly

2 cups fresh raspberries

1. Put chocolate chips in a small microwave-safe bowl. Microwave at 50 percent power for 1½ minutes; stir until chips are melted.

2. Cut cream cheese into cubes and add to melted chips; beat well until smooth. Place mixture in refrigerator for 10 minutes.

3. Spread cooled chocolate mixture in bottom of pie crust.

4. Put jelly in medium saucepan over low heat; cook and stir just until jelly is almost melted. Remove from heat and gently fold in raspberries just until coated.

5. Place on top of the chocolate mixture. Serve immediately, or cover and refrigerate until serving time.

Chocolate-Toffee Torte

This elegant torte is a wonderful finish for a company meal because you can make it up to 8 hours ahead of time. Use a serrated knife for slicing for best results.

INGREDIENTS | SERVES 10–12

1 (9-inch) round angel food cake
4 (1.4-ounce) chocolate-covered toffee bars
2 cups whipping cream
⅔ cup powdered sugar
⅓ cup chocolate syrup
1 teaspoon vanilla

1. Using serrated knife, cut angel food cake horizontally into 4 equal layers.

2. Place toffee bars in resealable plastic bag and crush with a rolling pin.

3. In large bowl, combine cream, powdered sugar, chocolate syrup, and vanilla. Beat until stiff peaks form.

4. Frost layers of cake as you reassemble it, sprinkling crushed toffee bars on each layer. Frost top and sides of cake and sprinkle with remaining crushed toffee bars. Serve immediately, or cover and chill for 2–4 hours. Store leftovers in refrigerator.

Mini Fruit Tarts

Your grocer's freezer section is a gold mine of prepared pie and tart shells.
Stock up on a few different types to make pies and tarts in minutes.

INGREDIENTS | YIELDS 24 TARTS

24 frozen mini phyllo tart shells
½ cup apple jelly
½ teaspoon chopped fresh thyme leaves
½ cup blueberries
½ cup raspberries

Herbs in Desserts

In the 1990s, using savory herbs in desserts became popular. Thyme, with its minty, lemony fragrance, is a natural partner with sweet and tart fruits. Rosemary is delicious with lemon desserts and in shortbreads, and lemon verbena is used in fruit jellies and cakes.

1. Preheat oven to 375°F. Place tart shells on a cookie sheet and bake according to package directions. Remove to wire racks.

2. Meanwhile, heat apple jelly and thyme in a medium saucepan over low heat until jelly melts. Remove from heat and stir in berries. Put a couple of teaspoons of berry mixture into each tart shell and serve.

Blueberry Crisp

A crisp is a baked dessert that has a crumbly topping made of flour, sugar, butter, and usually oatmeal and nuts. Using canned pie filling streamlines this excellent recipe.

INGREDIENTS | SERVES 6

1 (21-ounce) can blueberry pie filling
½ cup flour
½ cup brown sugar
½ cup oatmeal
½ cup chopped walnuts
½ teaspoon cinnamon
¼ cup butter, melted

Crisps, Crumbles, Grunts, and Cobblers

All of these old-fashioned, homey desserts are basically the same thing: fruits with some kind of topping. Crisps use oatmeal and nuts to form a crumbly topping; crumbles are the same thing. Grunts are more like a steamed pudding, sometimes cooked on top of the stove. Cobblers are similar to a deep-dish pie, with a thick biscuit-type crust.

1. Preheat oven to 400°F. Pour blueberry pie filling into 9" × 9" glass pan and set aside.

2. In medium bowl, combine flour, brown sugar, oatmeal, walnuts, and cinnamon and mix well. Pour butter into flour mixture and stir until mixture is crumbly.

3. Sprinkle over blueberry pie filling. Bake for 20–25 minutes, or until filling is bubbly and crust is light golden brown. Serve warm with ice cream or whipped cream.

Simple Cheesecake

Use any flavor of canned pie filling in this easy pie.
You could even top it with some fresh berries mixed with a bit of jam or jelly.

INGREDIENTS | SERVES 6

1 (14-ounce) can sweetened condensed milk

1 (8-ounce) package cream cheese, softened

¼ cup lemon juice

1 (9-inch) graham cracker pie crust

1 (18-ounce) can cherry pie filling

Cheesecake Toppings

There are many toppings that are delicious on cheesecake. Try mixing fresh berries with preserves or jelly, drizzling the dessert with chocolate and caramel ice cream toppings, beating whipping cream with chocolate syrup, or combining chopped nuts with chopped chocolate bars and marshmallows.

1. In large bowl, combine condensed milk, cream cheese, and lemon juice; beat on low speed until smooth and combined. Pour into graham cracker crust. Place in freezer for 10 minutes.

2. Using a slotted spoon, remove the cherries from the pie filling, leaving a lot of the gel behind. Discard the rest of the pie filling. Place cherries on cream cheese filling and serve, or cover and chill the pie up to 8 hours. Store leftovers in the refrigerator.

Strawberries with Sour Cream

There isn't an easier dessert on the planet, and this simple fruit recipe has the most wonderful sweet-and-tart flavor. You can make it with peaches, mangoes, grapes, or pears too; just use fruits that are acidic.

INGREDIENTS | SERVES 6

2 pints strawberries, stemmed and sliced
1 cup sour cream
½ cup brown sugar
¼ cup toasted pecans

In glass serving bowl, place ⅓ of the strawberries. Top with ⅓ of the sour cream and sprinkle with ⅓ of the brown sugar. Repeat layers, ending with brown sugar. Top with toasted pecans and serve, or cover and refrigerate up to 8 hours.

Chocolate–Peanut Butter Pie

This is such an indulgent dessert; it's hard to believe that it uses only five ingredients! Take it out of the freezer 15 minutes before serving for the best flavor and texture.

INGREDIENTS | SERVES 8–10

30 fudge-covered graham crackers
⅓ cup butter, melted
3 pints chocolate ice cream
¾ cup peanut butter
5 ounces peanut butter cups, chopped

1. Crush graham crackers and combine with butter; press crumbs into 9-inch pie pan and set aside.

2. In blender or food processor, combine ice cream and peanut butter; blend or process until combined. Fold in chopped candies and place in pie crust. Freeze until firm. Serve cold.

Graham Crackers

There are many varieties of graham crackers on the market. You can find chocolate-covered crackers, low-fat crackers, cinnamon-flavored crackers, and honey-flavored crackers. Choose any of them to make a wonderfully easy and quick pie crust by crushing the crackers and mixing the crumbs with some melted butter; then press the mixture into a pie pan.

Raspberry Fool

*A fool is a soft parfait usually made with a puréed fruit and flavored whipping cream.
Top it with more sweetened whipped cream and some mint sprigs.*

INGREDIENTS | SERVES 6

2 pints raspberries

1½ cups whipping cream

½ cup powdered sugar

½ teaspoon vanilla

½ cup chopped pecans, toasted

½ cup grated semisweet chocolate

Whipping Cream

Heavy whipping cream must contain at least 36 percent butterfat. To whip cream, chill the bowl and the beaters in the freezer for 10–15 minutes. Begin whipping slowly, and gradually increase speed as the cream thickens. The cream is done when peaks droop slightly when the beaters are lifted.

1. Place raspberries in medium bowl and mash some of them, leaving some whole. In large bowl, combine cream, powdered sugar, and vanilla and beat until stiff peaks form.

2. Layer raspberries with whipped cream mixture, pecans, and grated chocolate in 6 parfait glasses. Serve immediately, or cover and refrigerate up to 6 hours.

Flaky Peach Tarts

You should make these little mini tarts just before you plan to serve them for best flavor and texture. Top them with peach ice cream and some chopped cashews.

INGREDIENTS | SERVES 6

1 sheet frozen puff pastry, thawed
2 peaches
⅓ cup peach jam
3 tablespoons brown sugar
⅛ teaspoon cinnamon

Topping Tarts

Tarts can be topped with sweetened whipped cream, ice cream, or hard sauce. To make hard sauce, beat ½ cup softened butter with 1 cup powdered sugar and 1 teaspoon vanilla. Serve on hot desserts; the mixture will melt into the dessert and form a sweet sauce.

1. Preheat oven to 375°F. Roll pastry into a 9" × 12" rectangle. Cut pastry into twelve 3-inch squares and place on parchment paper–lined cookie sheets; set aside.

2. Peel peaches, remove pit, and cut into thin slices. Arrange peach slices on pastry and brush each with some of the peach jam. Sprinkle with brown sugar and cinnamon. Bake for 10–14 minutes, or until pastry is puffed and golden and fruit is tender. Serve immediately.

Lemon Angel Cake

Bakeries always have angel food cake available; also look for them in the bakery department of your supermarket. Lemon curd is available near the pie fillings and also in the gourmet foods aisle.

INGREDIENTS | SERVES 10–12

1 (9-inch) round angel food cake

1¼ cups whipping cream

2 tablespoons powdered sugar

1 cup lemon curd

1½ cups chopped candied walnuts

Recipe Variation

You can use just about any well-flavored, smooth, creamy filling, pudding, or custard in place of the lemon curd in this easy recipe. Try chocolate pudding, caramel pudding, or cream cheese frosting. You can also sprinkle the layers with toasted coconut, nuts, or chopped or crushed candy bars as you frost them.

1. Using a serrated knife, cut cake horizontally into 3 layers.

2. In a large bowl, combine cream and powdered sugar; beat until stiff peaks form. Fold in lemon curd until blended.

3. Spread mixture between layers, sprinkling each layer with some of the nuts, and then frost top and sides with lemon mixture. Sprinkle top with remaining nuts. Serve immediately, or cover and refrigerate up to 8 hours. Store leftovers in refrigerator.

Apple Crumble

Use the crumbly topping with any flavor of canned pie filling; peach would be very delicious.
Top it with some vanilla or caramel ice cream for extra decadence.

INGREDIENTS | SERVES 6

1 (21-ounce) can apple pie filling
¾ cup brown sugar
1 teaspoon cinnamon
¼ teaspoon nutmeg
½ cup flour
½ cup oatmeal
⅓ cup butter, melted

1. Preheat oven to 400°F. Place pie filling into 1½-quart casserole dish.

2. In medium bowl, combine sugar, cinnamon, nutmeg, flour, and oatmeal and mix well. Add melted butter and mix until crumbs form. Sprinkle crumbs over pie filling.

3. Bake for 15–20 minutes, or until pie filling bubbles and crumb mixture is browned. Serve warm.

Chocolate Velvet

You can pile this mixture into a baked and cooled pie crust or a graham cracker crust and freeze to serve it as a pie; top wedges with some whipped cream and grated chocolate.

INGREDIENTS | SERVES 8

1 cup chocolate syrup
1 (15-ounce) can sweetened condensed milk
1 (16-ounce) container frozen whipped topping, thawed
½ teaspoon vanilla
⅓ cup sliced almonds, toasted

In large bowl, combine syrup and sweetened condensed milk and beat until smooth. Fold in whipped topping and vanilla. Sprinkle with almonds and serve immediately as a pudding, or place in 1-quart casserole dish, top with almonds, and freeze until solid.

Toasting Nuts

To toast nuts, place them on a shallow baking pan and bake at 350°F for 5–10 minutes, shaking pan frequently, until nuts are fragrant and just beginning to turn light golden brown. You can also microwave the nuts at 100 percent power for 3–5 minutes, until the nuts are fragrant. Let cool completely before chopping.

Pumpkin Cake in a Cone

*Pumpkin cake made in an ice cream cone is one of the most creative favorites—
and hiding in the cone is a vast amount of beta-carotene cancer-fighters!*

INGREDIENTS | SERVES 18

1 package prepared carrot-cake mix

1 cup canned solid pumpkin

3 eggs

⅓ cup canola oil

¼ cup water

1 teaspoon vanilla extract

2 tablespoons brown sugar

1 teaspoon ground cinnamon

18 cake cones

Frosting:

⅔ cup confectioners' sugar

¼ cup canned solid pumpkin

¾ teaspoon vanilla extract

1 (8-ounce) package low-fat cream cheese

1. Preheat oven to 350°F.

2. In a large mixing bowl, combine the carrot cake mix, pumpkin, eggs, oil, water, vanilla extract, brown sugar, and cinnamon. Beat with an electric mixer for 2–3 minutes, until well blended.

3. Place cones in the cups of a cupcake pan or on cookie sheets. Spoon batter among the 18 cones, filling about ⅔–¾ full.

4. Bake in the oven for 25–30 minutes, until toothpick comes out dry. Cool on a wire rack.

5. To prepare icing, mix together confectioners' sugar, ¼ cup pumpkin, vanilla extract, and cream cheese. Beat with electric mixer until frosting is smooth. Spread each cone with frosting before serving.

A Versatile Vegetable

Pumpkin might not be the first vegetable you would think to introduce to your children. Maybe it should be! In a soup, a pie, a hot casserole, or even a shake, pumpkin is one of the healthiest vegetables around. An incredible source of antioxidants, potassium (remember the muscle builders), and much-needed vitamins, being that bright orange color makes it a very special vegetable. The red, yellow, and orange vegetables are packed with nutrition power.

Lime-Almond Tarts

Ground almonds add a delicious texture to this tart.
Toast the slivered almonds for the best flavor and results.

INGREDIENTS | SERVES 8

½ cup, plus 1 tablespoon slivered blanched almonds, toasted

1 tablespoon lime zest

Sugar substitute equal to ½ cup granulated sugar

2 large eggs

6 tablespoons butter, plus extra for greasing

3 tablespoons freshly squeezed lime juice

½ cup heavy cream, whipped

Pleasing Presentation

Use hollowed-out halves of oranges and grapefruits as bowls for servings of freshly cut fruits and berries. Use hollowed-out halves of lemons and limes as bowls for any sauces. Cut a small disk from the bottoms to keep the bowls sitting flat.

1. Preheat oven to 350°F.

2. Place the ½ cup almonds in a food processor fitted with a metal blade and pulse until the almonds are finely ground. Transfer the almonds to a bowl and set aside.

3. Using the same food processor bowl, combine the lime zest and sugar substitute and process until evenly mixed, about 1 minute. Add the eggs, butter, lime juice, and 1 tablespoon ground almonds; pulse 2–3 times, and then process for 8–10 seconds, until well mixed.

4. Lightly butter the inside of 8 (4- or 6-ounce) ovenproof ramekins. Equally divide almond mixture between the ramekins. Lightly press the mixture into the bottoms of the ramekins and smooth the surface. Place on a baking sheet and bake until lightly browned, about 15 minutes.

5. Remove from oven and transfer the ramekins to a wire rack to cool. To serve, top the tarts with the whipped cream and sprinkle with any remaining toasted almonds.

APPENDIX A

Shortcut Ingredients

Companies introduce thousands of new convenience products into the market every year. It's worth your time to stroll through your grocery store every month or so looking for new products and advances in food preparation.

Shelf-stable grocery products can be stored at room temperature without refrigeration. Keep a good selection of these products on hand in your pantry, organized by type.

- ✔ Cake mixes
- ✔ Cookie mixes
- ✔ Prepared frostings
- ✔ Bread mixes
- ✔ Dessert mixes
- ✔ Soup mixes and bases
- ✔ Self-rising flour
- ✔ Flavored rice mixes
- ✔ Dried fruit
- ✔ Fruit pie fillings
- ✔ Flavored oils
- ✔ Canned soups and stocks
- ✔ Breads and crackers
- ✔ Dry seasoning mixes
- ✔ Flavored pasta mixes
- ✔ Seasoned bread crumbs
- ✔ Prepared sauces
- ✔ Pasta sauces and tomato products
- ✔ Pasta
- ✔ Prepared salad dressings
- ✔ Pudding and pie filling mixes
- ✔ Canned and jarred fruit salads
- ✔ Stocks and broth in aseptic boxes
- ✔ Rice mixes
- ✔ Flavored vinegars
- ✔ Marinades

The number of prepared meat products has skyrocketed in recent years. From cooked deli meats to heat-and-eat entrées, these products not only make quick work of the main dish, but they can be used as an ingredient in recipes. Excellent value-added meat products include:

- ✔ Preformed hamburger patties
- ✔ Precooked bacon
- ✔ Marinated meats
- ✔ Fully prepared entrées like pot roast in gravy, BBQ beef, and pulled pork
- ✔ Prestuffed and seasoned chicken and fish
- ✔ Chicken and turkey cutlets
- ✔ Chicken tenders
- ✔ Preseasoned turkey tenderloin
- ✔ Frozen precooked meatballs
- ✔ Fully cooked frozen shrimp
- ✔ Minute steaks and cubed stew meat
- ✔ Cooked ground beef in sauces
- ✔ Frozen stir-fry mixes
- ✔ Frozen seasoned burgers
- ✔ Fish fillets and steaks
- ✔ Smoked pork
- ✔ Cooked shredded chicken in sauces
- ✔ Marinated and smoked salmon
- ✔ Seafood dinner starters
- ✔ Breading and batter mixes
- ✔ Fajita kits
- ✔ Lunch kits
- ✔ Fully cooked sausages

The produce and dairy departments have perhaps changed the most over the past few years, with introductions of many value-added and prepared foods. Many of these items will keep after opening, under refrigeration, for several weeks. Be sure there is a "use by" date on them; if not, mark the date of purchase and discard after a few weeks. Produce and dairy products that will save you time include:

- ✔ Prewashed salad mixes
- ✔ Flavored tomato products
- ✔ Refrigerated hash brown potatoes, mashed potatoes, potato slices
- ✔ Vegetables from salad bar
- ✔ Sliced mushrooms
- ✔ Jarred minced garlic
- ✔ Preshredded cheeses
- ✔ Refrigerated pasta sauces
- ✔ Fresh pasta
- ✔ Pesto sauce
- ✔ Shredded coleslaw mix
- ✔ Shredded carrots
- ✔ Shredded cabbage
- ✔ Prepared polenta
- ✔ Fresh herbs
- ✔ Smoothie mixes
- ✔ Salad kits

In the frozen aisle of the supermarket, you'll find totally prepared meals as well as ingredients to make meals quickly. For instance, add some chopped chicken to any of the frozen vegetable combinations, especially those with sauce, and dinner is on the table in less than 15 minutes.

- ✔ Frozen chopped vegetables
- ✔ Frozen vegetable combinations
- ✔ Frozen chopped onions and pearl onions
- ✔ Ice cream combinations
- ✔ Frozen stuffed chicken entrées
- ✔ Prepared hash brown potatoes, mashed, French fries
- ✔ Pizzas
- ✔ Snack foods
- ✔ Prepared entrées
- ✔ Vegetables in sauce
- ✔ Meal starters
- ✔ Slow-cooker meal starters
- ✔ Frozen prepared garlic and cheese breads
- ✔ Breakfast pastries
- ✔ Frozen puff pastry and filo dough
- ✔ Frozen cakes and pies
- ✔ Frozen juices and beverages

And the deli department is bursting with wonderful precooked meats and vegetables, salads, cheeses, breads, and flavored oils and sauces. These ingredients do cost more than those you prepare yourself, but they are excellent time-savers. Not only can you serve them as is, but they are great components in many five-ingredient recipes. Deli ingredients to look for include:

- ✔ Fully cooked rotisserie chicken
- ✔ Fried chicken
- ✔ Fully cooked roast beef
- ✔ Fully cooked ham
- ✔ Corned beef
- ✔ Unusual cheeses
- ✔ Sandwiches
- ✔ Fondue mix
- ✔ Pastrami and other sandwich meats
- ✔ Vegetable salads
- ✔ Potato salads
- ✔ Pizza
- ✔ Relishes
- ✔ Mashed potatoes
- ✔ Fruit salads
- ✔ Rolls
- ✔ Flavored oils
- ✔ Desserts
- ✔ Prepared breads
- ✔ Party trays
- ✔ Gelatin salads
- ✔ Cold cuts
- ✔ Soups
- ✔ Wraps and unusual breads

There are many products on the market that will help you organize your kitchen and cook safely and more efficiently: from lazy Susans to spice racks, pot racks to storage containers. Think about investing some money in new products to help keep your kitchen in order. If you have a kitchen with little counter space, purchase a center island or work island on casters that can be pulled out when cooking, then rolled away into a pantry or closet after use.

- ✔ Pull-down cookbook holders
- ✔ Pull-down knife racks
- ✔ Door organizers for cans and bottles
- ✔ Lazy Susans for large, deep cupboards
- ✔ Pot racks and hangers
- ✔ Under-cabinet lighting
- ✔ Nested storage containers
- ✔ Over-the-door racks and organizers
- ✔ Baker's racks
- ✔ Bread boxes
- ✔ Cutting boards
- ✔ Dish drainers
- ✔ Tiered shelves
- ✔ Drawer organizers
- ✔ Microwave carts
- ✔ Salad spinners
- ✔ Spice racks
- ✔ Timers
- ✔ Instant-read thermometers
- ✔ Silicon hot pads and gloves

Glossary of Common Cooking Terms

al dente:
An Italian term literally meaning "to the tooth," al dente is used to describe the state to which pasta should be cooked. Pasta that is cooked al dente has no taste of flour remaining, but there is still a slight resistance and chewiness when it is bitten into. Like Italian pasta, Chinese egg noodles should be cooked al dente.

baste:
To spoon liquid over a food while it is cooking. Meat, seafood, or poultry may be basted with a marinade during broiling or grilling, while meat or poultry is frequently basted with drippings from the bottom of a pan during roasting.

blanch:
To partially cook food by plunging it briefly into boiling water. Blanching is used to loosen the skin on fruit or nuts, or to partially cook food before finishing cooking by another method (such as stir-frying). Normally, blanched food is immediately plunged into ice water to stop the cooking process. Depending on the purpose, blanching times will vary from a few seconds to minutes.

blend:
To thoroughly mix two or more ingredients together until they are smooth and indistinguishable from one another. Liquid or wet ingredients are blended together, as in a shake, salad dressing, or sauce.

boil:
To cook food by immersing it in water that has been heated to the point where bubbles are regularly breaking on the surface. Although boiling is an excellent quick-cooking method, it is less healthy than steaming, as some of the nutrients may be lost in the cooking water.

braise:
To cook meat in a small amount of liquid in a tightly covered pan. Normally, the meat is browned before braising. Popular braising liquids include wine and broth.

broil:
To cook food by radiant heat (the transfer of heat from a heated surface). In the case of broiling, the heated surface is located above the food.

brown:
Browning food consists of heating it in a small amount of oil to seal in the juices. Browning food is not stirred, but is turned over halfway through cooking. Normally, the food is not browned for more than five minutes on each side.

caramelize:
Caramelization comprises heating sugar until it liquefies into a caramel-colored syrup. Carmelizing vegetables refers to heating vegetables (such as pearl onions) until they release their natural sugars.

chop:

To cut food into small pieces. While the chopped pieces of food don't need to be uniform, they should be roughly the same size to cook evenly.

dash or pinch:

A inexact measurement, equal to approximately 1/16 teaspoon.

deep-fry:

To cook food by immersing it in hot oil. Once the food is deep-fried, it is removed with a slotted spoon or a mesh container and drained. While deep-frying is very quick, it can take several minutes for the oil to heat to the correct temperature. An electric deep-fat fryer heats the oil more quickly.

deglaze:

To heat liquid in a pan or roasting pan that has been used to cook meat or poultry. A rubber spatula is used to scrape up leftover browned bits from the cooked meat. The browned bits gradually mix with the liquid, adding extra flavor. Deglazing does not take much time, and is a great way to add extra flavor to the dish.

dice:

To cut food into half-inch cubes.

dredge:

To coat food with a dry ingredient, such as flour or bread crumbs, before it is fried. Dredging the food before frying gives a crunchy coating and seals in flavor.

grill:

Like broiling, grilling consists of cooking food through the transfer of heat from a heated surface. Unlike broiling, however, the heated surface is located below the food.

marinate:

To soak food such as meat or poultry in a liquid before cooking. Marinating tenderizes food and adds flavor. Since marinades used to flavor raw food can carry bacteria, it is best not to add leftover marinade to food while it is cooking. Instead, prepare more marinade than you need and set aside a portion to add to the food.

mince:

To cut food into very small pieces. Minced food is cut more finely than either chopped or diced food. Garlic and ginger are frequently minced before being added to stir-fries.

sauté:

To quickly cook food over high heat in a small amount of butter or oil.

simmer:

To cook food in water that has been brought almost to a boil. When water is simmering, the bubbles are rising slowly, and often breaking before reaching the surface. In cooking, liquid is often brought to a boil and then simmered at a lower heat.

steam:

To cook food by placing it over water that has been brought to a boil. The steam produced by the boiling water cooks the food.

stir-fry:

To quickly cook food over high heat by stirring it continually in a small amount of oil. Unlike sautéing, food is cut into smaller, uniform pieces before it is stir-fried.

Index